SHARING L
TO M
FAVOURITE FILMS

C000151387

DEAR MOVIES

PETER MALONE

COVENTRY
PRESS

Published in Australia by
Coventry Press
33 Scoresby Road
Bayswater Vic. 3153
Australia

ISBN 9780648725183

Cataloguing-in-Publication entry is available from the National Library of Australia http://catalogue.nla.gov.au/.

Cover design by Ian James - www.jgd.com.au
Text design by Megan Low (Filmshot Graphics FSG)
Text set in Caladea

Printed in Australia

CONTENTS

FOREWORD

Many years ago – thirty to be precise – I fell into film reviewing after a varied career as a journalist, teacher, and Early Music aficionado and entrepreneur. It's not often that one remembers the very moment that a strong bond is formed – by chance or in the course of one's work – with someone who becomes a friend for life. For me this moment came in a cinema aisle after a preview screening, listening with pleasure and some amazement to a man with a gentle voice whose take on films was virtually the same as my own.

'How long have you been reviewing films?', I asked this kindly man with a beard, and as a novice was blown away by the reply which came with just the barest hint of pride: 'Twenty years'. It was in that moment that I learned that Peter Malone was known in Australia at the time as a 'movie priest', one of a small handful of ordained Catholics whose mission in life is not only to enjoy movies (which Peter does enormously as witnessed by this book), but to spread the humanism at the heart of the Gospels through the power of pictures projected onto a screen.

My understanding of why I found it so enjoyable discussing movies with Peter, then as now, comes from my own religious background which is Jewish. There is a deeply pastoral element in Peter's nature and I discovered this when he began inviting me to write articles and reviews on films for Catholic journals and books. In a theological sense, both Jews and Catholics understand the importance of metaphor in storytelling, sometimes to the point of addiction. Nothing is simply what it seems. More is to be learnt and understood through scratching the surface of things and plumbing the depths.

Federico Fellini once said that watching films is 'dreaming in the dark with our eyes open', and this, I think, is the secret to why Peter's latest book is for me his most personal and revealing. At the heart of *Dear Movies* is his intellectual ability to interpret through a humanistic and religious lens, the dreams and nightmares of an often suffering humanity, conveying his profound interpretations with simplicity and clarity.

In this book, Peter the man as well as Peter the priest is writing love letters to movies which have transformed his life and given him aesthetic and intellectual access to cinematic meaning. He confronts realism without blanching and withholds judgment of human motivation, often finding great good amongst the bad.

An example of this, energised by his innate empathy, is the letter Peter writes in praise of *Bad Lieutenant*, directed by Abel Ferrara in 1992. About a corrupt New York detective addicted to drugs, gambling and sex, Peter sees through the film's graphic nudity, drug use, language and violence (it was rated NU-17 in the US), to the very heart of the bad lieutenant's self-loathing, which is his longing for transcendence and redemption.

Another joy that comes from reading Peter's book is the freedom with which he allows his thoughts to roam with a 'stream of consciousness' logic. In the case of *Bad Lieutenant,* this links in an affecting way to Oscar Wilde's letter *De Profundis* – written while incarcerated for homosexuality in Reading Gaol – to Psalm 130 (called in Latin *De Profundis,* 'out of the depths'), and a decision by Catholic theologians that not only films about good people are good.

There is evidence in *Dear Movies* not only of Peter's enjoyment of all genres of films (from art house to factory with a broad spectrum in between), but also his deep understanding of the art and craft of filmmaking which comes from viewing thousands of films over a lifetime.

One of my own beliefs about film reviewing is that a critical judgment of movies is largely dependent on 'informed taste'. Taste is what makes us like a film or not, and my own taste in movies being rather on the dark side (I was converted to 'Continental' cinema and films by Hollywood dissidents when I was still very young), I was initially shocked and then delighted to discover that films that I couldn't connect with or actively disliked (*Interiors, Singin' In The Rain*) took on an entirely new meaning and significance through Peter's perspicacious eyes and mind.

Reading Peter's *Dear Movies* is more than a joy and revelation. It is a reminder of the power of pictures, and the important role movies still play in all our lives today.

Jan Epstein
Broadcaster ABC, journalist *Jewish Times*,
film reviewer *Australian Film Critics Association*

INTRODUCTION

Dear Reader,

Have you ever written a letter to a movie? Perhaps not. Probably not. And, up till now, neither have I. Plenty of reviews, over fifty years of them, but up till now it has not occurred to me to write any of them a letter.

Let me tell you a story. I had been wondering whether there was another film book in me. There had been quite a number, some I had written, others collections of chapters by different reviewers, material for study and discussion as well. And, I was not getting any younger.

I like to use the word 'providence' for my life. There I was, driving home on Boxing Day night, listening to ABC Radio National. It was a book review program. As I tuned in, there was a conversation between the host and an American lady. It emerged that she had been a librarian and one of her tasks was to cull the library, getting rid of books that were physically deteriorating, eliminating books that were no longer relevant (her example was from 1981, a volume on how to use a calculator!). So far, so interesting.

But, the reason she was on the program was that she herself had written a book. And, not just a book. It was a book of letters to a variety of books that were significant to her. She had quite a long title in fact, *Dear Fahrenheit 451: Love and Heartbreak in the Stacks: A Librarian's Love Letters and Breakup Notes to the Books in Her Life.* The title itself was an exercise in reading! The author's name was Annie Spence and her book was published in 2017.

I forget whether it was love at first hearing or whether I was mulling over her idea for the rest of the drive home, but, when I arrived, I had made a life choice, so to speak. What about a book of letters to movies?

Titles started to invade my mind. Better to calm down and try to get a bit of order for a selection, some credible criteria. Obviously, films that were important to me were for the top of the list. The first was obvious, *2001: A Space Odyssey.* For years, people have been asking me what my favourite film was and *2001* was my reply. But then, more titles came flooding in.

It seemed to me that I had to pick from the many films I had enjoyed and appreciated, those that had had some personal significance for me, at a particular time in my life (and they may not have had the same significance and impact later), films that I had enjoyed and cherished, films from filmmakers whom I admired. At least! This meant films for which I had a 'soft spot' – actually films for which I had affection.

The initial plan was to write a letter, addressing the film itself, my side of a personal conversation. And, best for the length of the letter to be fewer than 1000 words, not only for the film itself to absorb the letter, but enough for any reader to get something out of the letter but for it not to outstay its welcome. That was the plan, anyway – though only one, the letter to *2001,* is over 1000 words (1014!) and the letter to the film *Jesus* has some words on the cutting-room floor at 999.

The next part of the plan was to arrange them in chronological order. I have an enthusiasm for history, for placing events and characters in their time and place (overdone, some people advise me). That meant that my letter to *Anna Karenina* (the 1948, Julien Duvivier version with Vivien Leigh) would be the opening letter, my having seen it at age eight or nine – how could we have been there and the theatre putting it on as a Saturday matinee!

But, my friend, fellow-reviewer, Jan Epstein, who kindly read some of the stories to give advice as to whether they worked or not, suggested that this method for contents was a touch straight-jacketing. She preferred to read them in the order in which I wrote them, random dates, random memories, certain recollection of a title that had been previously overlooked, some deliberate choices for films that I thought should be included...

So, I decided to follow Jan's advice and that is the order in which you will find them. It was a matter of the coinciding of memory, inspiration, opportunity.

In case you wondered, I have spoken all these letters rather than writing them, using Dragon Speech Registration (a bit of product placement). This means that the letters come from me directly, without the extra mediation of fingers tapping keys and the longer time that it takes compared with speaking. (And, of course, there is the pleasurable time of aftermath with editing, word changes, tweaking, punctuation.)

Looking back over the selection of titles for the letters, I realise that, while I have seen so many arthouse/festival films over the decades and admired so many of them, this selection is rarely 'highbrow'. Seems as though I am steadily 'middlebrow'. Is that where most of us are? At least in our actual watching and enjoying?

I took the opportunity some years ago to go back over my life in a rather long memoir – and found a title that suited, *An Everwidening Screen.* It seems to me that *Dear Movies* shows something of when and how my screen widened. When I screened *Nashville* (as I will recount later), amazed that everyone did not admire it as much as I did, one of the participants asserted (that's the word) that this said more about me than about the film. This time, I hope my letters say more about the films, although I now realise they say quite a deal about me. I like the serious but am a bit selective about comedy. I can be absorbed by the sombre but appreciate some lighter moments. I can immerse myself in history, but do not neglect current issues. I can get lost in fantasy of the mythological kind, not so much science-fiction. And I am comfortable with both religious and secular narratives. Narrative is key for me.

One final thought before the letters. Many people have asked me how I can possibly remember so much detail from the films, explaining that if they had seen more than one film on the same day, they would have mixed up the details by nightfall. That actually doesn't happen to me. I try to explain that seeing and appreciating a film (or not really liking it) is very much like meeting people. I would like to think that I meet people on their own terms, some immediate connections, some slower developments, acknowledging individuality, appreciating different styles, ways of communication (or not), idiosyncrasies, and valuing time spent with them, mostly anticipating more time with them. So, the same with the film – and some have remained powerfully present in my memory and imagination, even over many decades.

One other point: I tend not to have a photographic memory for particular sequences. Rather, I remember situations and themes. Different qualities of visuacy, as there are of literacy.

And 101 titles? Everybody has their top 100! In fact, glancing at my lists and noting omissions, there could easily be *Dear Movies 2.*

And that is something of why I embarked on this project of *Dear Movies.* Whew.

By the way, this is not a book you have to read from cover to cover. Of course, you could. But it is one of those books that you can dip into as you wish, at leisure, easily. On looking back at some of the letters, some sound a little preachy. I hope not too much.

I wanted to add some supportive thoughts from an actor/playwright/director who was also a cinema fan.

The cinema can become the interpreter of this natural propensity and be a place for reflection, for appeal to values, for invitation to dialogue and for communion... a cinema that considers only some aspects of the amazing complexity of the human being inevitably ends up being simplistic and does not provide a useful cultural service.

The cinema enjoys a wealth of languages, a multiplicity of styles and a variety of narrative forms that are truly great: from realism to fable, from history to science fiction, from adventure to tragedy, from comedy to news, from animated cartoon to documentary. It thus offers an incomparable storehouse of expressive means for portraying the various areas in which human beings find themselves and for interpreting their inescapable calling to the beautiful, the universal and the absolute.

The cinema can thus help to bring distant people together, to reconcile enemies, to promote a more respectful and fruitful dialogue between different cultures, by showing the way to a credible and lasting solidarity, the essential premise for a world of peace.

(John Paul II, Address to the International Cinema Conference, 2 December 1999.)

Earlier in the year (4 April 1999) he had addressed a long letter to artists. It included this statement: '...even when they explore the darkest depths of the soul or the most unsettling aspects of evil, artists give voice in a way to the universal desire for redemption'.

Uh-oh. I just used the word count and discovered that despite good intentions, this letter to you, dear reader, is already well over 1000 words. 1575! My apologies.

Peter Malone msc

Dear

2001: A SPACE ODYSSEY

A special confession for you, the confession you and director, Stanley Kubrick, would, I trust, like to hear.

You have been the constant answer for over fifty years to friends and associates who succumb to the friendly curiosity temptation to ask, "What is your favourite film?". And, in case I didn't get the point, they frequently add, "of all time".

As I confessed, the answer is you.

In fact, you are one of the first films I ever reviewed, going to the premiere at the Plaza Cinema in George Street, Sydney, April 1968. There was quite a crowd, one of the attractions being the screening in Cinerama, vastness even before the curtain opened. Our seats were very near to the screen, which means that I felt enveloped by you almost immediately and you never let up.

The trip home on the bus was rather anticlimactic. My very rational struggle with my rationalist confrère who really did not get you much at all but was open to any explanation that could help him come to terms with what he just sat through. A rational approach was not quite how I wanted to respond. In later writings, and in those justifications and/or explanations for that enquiry "of all time", I have always relied on the phrase "a cinema poem". And, if you simply or complexly describe/analyse a poem, you have done an academic exercise but not necessarily expressed appreciation of the poem.

It has to be suggestions, visual images, sounds and music, emotional moments (and, yes, finally, some ideas).

I had better admit disillusionment with your middle section when the real 2001 eventually came round. The reality was not at all like the cinema-poem! In fact, despite all the advances in technology, the world turned out to be much the same as ever. There was no space travel to provide those luxury space stations, no need to train flight and lounge assistants or dress them in what we were used to seeing in a futuristic way. That kind of 2001 is still a long way away.

And, of course, 2001 now has the touch of apocalyptic terror, 9/11.

But, the first section was wonderful, in emotion and in the imagination of evolution rather than a palaeontological checklist and identification of the various "ages". It was more than sufficient that you provided those sequences of the apes, attempts at community, hopes for a better future that might develop, but the reality of what we could call, or have called, "original sin". The great ape tossed his murderous bone into the air. One of the main products, not a by-product, of evolution is that human beings seem not to be able to live in peace. Rivalry, competitiveness, violence, brutality.

But, you are not without hope after this first wonderful section. Up went the bone into the air and, a moment that stays in many imaginations of cinema history, the bone transformed into the spacecraft and the stratosphere was as calm and melodious as the Blue Danube.

I won't remind you again of the 2001 section – that has gone into the cinema archives of non-fulfilled prophecies.

But, before venturing out into the extraordinary future, the vision of space and time that you suggested, once again poetically, (not to be mistaken for scientifically), I want to commend you on one of the most wonderful cinema symbols for me, the monolith.

Stanley Kubrick and Arthur C. Clarke in their pre-production musings and plans, came to grips with the reality of transcendence, of reality beyond our universe and our consciousness, something like what Thomas Aquinas said in the Middle Ages, "which we call God". Not that many of those millions who admired you identify the monolith with God but that, in retrospect, seems to be one of the most important things it did. You were a God-occasion for me.

Your monolith was certainly not the product of any evolution. It was too finely crafted. And it kept appearing in that planet of the apes. It was there. It was mysterious. Its presence took us symbolically beyond realism.

And there it was in your futuristic sequences. Many of the comments, including my own, marvelled about the space travel in the future, the speed through space, the beautiful lines of colour (which I realised had been there in black and white already in Kubrick's *Dr Strangelove*), the overwhelming rush to... ?

But, before you feel like accusing me of rhapsodising, I will admit to the fascination of the ape inheritance of rivalry and brutality continuing on in and beyond 2001. But, and this is the true fascination, the equivalent of the apes in the future is that cinematic arch-villain, HAL (and, yes, somebody did have to tell me that each of those letters follow IBM). There is rivalry from technology, the human-made machines with capacities beyond the human and a malevolence that has provided opportunity for continuing to overwhelm human benevolence.

You did want to be puzzling and challenging back there in 1968 with imaging a future that looked a great deal like classical 18th century settings, furniture, costumes... Was it the continuity of human nature but using a circular time span? Whatever it was, you suggested evolutionary continuity but also an experience of cultural recycling in future centuries.

And, of course, there it is again, the monolith, the transcendent in space, the transcendent in a savage past, the transcendent in a room in an elegant future. I remember that one of the divine qualities is omnipresence.

Hope. That is your final image and message. No matter what stage of evolutionary experience, cultural development, humans have lived in and no matter what the evil and malice, our universe and the human presence are continually reborn, the past being the womb of the future, and with the star child, huge up there on the Cinerama screen back then, promising re-birth.

I really hope this letter to you, 2001, shows you why your cinema-poem on the vastness of this Space Odyssey from the past to the future is my favourite "of all time".

Dear

THE OUTLAW JOSEY WALES

Not sure whether you are my favourite Western or not, but you could be. Of course, you have to stand in comparison with Clint Eastwood's other westerns, particularly those he directed.

What attracted me to you first of all was your presentation of Josey Wales as a Christ-figure. It still amazes me when I tell you that in 1976, when you were first released, I put it to some theology students that your first three minutes – the story of Josey's wife and son being killed by the marauding raiders and the pathos of his burying them – that these were significant indications that they should see him as a Christ-figure.

I suppose you appreciate what a Christ-figure is. While there are many portraits of Jesus himself in various biblical films, that Jesus is seen throughout various dramas, as an image, as a mysterious figure, and, of course, Jesus on the cross, these are what are called Jesus-figures, figures of Jesus himself. So, in novels, plays and films, characters who resembles Jesus – and you would want me to add "significantly and substantially" – could be called Christ-figures. I should mention to you that one of the benefits of leading workshops on Christ-figures is the revelation to the students themselves of what it is in Jesus that they admire, what words, what episodes, they are reminded of because of the Christ-figure they recognise.

And, just in case you are tempted to say that this is reading Christ-figures into the screenplay, I remind you that identifying Christ-figures and commenting on them is exegesis, reading the meaning out of the text (and I'm presuming you know the word 'eisegesis', which I am not promoting, the word for reading meaning into the text).

You were released three years after the first of the Christ-figure Clint Eastwood-directed westerns, *High Plains Drifter*. Actually, you might remember that there is a complication there. On the one hand, the figure that Clint plays, emerging as the spirit of a murdered man in a vengeful West, acts in the manner of Jesus by rescuing the poor and the lame, the widows and children in the town which he later calls 'Hell', the name painted on a sign at night, this sign painted red, the town set alight, all aflame by a burning lake. Which means that the high plains drifter is a complex character, a Christ-figure and saviour on the one hand; and on the other, a devil, Lucifer/Satan-figure wielding an angry whip on those he is destroying.

In fact, Clint followed up these themes more directly as the minister-gunfighter in *Pale Rider* with its biblical quotations and overtones – and then won an Oscar for the complexities of *Unforgiven*. It seems significant that he cast himself as the central character in all these films.

You will appreciate the comment made by the Archbishop of Melbourne at the time, Frank Little, who would enquire whenever I met him whether Clint Eastwood had made any soteriological westerns lately!

Looking back at yourself, you are probably puzzled why students in those days did not immediately pick up on the religious symbolism of those opening three minutes. What happened was that Clint – in grief for his wife and child – as he drags one of the bodies, a hand slips from out of the cover and, literally touchingly, he gently places the hand back at peace. At the graveside, he has made a makeshift cross out of two sticks. He says "Ashes to ashes, dust to dust" (and these written words don't do justice to his American accent and his distraught muttering and mumbling which means that local audiences often have to ask, "what did he say?"). And he adds, "The Lord he gives, The Lord he takes away". And, as he does so, he bends over the grave, the cross falling on his shoulders.

Nowadays you might say, "that was a bit obvious". It wasn't then.

As you continue, there are other indications of the Christ-figure. While Josey Wales is going on a quest of vengeance, his journey becomes something of a pilgrimage to salvation. He attracts such a rag-tag band around him, especially an old Indian chief who says that he has lost his edge because he can't creep up silently on people, escaping detection. There is a young woman who has mental limitations. There is a young soldier who has failed during the Civil War. They and others follow Josey (and just pronouncing 'Josey' does remind us more than a little of 'Jesus').

So, you showed Josey going about with evil intent but doing good. To that extent, he is clearly a variation on the high plains drifter.

Later in the film, Josey will exchange "words of life" with another chief. And, when the inevitable confrontation arises, Josey and his band against the raiders, his base is in a deserted church, the rifles pointing out from windows that are, in fact, cruciform.

Over the decades, I have been trying to do a bit of proselytising work for you and your reputation, urging people to watch you, definitely urging them to notice the Christ-resemblances. And, you will be pleased to know, that there has been considerable success.

After *Unforgiven*, Clint Eastwood has not neglected religious themes, his consideration of each side in the American war with the Japanese, *Flags of Our Fathers/ Letters from Iwo Jima*. He dramatised the mysteries of life and death, especially death, in *Hereafter*. And you might let *Gran Torino* know, Clint giving a wonderfully crusty performance, tangling with and helping to pastorally form a young priest, and Clint giving his life for his Asian neighbours, that it is near the top of my list for another *Dear Movie*. And, since I initially wrote to you, I have seen *The Mule*. Letters to come.

ANNA KARENINA

You were actually the first film to come to mind when thinking about a project of letter writing to films which had been (and still are) important to me, formative films so to speak, films that were enjoyable, films that were likeable.

Actually, likeable is not the first word that comes to mind concerning you. Tolstoy created a very serious novel with Anna at the centre, a story of love, fidelity and infidelity, the thwarting of love – even to death. No, likeable is certainly not the first word to describe you. But, you were and are a most powerful film.

One of the main points to bring to your attention is that I actually saw you on first release, 1948, which means that I was eight years old or turning nine. Not exactly the age to be going to see *Anna Karenina*. So, what we were doing at the *Amusu* theatre in Anzac Parade in Sydney's Maroubra Junction, I don't know. I was not there by myself. Philip was there. And so were several cousins who were living in the house with us after our mother's death. And why was the Amusu showing Anna Karenina at a Saturday afternoon matinee? Who knows!

When checking my conscience and moral sensitivities in the past, I have had to acknowledge my selfishness while watching you. Some of the youngsters needed to go out to the toilet. I certainly did not want to go – and rationalised my situation by delegating, perhaps to Philip, that he should accompany them to the toilet and leave me unimpeded fully free to stay in Russia.

But, for me, you will always be most powerful. Looking back, I have little idea of how well I understood the characters and the plot. I'm now thinking about your plot in hindsight because not only did I read the novel in 1959 but it was on our syllabus for English I at the Australian National University in 1960. And, of course, there have been several versions. But, for me, you are the Best. And Vivien Leigh is Anna Karenina brought fully to life. (I knew there had been Greta Garbo as Anna in the 1930s but saw her later in life. And, in reviewing days, there was Jacqueline Bissett in the 1980s, Sophie Marceau in the 1990s (my least liked), very young Keira Knightly for the 21st century as well as the Russian film set at the beginning of the 20th century where Karenin and Vronsky find themselves at war in the Crimea together, memories of Anna and her influence on their lives.)

One of the side benefits of seeing you at a young age is that czarist Russia was present in my imagination quite early in my life – so there was no difficulty in my being at home in the world of *War and Peace* (reading the novel, seeing the Audrey Hepburn and Henry Fonda version, watching the Russian Sergei Bondarchuk's version, the 2016 BBC miniseries), in the world of Rasputin stories, Nicholas and Alexandra, and their deaths.

But, it is your image of Anna deciding to go to her death. The black-and-white photography is still powerful. Vivien Leigh as Anna is on the rail tracks. The train is behind her, the steam engine ready to leave the station, her standing with a mixture of emotions that the performance and the director ask and persuade us to empathise with as we imagine them. I can't remember how much of the train actually hitting Anna there is in the film – but, that does not matter, it did and Anna is dead.

In fact, this sequence was already so vivid in my mind that when I read the novel about ten years later, during our seminary holiday together at Shoreham on Victoria's Westernport Bay, the sun shining brightly, the atmosphere of quiet under the trees, reading the episode of Anna's death for the first time had such an effect on me that I just could not sit in the chair. I had to stand up. I had to walk around. I had to deal with my now older impression of Anna's death and her reasons, the consequences for her, for her children, for her husband, for Vronsky.

But, as I read, as I wandered around trying to deal with what I had read, there again was Vivien Leigh, in black-and-white, standing on the tracks, bringing Tolstoy to life – and too overpowering death.

Sometimes I wonder what my impression would have been had I seen you later in life. Would you have had that overwhelming impact? Would I have been able to absorb Tolstoy's themes in a more cerebral way, allowing for the emotions?

That is, of course, something I'll never know. What I do know is what I felt in 1948 and how that initial impression has stayed with me even as I write you this letter.

Dear

THE MAN WHO KNEW TOO MUCH

Yes, the reason I'm writing to you is Alfred Hitchcock. I suppose I'm wondering why I look back upon you with the most affection for a Hitchcock thriller. After all, you would be considered average, I suppose, on lists by the respected movie critics.

Of course, I have enjoyed seeing practically all of Hitchcock's films over many decades, some of the silents from the England-Germany days, the range of British thrillers from the 1930s including, of course, *The 39 Steps*. The range of American thrillers from the 1940s, starting with *Rebecca*, are also highly enjoyable as well, including *Spellbound* with the touches of Salvador Dali Surrealism.

Actually, I'm rather stuck in the 1950s. Robert Walker focused on Farley Granger playing tennis while everybody's heads swivelled to watch each return of the ball in *Strangers on a Train*. And Grace Kelly. A touch hard to believe that she could be part of a murder plot in *Dial M for Murder*. Easier to watch her cool glamour in *Rear Window*. And, a group of us watched *To Catch a Thief* at the Lyric theatre in George Street and proceeded to sit through the next screening.

But then you were screened at Paramount's prestige cinema, the Prince Edward, when Noreen Hennessey rose from the depths smiling and glowing, playing the organ, *The Man Who Knew Too Much.*

Was it just the right time? I was turning 17, preparing to do the Leaving Certificate, the final exams at the end of school – and, I remember, that I read an Agatha Christie novel every afternoon during that exam month. So, a bit of a blend of Hitchcock and Christie. (I hadn't seen the 1934 version with Peter Lorre, something to come later.) So, you made an indelible entry on my imagination – enhanced by *Que sera, sera.*

You fitted well into my enjoyment of the big-budget films of these years, the introduction of Cinemascope, experiments with three-D, and Paramount using the clarity, as here, of Vistavision. The settings were a mixture of the exotic and the mundane, a dramatic blend, scenes in the Middle East for tourists James Stewart and Doris Day, a black-faced Daniel Gelin stabbed, struggling along the sand towards them, reaching out, James Stewart bewildered, touching the man's face and the make-up coming off, smearing on his hand. Who could resist this opening?

And the mysterious London settings? Bernard Miles, with his distinctive accent, and Brenda de Banzie had been in so many British films, character actors. So, what were they doing here, ministering in a church, connected with spies – and the memory of Brenda de Banzie coming to the front of the church, staring at her husband, just moving her eyes to the side to indicate dangers...

By that stage, James Stewart had become part of our going to the pictures, his appearing in the number of films we screened at school. I hadn't seen *Rope* yet but had been thrilled by *Rear Window* (and had better remind you that most of those critics who don't give you such a rating usually rate *Vertigo* very high on their list for some Hitchcock achievement – but there is that sudden, and, for me, too brisk ending of *Vertigo* with the nun and the belltower, frightening Kim Novak, which brought the contemplation of passion, questioning of identity to a too-dramatically hasty conclusion.

Having lived in London for many years and, travelling by bus from Hammersmith to central London, routes 9 and 10 (10 now abolished), I passed the Albert Hall countless times, going in and coming out. In the 1960s, I had gone with a friend from Australia to the end of the finale of *The Proms* and we snuck in the open doors as the audience was trailing out. I didn't think of you every time I went past the Albert Hall but this happened many, many times, a fleeting memory, a conscious recollection, a satisfaction, one of your key scenes. My eyes looked up for Doris...

It was Doris Day, who had brought 'Que Sera, sera' to life. Now she was desperate to warn the victim of an assassination attempt, sitting there in a box in the Albert Hall. What could she do? What was she going to do? And then there was that dramatic silence, the unapplauded pause between music movements – and Doris and her resounding scream that alerted the target and threw the assassin off-balance as he fired his shot. Marvellous.

I'm glad to be able to tell you that four years later, on summer holidays at Chevalier College in Bowral, we saw a number of films. And there you were, *The Man Who Knew Too Much*, bringing back wonderful memories, re-living the past and, I can assure you, enjoying the screening and screaming anew, seeing you once again.

Dear

INTERIORS

From the very first time I saw you and then started to read the hostile reviews, I have had a great sympathy for you. This might be something of a consolation: I can say that you are my favourite Woody Allen film. I do like the comedies, of course, the "gub" in *Take the Money and Run*, the absurdity of Latin American dictators in *Bananas*, Jeff Daniels coming down from the screen in *The Purple Rose of Cairo*, expatriates in the 1930s, *Midnight in Paris*... at least, one film a year for fifty years.

So, what is it with you that makes you so special? Your title indicates that Woody Allen is trying to explore something beyond the jokes, beyond the wit, beyond his everlasting cleverness (which I do enjoy). Sometimes, when Woody Allen tries for the serious, he is not so well appreciated. Do you remember the film that came after you, *Stardust Memories* (another film, Fellini-esque, that is high on my list) where there is the complaint voiced that people preferred Woody Allen's older funny films? Perhaps the best combination was in *Crimes and Misdemeanours* (and one could write a thesis on this film and its many variations he used in subsequent serio-comic ventures).

I actually saw you in the United States, an outsider appreciating what you were trying to do, rather than just wishing for American humour. And outsider is a key word. You were acknowledging your debt to a Scandinavian outsider, Woody Allen's admiration for the Swedish master-director, Ingmar Bergman. Some years later, he was to continue this homage in *A Midsummer Night's Sex Comedy*.

Would you have an opinion on which Bergman films are key for understanding and appreciating you? One thought would be that it is some of his films of the 1960s, his trilogy with their evocative names, *Through a Glass Darkly, Winter Light, Silence*. These could well be used as subtitles for you, aspects of *Interiors*. Another Bergman film from the 1960s that comes to mind is *Persona* (and some of the stills, especially used for advertising *Persona*, seem to be the model for some of your posters).

I should commend you for your colour photography even though at this time, Woody Allen was experimenting with black-and-white in *Manhattan* and *Stardust Memories*. The reason that I note this is that my favourite Ingmar Bergman film (and surely due for a letter like this) is photographed in vivid and beautiful colour, emphases of red, black, white, *Cries and Whispers*.

While I liked you very much right from the start, something else happened in my life at this time which connected me to your characters and themes. About a month after seeing you, while doing a sabbatical at Graduate Theological Union, Berkeley, and being an enthusiast for themes in Jung's psychology, I was introduced to an American application of Jung's theories, the work of two American women, mother and daughter, Katherine Briggs and Isabel Briggs Myers (whose names are incorporated with the psychological type indicator that they developed).

Let me tell you what I mean. By way of an example. I found it something of a revelation to realise that I identified more with introversion than extroversion (generally something of a minority position). I also identified with being intuitive, relishing intuitions, hunches, making connections (like the epigraph for E. M. Forster's *Howards End*: Only Connect). Another realisation-discovery was that I much preferred the approach of let's get on with the job rather than asking (and delaying) whether there is any more information or data that I should consider before making a decision!

And, so, the example from you. Several of the characters in your screenplay are introverts. And some of the daughters, especially one played by Diane Keaton, are also intuitive. The father of the family, E. G. Marshall, is separating from his somewhat neurotic wife, Geraldine Page. He has taken up with a new friend played by Maureen Stapleton. And the thing is that she is not introverted (to say the least). She is exuberantly outgoing, enthusiastic about living, intuitions don't bother her because she is definitely alive in the present and enjoying it. She begins to transform the lives of the family – and the superior daughters, perhaps taking refuge in the ivory tower of introversion, do not take kindly to her interventions.

And, doesn't it seem to you quite amazing that of all people, Woody Allen could write such an extroverted character!

And that is one of the fascinations of watching you over again. The psychological portraits of each of the characters are so well delineated, their strengths, their lack of development of other characteristics. And the image from a poster keeps coming back, the profiles of three sisters standing inside a room, inside their personal and family interiors – but at a window, looking out – at what?

Dear

SILENCE

For me, one of your great qualities is the Catholic sensibility. I don't want to be patronising but I do want to say that I am very glad you were released in 2016, a contribution to the development of Catholic sensibility in film, acknowledging the sins of the church's past and its sometimes groping for the truth, acknowledging that there is a deep sense of the transcendent, and a profound faith that underlies the experience of so many individuals and communities in our fractured church.

One of the advantages was that the press preview took place almost three months before you were released. This meant responding to you without any influence from critics and reviewers, either for or against. The preview was an opportunity to see, feel, reflect, absorb... and time to form a personal response before writing a review.

One of the things that occurred to me is that the first two hours of your drama reflected a Catholic Church of the past – and not such a dim distant past either, a past that I grew up in. There was a sense of the inevitability of martyrdom in so many of your characters, and not just the

Jesuit missionaries, but also the lay converts with their deep commitment, no matter what the trials and tests.

In what can be now called the days before the Second Vatican Council, there had been an underlying spirituality of willingness to die for the faith, perpetual commemoration of the early martyrs, the victims of anti-church politics throughout the centuries, from Thomas a Becket through to those who were persecuted and killed during the Soviet Communist regimes. The heroes when I was at school included Cardinal Mindszenty of Hungary, Archbishop Beran of Czechoslovakia, Cardinal Stepinac of Yugoslavia. In that anti-Communist atmosphere of the 1940s and 1950s, there were many films that reinforced the stamina of our faith, Charles Bickford as Cardinal Mindszenty in *Guilty of Treason* (and the fictionalised version by Bridget Boland in *The Prisoner*, with Alec Guinness as the prisoner).

And, as I watched your first two hours, it occurred to me that this was the spirituality in which Martin Scorsese grew up, part of his movie-going, part of the reading in which he was encouraged by the young local priest he admired. They say that Scorsese used to sketch film storyboards for different scenes, imagining movies about Rome, the martyrs and the early church. But, despite his time in the junior seminary in New York and his pondering the possibility of being a priest, he lost his church practice (perhaps not beliefs) at the very time that the renewal was starting for the Council, in the early 1960s.

I don't know whether you would agree, but there has always been something old-church about Scorsese's theology and spirituality, his use of cross icons in *Boxcar Bertha* and *Cape Fear*. And there is that American-Italianate focus on blood in *Last Temptation*, flowing from the pierced heart of Jesus, flowing from the Eucharistic bread as the disciples bit into it.

So, what was really challenging about you is the last forty minutes, very much the sensibility of the 21st century church, issues of faith, confession of faith, denial of faith, the witness to faith even in denial. (And there is always a distraction to think about some of Graham Greene's theology in such novels/films as *The Heart of the Matter*, Scobie willing to risk damnation by going to Communion in the state of mortal sin for the peace and love of his wife.)

Scorsese had been a fan of Endo's novel for many decades, fascinated by its themes of faith and church. I am glad that he made you later than he intended, drawing on his own personal religious experience in his later decades, on developments of thinking within the church (especially fostered by his friendship with James Martin SJ, advisor for the film).

I became especially conscious of this when SIGNIS, the World Catholic Association for Communication, hosted the director at their Québec International Congress, 2017. There was a screening. Scorsese was interviewed on stage, not only talking about the film but also going back into his childhood and adolescence, his awareness of church, admiration for clergy, that was part of his making this film. In fact, he attended the Mass with us at Québec Cathedral, came to a dinner, praying the grace before the dinner, recipient of an award, and acknowledged by a worldwide Catholic organisation for his contribution to film-making and the Catholic sensibility.

Your last section focuses on the faith, not just of the Jesuits, though that is central, but on the faith of the Japanese converts, their fidelity, the attempts by the authorities to scandalise them by pressurising the priests to deny their faith, to stomp on the image of Jesus. The laity remained faithful – a deep pocket of Catholics for 200 years around Nagasaki.

In recent times, there have been many "Faith-based" films from the US. They are dramatisations of Christian values, interpretations of the Scriptures, taken literally, dramatic exhortations to belief and commitment and values-oriented lives. They could be called "worthy". However, you are quite a different faith-based film, probing the nature of belief, commitment, understanding, grappling with the complexities of persecution, pressures to denial, schemes to undermine faith.

You don't have a black-and-white conclusion. Faith and commitment to you Indicate that they are not cut-and-dried matters – and that we humans are always involved in the struggle between belief and the expression of belief, sometimes taking mis-steps, sometimes making mis-judgments, sometimes scandalising as we try to exercise our conscience between the demands of experience and the nobility of authenticity and integrity.

Much appreciated.

Dear

CRIES AND WHISPERS

You may be surprised, perhaps even shocked, when I tell you that you are my choice for my Ingmar Bergman film. Over many decades, with such a vast canon of cinema masterpieces, Bergman was one of the greats of the 20th century. Critics are always referring to *The Seventh Seal* or *Wild Strawberries*. They often enthuse with amazement at the many powerful dramas, especially focusing on the silence of the divine in our world, from the 1960s. Then there are the wonderful family sagas where he remembers Swedish society and his upbringing.

Accepting all that and agreeing with it, I still choose you.

In my memory, I am still drawn into the world that Bergman has created through you. It is a world of beautiful and striking (and Oscar-winning) colour. There is so much red. There is so much white. And there is also black. And, because you are a period piece, the costumes, hairstyles and make up, decor, make an impact and are memorable. One also has to mention, more than mention, your outstanding cast, Bergman's admired actresses, Ingrid Thulin, Liv Ullman,

Harriet Andersson and the very moving performance by Kari Sylwan as Anna, the maid.

You are a film about illness, suffering and death. You are also a film about selfishness, raising the question as to whether the selfish can be converted, even in the face of self-sacrificing suffering. In a world of film violence and brutality, the death of Agnes, Harriet Andersson at her most moving, with overtones of the title for Jesus, Lamb of God, Agnus Dei, is extraordinarily harrowing, a reminder of how devastating death can be.

While Bergman had a Lutheran and religious background, his interest in religion was far less explicit. However, the prayer by the pastor during Agnes' funeral is a profound expression of faith, questioning faith. In case there are other readers of this letter to you, I include the text.

If it is so that you have gathered our suffering in your poor body, if it is so that you have borne it with you through death, If it is so that you have gathered our suffering in your poor body, if it is so that you have borne it with you through death, if it is so that you meet God over there in the other land, if it is so that He turns His face towards you, if it is so that you can speak the language that this God understands, if it is so that you can, then speak to this God, if it is so, pray for us... Pray for us who are left here on the dark, dirty earth under an empty and cruel Heaven. Lay your burden of suffering at God's feet and ask Him to pardon us. Ask Him to free us at last from our anxiety, our weariness and our deep doubt. Ask Him for a meaning to our lives. Agnes, you who have suffered so unimaginably and so long, you must be worthy to plead.

And Bergman, further to his way with words, drawing on his skill with images and symbols, offers great meaning to the life and death of Agnes by her being laid on the lap of Anna, the maid, her caring and maternal nature dramatised by her full breast. It is the parallel of Jesus on his mother's lap, a Pietà.

It is no wonder that you would have a place of honour on any list of religious films.

Like Jesus, Agnes came into a world of sin and selfishness, embodied by her two sisters, elegantly coiffed and dressed in immaculate white, superior in manner, wilful, self-absorbed. Which means that you are very much a Good Friday religious film, Agnes very much a suffering Christ-figure, a figure for possible redemption of others. And, while Bergman admires Agnes, he does not seem to be optimistic as regards her sisters' hearts being touched.

While Bergman's use of the colour white may not indicate either holiness or purity, he did make a comment about his use of the colour red. He noted that the soul was like a damp membrane, all red.

A final compliment. At the time of your release, the expectations for a Christ-figure were that it would be male. Agnes is a powerful reminder that a Christ-figure is also female.

Dear

SINGIN' IN THE RAIN

First of all, I want to reassure you that I did not have a deprived childhood. We were a more or less middle-class family in Sydney, not too much money, but enough, enough to go twice a week to the pictures during school holidays home from boarding school. We also had a film almost every week at school. Which means that we did see quite a few. But that is just a prelude to what I wanted to tell you.

It was very popular in the late 1940s and early 1950s to enjoy the MGM musicals. Off we went to the St James Theatre in Elizabeth Street, but for the slightly more highbrow musicals (think *The Bandwagon*) to the Liberty in Pitt Street – or else up to Bondi Junction to the Regal. I think we saw most of them, plenty of Fred Astaire (*Easter Parade*), plenty of Gene Kelly (*Brigadoon*), Kathryn Grayson, Jane Powell, Ann Miller, Ann Blythe and Mario Lanza – and, of course, Betty Hutton and Howard Keel pounding it out in *Annie Get your Gun*.

Actually, that sounded like a second prelude to what I've been hesitating to say: during our school holidays, we never saw you. I don't know how we missed out, but we did.

In fact, I didn't see you until I was in my 30s, 20 years later, when those critics who like to contribute to lists of their best films usually nominated you as the best musical.

Not that you aren't!

However, seeing you in the 1970s meant that I was probably much better prepared to enjoy and to appreciate. So, what is there to say, except quite an amount of indulgence in reminiscing about all those wonderful ingredients that make you such an entertainment.

I realised later that the song by Arthur Freed and Herb Nacio Brown had been around for over twenty years before the film was made. In fact, several of the songs had already made an appearance in *Broadway Melody of 1929*, one of the earliest Oscar-winners for Best Film. But, with the popularity of the musicals by 1950, it seemed to MGM that it would be good idea to find a vehicle for those songs. So there we were with *Good Mornin', I Was Meant for You, Make' em Laugh...* As songs with tunes go, you were really very fortunate to have this selection.

Well, we all expected the best from Gene Kelly, dancing, choreography, co-directing with Stanley Donen (and pleasantly passable singing voice). But, when he took things literally and began singing and dancing in the rain, it was a showstopper – and, twenty years after that, it was a showstopper, show-shocker, with Malcolm McDowell as the droog, Alex, singing and dancing mayhem, re-immortalising the song, with some touches of "ultra-violence" for Stanley Kubrick in *A Clockwork Orange.*

But, back to the bright side. Debbie Reynolds full of chirp and energy turning 20, singing and dancing, keeping pace with Gene Kelly. And, very high on the list, is Donald O'Connor's presence but, especially, his hilarious blend of athleticism and pratfalls, clowning in *Make 'em Laugh.*

Actually, the plot was entertaining in Hollywood sending itself up, about how the studios responded to the coming of sound. And the success of this part of the plot is very much due to Jean Hagan using the most awful squeaky, scratchy voice that made her the literal laughing stock of audiences for the costume drama they were watching – and for Debbie to have to lip sync behind the screen. Jean Hagan was nominated for a Best Supporting Actress for this role and, with all respect to Gloria Grahame, who even did have a film produced about her, *Film Stars Don't Die in Liverpool*, Jean Hagan should have won.

And, whether it was for box office insurance or just that Gene Kelly liked to have a Cyd Charisse dance number in his films, quite outside the main thrust of the plot, she also does a showstopper, reminding audiences what a talented dancer she was.

Of course, I'm not telling you anything you don't know. It's just a brief summary of who you actually are and a reminder to anyone who should find themselves reading this letter just how good a Hollywood musical should be – and can be, and is.

Dear

MURIEL'S WEDDING

I hope no Australian is surprised to find a letter to you. In fact, I would hope that every Australian would have you close to the top of any list of films that they enjoyed and admired. At the time, 1994, I did not have high expectations of you. Apart from a supporting role in *Spotswood*, what had Toni Collette been in! And Rachel Griffiths! Plenty from Bill Hunter – and we always expected the best from him.

I had better tell you that I actually saw you twice within a few months. And the reaction and response was quite different each time. That doesn't often happen – but it was the circumstances for each viewing that made the difference and helped develop a great appreciation for what you presented and how you did it.

In fact, over the decades I have been sitting in my room, working at the desk, television on, and your opening credits begin. I stop. I begin to watch, continue to watch, enjoy you all over again, and remembering the initial effect you had me – and how much in P. J. Hogan's screenplay there is to reflect on.

So, the two viewings.

The first was particularly festive. You had been selected to be the opening film for the Melbourne International Film Festival of 1994. The audience was in a cheerful mood, pre-screening drinks, ready for some laughter, not quite as ready for some ironies that were to confront them, forewarned, however, that there were to be some Abba songs (and, you will remember, that at much the same time Australian audiences responded to elaborate and colourful (and send-up) songs and dancing in *Priscilla, Queen of the Desert*.)

There were quite a few, relying on the continued popularity of Abba (and this was a couple of years before *Mamma Mia*) but Toni's and Rachel's enthusiasm (and the louder than loud costumes) did them justice. If you had stood outside the screening and questioned those coming out for a mini-review, there would have been unanimity in audiences happily commenting on how much they enjoyed the film, how funny it was, a good old send-up Australian story. And it was.

An opportunity offered itself some months later for another viewing. Up at the Village Cinemas at Doncaster's Shopping Town, I had been watching *Ace Ventura, Pet Detective*, not having been acclimatised at this stage to Jim Carrey and his faces and antics (though coming to accept them as time went on) and feeling quite isolated, unable to raise a laugh to join in the hilarious mood of the rest of the audience.

I came out a bit disheartened and noticed that there was a session featuring you about to start in a few minutes. As reviewers, we have been blessed with passes to go into most films at most cinemas (complimentary tickets, that is), so in I went.

Maybe it was the non-response to Jim Carrey and the zany activities of *Ace Ventura*, but it was not your funny side that I began to notice, the poking fun at Muriel's ingenuous attitudes and awkwardness ("Muriel, you're awful"), not the Abba performances, but your permeating sadness. Yes, you had a great deal of humour, a great deal of critical humour especially through Bill Hunter and his character, two-timing, putting down his daughter, neglecting his wife. There was also the send-up of Muriel's bitchy, alleged-girlfriends.

I'm sure I noticed her the first time I saw you but she made a powerful impression this time. I'm meaning Muriel's mother, Betty, played with enormous pathos by Jeannie Drynan. Her humdrum life as a housewife, her having to support her frequently insufferable husband, her care about her children but their not responding to her becomes your core. And, by the time the final part of the film comes and Betty kills herself, I was wondering why I found you so funny in the first place and that that was what I remembered most strongly. How could I have missed Betty, her sadness, unrequited, opting out of that sad life?

I did want to tell you that because it is very important to me back then and still is whenever you turn up on the television or when people comment about your place in Australian cinema.

There is one other thing I wanted to tell you that also has a great deal of pathos. It is about Muriel herself. She has hopes and dreams but is not the type of woman who will fulfil them. Rather, marriage had become such a rainbow goal in life, that she did not realise that walking down the aisle, Toni Collette memorably glowing and smiling at everyone in the congregation, was just a wedding – the first step in the life of marriage.

Why I mention this, and you may be surprised, is a connection with men and women who are eager to be engaged and married, but also priests and members of religious orders who go through years of training and, when they are ordained or make their first religious vows, may not realise until it is too late that their whole goal was not living out of any priesthood or religious service but simply to have a wedding ceremony, to be ordained, to make a profession. Like Muriel, they hadn't given much attention at all to what was to happen afterwards. They had achieved a goal, but…

Separation, divorce, annulment, or dispensation from religious commitment and bonds and a somewhat disillusioning discovery that there was more to life than they anticipated.

This makes you sound like a very serious film – and funnily enough, you are.

Dear

JIRGA

The first news I heard of you was from the publicist who contacted me because of the religious connection. She pointed out that the father of your director, Benjamin Gilmour, was a minister of religion and that this could be a significant point for promotion. Press notes include the fact that your director himself had worked as a medical attendant and, for a time, worked with Mother Teresa in Calcutta.

There was a Vimeo link for me.

My desk and computer were not the easiest locations for watching you. However, you did, one might say, transcend the limitations. The location photography in Afghanistan itself (and later interviews revealed how difficult it was for your director to film, moving from initial attempts in Pakistan, concealing movement and the filming) was really very beautiful. There was also the authentic feel in the crowded Afghan cities, as if we had visited Kabul itself, but also the sweep and freedom beyond the cities, mountains, rivers, deserts and local villages. We were there.

You have also been important for Australian awareness and conscience. Your opening raid sequence, filmed in green nightlight, the uncertainty of who was who, where the threat to the military, decisions to shoot, was powerfully atmospheric. But, then there was the transition to the Australian soldier, Michael Wheeler, coming to Afghanistan, making contacts in the city, staying at a hotel, going to the bazaars, trying to persuade a taxi driver to take him into the countryside. This all sets up a puzzle for the audience. Who? Why?

When the members of the Australian Catholic Office for Film and Broadcasting held their annual meeting in 2018 to make an award for the Australian film of the year, I thought it important to nominate you, if not for the prize (which, in fact, went to indigenous issues for *Sweet Country*), then for a special commendation. And this was accepted. So, you are on our list of honours.

And then, at much the same time, you won an AACTA award for the best independent film. A good example of like minds, religious and secular.

While the scenes out in the countryside with the taxi driver were happily humane, despite the taxi driver's reluctance, but with moments of joy, moments of prayer, music and song, moments reflecting the long traditions of conflict in the area, it was the mission of Michael that arrested and held our attention.

As Mike Wheeler continues his journey on foot through the desert, we realise that he is on a pilgrimage, to go back to the village, to confess, appear before the Jirga, the Council of Elders, for them to decide his fate.

For a Catholic watching the film, the parallel with the Sacrament of Penance becomes ever more clear. In this sense, the film does serve as a paradigm for the Sacrament. There is the offence, the perpetrator of the killing deciding that he has "sinned". He has examined his conscience quite profoundly which leads him back to the Jirga meeting which is his confessional. He is sorry for what he has done. He has repented. But this is not enough. He needs to confess aloud, to acknowledge his sin. He certainly has a firm purpose of amendment. He wants to atone – although some of the locals note that the money he has brought is something of a curse and we see some of it blowing, blowing away, in the wind. He wants to make reparation and to perform a penance.

He experiences both condemnation and forgiveness – and, in the ritual styles of the Middle East, an animal is sacrificed, shedding its blood, symbol of the suffering and reconciliation.

So, you are well worth seeing as a film, brief, some beauty, some dread. A non-religious audience watching you would appreciate the humane themes while the Christian audience, especially those with a sacramental tradition, would appreciate how the pattern of penance and reconciliation is played out before their eyes.

An unexpected joy, a profound values-challenge.

Dear

GALLIPOLI

You have an important title, an important name. At least for us Australians. Most of the rest of the world does not immediately recognise you (and many mispronounce you). But, since 1915, World War I, Turkey, young Australian and New Zealand soldiers, poor British strategies and misjudgments, a military defeat, you are a hallowed name.

Most of us who are older grew up with the name Gallipoli, a powerful awareness of Anzac Day, the commemoration of Anzac Day, Dawn Ceremonies, veterans in procession in the city streets, at small town war memorials. It quickly became a national day, a day of national pride, especially with World War II coming only twenty plus years later.

But, even before Australia's involvement in the Vietnam war, something had happened. Questioning, criticism, disillusionment, mockery. Many said it was the 1960s. But, even before that, some changes in attitude. As regards Anzac Day, sixty years later it was a mixed celebration. A post-World War II generation who read this letter, might remember a significant play, quite popular (even scandalous) in the early 1960s, Alan Seymour's *The One Day of the Year*. It incorporated the Dawn Services, re-living the memories, the acknowledgment of the sacrifices made – but, in the play, there was a younger generation, university students, who were disillusioned, mocking the oldies, especially from World War II who used the occasion to meet old friends but also to get grossly drunk – and loud. However, Seymour also paid a great tribute to the initial Anzacs, his old character, Wacka, who was indeed present and has a powerful scene for himself, his reminiscing about the night, the day, fears, action, almost mystical memories.

During the 1970s, sometimes it seemed that the actual events might be obliterated from memory. I would like to tell you that during an introductory theology course I taught for those beginning seminary or training in a religious order, *The Mystery of Christ*, we had a play reading of Seymour's drama in the first term, an attempt to get to grips with our national theme.

But, we were somewhat unprepared when you were released in 1981. You made a huge impact. You contributed to the altering of the perspective on the Anzacs, a renewed meaning for Anzac Day. I remember being very much affected by the screening for the Australian Film Institute awards, sitting stunned at the end when Mark Lee goes over the top, shot, body halted in mid-air, freeze-frame... A very well-dressed gentleman sitting next to me then bent over and, partly under his breath, desperately muttered "shit". Yes.

In interviews, director Peter Weir, spoke of his deeply personal experiences as he walked the beach of Gallipoli, remembering the past, discovering a bottle of Eno's Fruit Salts from over sixty years earlier, recounting something of a mystical awareness, the sense of the spirit of the Anzacs still present on the beach.

You certainly contain that spirit. Actually, David Williamson's screenplay also injects a great deal of realism into the events, the atmosphere and experiences leading up to the events, the freedom of the young Australians abroad, a capsule of the history that should be remembered in later multicultural times. Only fifteen years after Australia's federation, who were these young men, particularly from Western Australia, coming in from the farms to enlist – and explaining to the old bloke wandering the desert that the Germans were coming to take the land and he nonchalantly remarking that they were welcome to it! Lies about age, the enthusiasm of Mel Gibson and Mark Lee, the middle section in Cairo, larrikins abroad, football under the shadow of the Pyramids, and enthusiasm of patriotic youth.

Your final section is most moving. The men at play swimming in the ocean. The basic elements of the trenches.

Talk amongst the men, praying the Our Father. The officers making the decisions, their subordinates reluctant, the tension before going over the top, the whistle, the men climbing, shouting, killed.

In trying to get to grips with Gallipoli, I was introduced at that time to a word coined by J. R. R. Tolkien. It was "Eu-catastrophe". By that he meant a disastrous experience which somehow rather leads to good. That "Eu" is from the Greek word for "well". Was nationalism born at Gallipoli? The national spirit? Does this mean that the Anzac experience is a "Eu-catastrophe"? In fact, for Tolkien himself, the passion, death and resurrection of Jesus was a "Eu-catastrophe". The linking of Jesus' experience to that of Gallipoli is important to a Christian response to Anzac Day.

Australians and New Zealanders are grateful to you,

Dear

BORN ON THE FOURTH OF JULY

It is a bit embarrassing to tell you (although there is something good at the end of this confession) that during the 1990s when so many people were criticising Tom Cruise (not that that this has necessarily stopped – a good friend of mine can refer to him only as "Midget Impossible"), I used to praise you as the film in which Tom Cruise acted! He certainly did, and quite powerfully.

While my favourite Vietnam war film is always *Apocalypse Now*, my favourite Vietnam war and post-Vietnam America has to be you, although your director, Oliver Stone, opened up the war in *Platoon*, took it further in *Heaven and Earth*. I'm going to tell you about a favourite scene later, one that I find most moving, even tearfully, and that I've used in workshops with parents. But, I want to pay a tribute to Oliver Stone (and his gallery of cinema portraits of US presidents) for bringing so much of Vietnam, the experiences and the consequences, to our memories and concern. I can't quite believe it when I tell you that I actually joined a group outside the Canberra Rex Hotel in 1966 to protest Lyndon Johnson's presence and our conscription commitment to "All the Way with LBJ". That year and the next I was teaching senior students English literature and the year after that some of them were already in Vietnam.

So, looking at the story of Ron Kovic and the enthusiasm of those young high school students enlisting, believing that the good old US was always right, training, going to war in a faraway and almost mysterious country, certainly with a mysterious enemy, the shootings, the disasters of friendly fire, injuries, wounds, the painful struggles for physical and psychological rehabilitation, became real and vivid for me.

I suppose I was disappointed to find that the Kovic family was Catholic, and that Ron's mother was such a hard Catholic, harsh in her exasperation at the behaviour of her wounded son, her anger in response, wanting to oust him from the house, and his desperation in pointing to Jesus on the cross, telling her that Jesus could come down and rise again but that he was stuck in his wheelchair. But if ever there was a powerful scene of family conflict, you provided one in that encounter between Ron Kovic and his mother.

Kovic experienced what the psalm despairingly prays, "Out of the depths, I cry to you, Lord hear my voice". But, whatever providence there was for him, he was able to come to life again. You provided great scenes of Ron Kovic and his commitment to anti-war campaigns.

But, I want to tell you about the scene that always comes to mind when I hear your name mentioned. Ron has come to admit to himself that he killed a soldier in friendly fire. He summons courage for a visit, wheels himself up the driveway to the house of the parents, talking in a quiet way about the dead boy, his life and the family pride, his widow and the young baby, appreciating their hospitality. And then – and I feel quite emotional now as I say this – comes the parents' response, the father being stoic and telling him that they don't have to go into this conversation, the widow says she understands but she cannot forgive. When Ron Kovic admits that it was he who fired the shot, you show a close-up of the mother's face collapsing, in grief-awareness, and, if ever there was a scene of forgiveness, she sympathetically tells him that she realises the pain he's been going through. One of the great emotional film sequences.

You might like to know this as a postscript about this scene. In the 90s, I was invited to do a seminar for the parents of youngsters who were about to make their first confession, the parents not too hot in their knowledge of the sacraments at all. I showed them some catechetical clips but it was your scene, this scene that brought home to them realities of confessing, forgiving, trying to atone that meant the most to them.

Dear

FIRST REFORMED

It is only just four hours since I finished watching you, so much to reflect on. In fact, sitting in the cinema before you opened, I had something of a premonition that I would be writing you a letter and it was not too far into the screening before this was confirmed. I had heard that critics were very praiseworthy about your approach to Christianity, Paul Schrader's approach, remembering his Michigan Calvinism from long ago, incorporated into *Taxi Driver* and into his interpretation of *Last Temptation*. He certainly hasn't forgotten his Christian past through an up-and-down career.

There had been some comment that you offer a portrait of a Reformed Minister, a contemporary interpretation of priestly ministry. Certainly that – but more, increasingly unexpectedly so. I was ready for comparisons, similarities to and differences from a Catholic tradition.

I was very taken with the opening, the camera crawl towards the door of the church facade, iconic. But then, John Toller was writing a journal, commenting on what it could mean to him in his life and ministry, musing on the nature of words to communicate a life. I certainly resonated with that, agreeably confirmed when amongst his books was one by Trappist Thomas Merton (quoted significantly about life, prayer, hope later in the film) – and the title was *A Life in Letters.*

Ethan Hawke is excellent in the role – evoking memories from long ago of his bewildered boy in *Dead Poets Society*, a poem being cajoled from him by the education-magician, Robin Williams.

So, here I was a priest, for almost fifty-four years, looking at a priest from an entirely different tradition, inheriting a Dutch Reformed 18th century church, only half a dozen attending services, a tourist church, family tours and explanations, children learning that it had been a refuge for the underground railway.

Gradually you revealed the life of the priest, a vivid evoking of Calvinist priesthood, marriage, exhorting his son to enlist, his death in Iraq, wife unable to cope and leaving, the leader of the choir needing his affection and fussing over him, the local church leader offering him this job – but, intimations of ill-health, tests and confirmation, drinking.

Perhaps nothing new, but Paul Schrader was able to invest this portrait with all kinds of theological reflections, explorations of discernment of God's will, the struggles with the nature of prayer and praying, not just saying prayers, a deeper experience of God which Toller certainly had but was not always able to articulate. Gospel references. Pauline references. And his pastor commenting that Jesus had a life outside the Garden of Gethsemane while Toller seemed to remain there.

While there were several scenes of pastoral concern, you showed Toller as an empathetic listener, some background as a military chaplain, sensible in his encounters with an idealistic protester who was filled with environmental ideals, pessimistic about the disaster-bent future of the world, not wanting his child to come into this world. Toller said that wisdom is coping with two different ideas in one's head at the same time and declaring that reason is not always the answer. The answer is courage.

One of the things that occurred to me while watching you is that I would very much like to have the text of Paul Schrader's screenplay to read, lots of wisdom, intelligent conversation, solid religious reflections.

The young idealist's wife summons Toller to the garage where they find a suicide vest. Toller doesn't give it to the police but discovers the body of the man, his head shot off, and conducts a scattering of the ashes near a polluted bay. And Neil Young's song encapsulating all these environmental issues.

By this stage I was not sure where you were going. There was a huge emphasis on the celebration of 250 years of the church, much of it being financed by a local energy baron. Paul Schrader obviously has no sympathy for such energy tycoons and gives him blatantly arrogant capitalist dialogue, urging Toller not to be political as if the industrialist's stand was not political in itself.

So, where were you going? And, in anticipation, I was thinking I was not going to like your destination. Could a Calvinist, Reformed Minister be so affected by his experience with the idealist and his wife to contemplate being an environmental jihadist?

Of course, you change tack and move into some moments of magical realism, Toller and Mary, one prostrate on the other, are seen floating over the landscapes of the United States, audiences thinking environment, and their final destination, skimming over contamination, over dumps, refuse, the flotsam and jetsam of progress.

One of the messages certainly is that love can overcome all fear, but the way that you show it in biblical symbolism and contemporary torture, images of blood, covered by a white alb, will have me pondering and wondering for some time.

Love, embrace and kiss. An instant stop. No real ending as such, just leaving me with the experience to sort out, sift, value...

Dear

BRAM STOKER'S DRACULA

Today I was searching my DVD draw for another film – and there you were, bringing back powerful memories. It may seem a strange word to use in connection with you as a film reviewer, but "breathtaking" is the effect you had on me.

Even if there had only been the first seven minutes, your prologue, the powerful sequence which culminates in the name of Dracula appearing on the screen through the fog to herald the rest of the film, you would have been something of a masterpiece. And, I'm very familiar with the prologue because it communicates a great deal of the supernatural atmosphere of your story, of Dracula's story, and of the 16th century background. It also offers a deep theological reflection on the symbol of Dracula, the symbol of blood, the symbol of resurrected life.

Some years before you were released, I wrote a book on images of Jesus, Christ-images and anti-Christ images on screen, the publisher suggesting the title *Movie Christs and Antichrists*. Your prologue dramatises both in one, offering some meaning to the understanding of why Dracula, and other vampire figures, might be seen as Antichrists.

I'm not sure that if there had been interviews with people coming out of the cinema when you were first released and being asked for their theological insights, that very many would have been articulate. Rather puzzled, maybe, wondering what the interviewer was talking about. But, in courses on symbols of evil, on aspects of religious experience, I regularly put you in the DVD player – and, because this is your opening scene, you are very easy to cue for those who do not have technological light fingers.

Before I do a bit of rhapsodising about the prologue, I would like to tell you that Bram Stoker would have felt very much at home in your screenplay. Your setting is the latter part of the 1890s, the period when Stoker wrote and published his classic. One of the things that really appealed to me on first viewing in the early 1990s is how you make a powerful contrast between the eerie atmosphere of Transylvania, Dracula's castle, his sinister power, the revolt of the people, his voyage to England, and the modern developments of the late 19th century, and an England of typewriters, ophthalmologists, even a visit to the newly invented cinema. This is not a remote, Hammer Studios Dracula story (exciting and admirable as they are, the atmosphere of Peter Cushing and Christopher Lee). Gary Oldman's Dracula might have come from an old world, but his pursuit of Mina (and the effective dramatic device of having Winona Ryder play both Elisabetta and Mina, objects of Dracula's desire), the exercise of his thirst for blood, takes place in a world which can be well recognised, an emerging modern metropolis.

But, as I've said, this all takes place in the context of the prologue. We are immediately arrested by the solemnity, depth and sinister undertones of the score and its chords. Then comes the introduction to the character of Vlad and the history of his impaling. The heavily Romanian-accented voiceover is by an uncredited Anthony Hopkins who will play the Orthodox priest who will later condemn Elisabetta, Vlad's wife who threw herself over a parapet, and condemns Vlad himself to his repetitive eternity.

The voice-over gives us the facts, Transylvania, the attacks of the Turks, Elisabetta's grieving as Vlad goes to war. Then you have the marvellous device of the stick-like silhouettes of the Turks, the Romanians, Vlad himself and close-ups in this Wayang artifice (for conflict and sound effects, and the red colour, no holding back on the impaling). The Turks deceive Elisabetta, a deceptive letter telling her that her husband is dead and she throws herself down the vast wall of the castle into the river.

And then, Gary Oldman appears as Dracula, eager to meet his wife, told of her death – and the imperious priest, solemnly robed, forbidding a Christian burial for Elisabetta because she has killed herself.

And then comes the theology! Dracula rages, seizes a lance, thrusts it at the huge cross dominating the chapel, piercing its heart, so to speak, blood immediately flowing out, the pounding music intensifying, Dracula scooping up the blood and drinking it, declaring that in its strength, he will not die but live on.

Not sure that Bram Stoker, despite his Irish background, actually gave thought to themes of the cross, the blood of Jesus, Dracula's blasphemy of having a resurrected life. If he ever watches you, I hope he finds the whole film, but especially this prologue, as exhilarating as I did.

BAD LIEUTENANT

Dear and bad juxtaposed! The Dear is for you – but the Bad is definitely your main character, corrupt in himself and in his work as a New York detective, despicable in his behaviour. So, you might wonder, why a letter about *Bad Lieutenant*!

You are a film that was most important to me in the early 1990s and has continued to be ever more significant. Your almost-finale, with the lieutenant desperate in the church, I might have seen at least fifty times.

Actually, I'd heard of you a year or so before I actually had the chance to see you. My interest was aroused because at a meeting of German theologians who were interested in cinema, they grappled with the question of films which were rather explicit about people who were evil. The reason for the question is that OCIC, the International Catholic Organisation for Cinema, was present at more than 30 film festivals around the world, both Catholic and Ecumenical. Some of the jurors thought that awards should be given only to edifying films, those obviously and explicitly good.

You became the example for their discussions. And the results of the discussions were quite exciting to somebody from the southern hemisphere, not always involved in such deliberations.

The main conclusion was to use a phrase from Psalm 130, usually its title, and immortalised by Oscar Wilde with his poem about his personal experiences, judgments on him, his prison experience and moments of despair. *De Profundis. Out of the Depths.* The theologians suggested that awards should certainly be given to *De Profundis* films because they dramatised the human cries, attempts to transcend despair into hope, from those who had sunk into the depths.

This was 1992 also and, rather interestingly, that enthusiast for Cinema, Pope John Paul II, wrote a letter in 1999 to artists, affirming that "... even when they explore the darkest depths of the soul or the most unsettling aspects of evil, artists give voice in a way to the universal desire for redemption".

So, how did you achieve this? What made an impact on the theologians and all those who embraced the idea of responding to *De Profundis* films?

Some of the responsibility goes back to the writer, Nicholas St John, who wrote screenplays for director, Abel Ferrara – with Ferrara referring to St John's religious preoccupations and his teaching catechetics! Abel Ferrara had a Catholic background but got tangled in the many webs of life, especially drug addiction. You might be interested to hear that I glimpsed him twice, once in Berlin, high and somewhat deranged on stage, as he introduced *The Addiction*, 1995. A year later, in Venice, he looked much better, and OCIC was awarding its prize to his gangster film, *The Funeral*. In fact, the jury, of which I was a member, was split between *The Funeral* and Jacques Doillon's charming film of a little girl, *Ponette*. This was the kind of voting that split juries, to make an award to an obviously beautiful values-film or to one from the depths and darkness. The head of the jury declared that he liked both films – which meant an official *ex aequo*! I suppose there are still the divisions between jurors who prefer dramatising goodness and those who like to have a cinematic wallow in harsh realities and the possibilities for redemption.

Redemption doesn't seem to be the top priority of the bad lieutenant. It is a marvellous performance by Harvey Keitel. While he is a detective, working on the job, his private life is a mess, prone to corruption, on the take, gambling, drinking, unfaithful – and then drug-addicted. This is your first half.

But then, all the more interesting, he visits a church where a nun with a traditional Catholic background, from Poland, has been raped. He is desperate in his interview with her because she won't name her assailants. She is prepared to give them another chance. He becomes exasperated with her and her reluctance, frustrated with not being able to move along with the case, dissatisfied with himself, disgusted with himself.

And then comes your great scene. He is left by himself in the church. He is sitting on the floor, a kind of crouch, just below the altar, at the head of the central aisle. And what comes out of his mouth, from the depths of the feelings in his heart, is a startling, even shocking, primal scream. He weeps and curses. He inveighs against his fucking God. He swears, groans, moans, interrogating God, where the fuck were you? He pleads, cajoles, demands an explanation of God, exasperated at God's seeming absence.

As you might imagine, showing this particular scene, with its desperation and language, with only a verbal explanation for the context, certainly has a dramatic impact, especially for a group with a touch of refinement, perhaps a little sheltered. (Which reminds me that a priest suggested I show it to a group of seminarians in Birmingham years ago – they managed.)

And then the lieutenant sees Jesus, a crucified Jesus, loincloth, blood, crown of thorns, standing halfway down the aisle. The lieutenant begins to crawl along the floor, still cursing, still weeping, until he reaches out and puts his hand on the foot of Jesus.

Then he looks up, it is the church; a janitor standing there, puzzled. But, he has undergone a catharsis of some spiritual kind, a gift from God, so to speak, not self-generated: redemption.

Which – spoiler for anyone else reading this letter who has not seen you – is just as well for the bad lieutenant's ultimate fate.

Re-reading this, I wonder whether it does explain why I hold you in such a high regard (unlikely as this might seem at first sight). I really hope so – and I would even hope to make some converts for you!

Dear

MY FAIR LADY

And I really mean the "Dear". You are a film experience that I treasure.

A great deal of preparation, over years, went into being ready to see you at the Dominion Cinema, Charing Cross Road, London, August 1965 (now dedicated to live theatre which Queen and *We Will Rock You* occupied during the naughties). Even though it was just a matinee session, it was built up as a special event, higher prices, even the matinee, 15 shillings – but it was a gift from an Australian friend from Wagga. Not just any old show on any old afternoon in jolly old London!

From school days we had known and read *Pygmalion*, compliments to George Bernard Shaw. We even knew what Eliza exclaimed at the Ascot races, "Not bloody likely!" – and the story of the school in Sydney in the mid-1950s who put on the play but – ultra-sensitive to audience delicate sensitivities – rendered this line, "Not (long and meaningful pause) likely!". So, *Pygmalion* had a little frisson for us in the 1950s.

We had a very enjoyable afternoon in the seminary in 1958. One of the senior students, very good singer with a knowledge of music, had obtained a copy of your text. He organised a reading of the text for those who were interested, playing an LP, all the songs at the right moments, Rex Harrison and Julie Andrews. This meant that we were really upset when Jack L. Warner didn't cast Julie Andrews as Eliza Doolittle in the film, but very pleased with her ironic thanking of him when she received the Oscar that same year for *Mary Poppins* – and Rex Harrison did the right thing by standing on stage with Julie Andrews and Audrey Hepburn, his "two fair ladies".

The reading also meant that we were more familiar with the songs, wonderful melodies of Frederick Loewe and the witty adaptation of Shaw, especially in the smart lyrics by Alan Jay Lerner (and acknowledging their achievements in *Brigadoon, Paint Your Wagon, Camelot* and *Gigi*).

We were ready for the film version, visualising the songs, relishing the lyrics once more, but also caught up in the atmosphere of the widescreen, the Edwardian decor, Cecil Beaton's costumes and sets for the Ascot races, far vaster than George Bernard Shaw might have imagined.

While Leslie Howard was very effective in the 1938 film version, Professor Higgins will always be Rex Harrison, pedantic, initially misogynistic, intrigued more by Eliza

Doolittle's accent than her appearance or personality. "Look at her, a creature of the gutter...". He wanted a challenge and he got one, Eliza dreaming "Wouldn't it be loverly...?". Each of them came to life in melody and words, "Words, words, words, I'm so sick of words". But, eventually "The Rain in Spain stays mainly on the plain". "By George, she's got it." Eliza could have danced all night, Freddie wanted to woo her on the street where she lived. While Higgins and Colonel Pickering forgot all about Eliza at the ball and the test case where Zoltan Karpathy "oiled his way across the floor" to denounce Eliza as a fraud, Higgins at last had to admit "I've grown accustomed to her face...". Certainly makes you want to listen to the songs all over again.

Acknowledgment as well to Stanley Holloway who brought Shaw's Alfred Doolittle to vividly comic life with a little bit of luck and his plea to get me to the church on time....

But, not forgetting "Ascot opening day" and how you dealt with "not bloody likely" in the 1950s and 1960s. It's hard to remember whether "Move your bloomin' arse" sounded particularly vulgar at the time or not. (And the dreaded thought arises: what four letter equivalent might be substituted for a 21st-century version!)

Dear

THE DEVILS

Dear is certainly not the first word that springs to mind in connection with you, *The Devils*. Something like "delirious" would be more appropriate. And yet, you are one of my favourite films. And not only when I first saw you in 1972 in the context of Australia's changing film classifications, but many times afterwards in the later 1970s and into the early 1980s. In class. In a theology course.

But, to go back to initial impressions. In a way, we were all ready for whatever Ken Russell might create, delirious or not. He certainly made a television impression with his sometimes wild and unanticipated portraits of composers and musicians. And he certainly did that with his Tchaikovsky extravaganza, *The Music Lovers*, seen by several unsuspecting audiences who assumed it was something like *The Sound of Music!* He had brought D. H. Lawrence to the screen, including naked wrestling, with (at that time) startling frankness, *Women in Love*. And, although he continued with delirious films (*Lair of the White Worm*, anyone?), The beginning of the 1970s was his heyday.

One of the intriguing bits of information was that Russell had become a Catholic convert, making a documentary on Lourdes. But his principal cinematic interest in Catholicism was you, going back to a weird period in the French church, the early 17th century, a period of some bizarre spirituality, Russell himself writing the screenplay based on a novel by Aldous Huxley and a play by John Whiting.

The immediate impact was strengthened by the highly stylised sets designed by Derek Jarman. While the audience was plunged into French history, the atmosphere was highly-charged, different, physically disorienting, putting an unsuspecting audience (and a suspecting audience as well) offguard, off-control.

There have been various movements in the history of the church where, in the name of spirituality and sometimes with earnest motivation (but ultimately self-deceptive) men and women have devoted themselves to prayer, claiming God's responsibility for their spiritual life, while they passively allowed themselves more permissive, even licentious behaviour – all in God's name. This was one of those periods.

And, it took place during the time of that political cleric, Cardinal Richelieu, who could exploit bizarre religious experience for power-gaining purposes – especially if some Jesuits were the target.

The background is the convent of Loudon, women forced into the convent by parents who didn't want them, couldn't afford them, suppressed in all ways, and sexuality becoming deliriously repressed and uncontrollably bursting out. What better to do than to send inquisitors and exorcists, accusing the nuns and their confessor of diabolical possession, witchcraft? And, Vanessa Redgrave's chilly, eerie performance as the hunch-backed superior, Mother Joan, certainly reinforced this.

When you were first released in Australia, several politicians objected to your release, dismayed at what they thought was licentiousness. The R, Restricted, certificate had just been introduced but the chief censor at the time still thought it necessary to justify your release by referring explicitly to the historical basis. Being rather overwhelmed when I first saw you, and walking up the steps from the basement Australia Cinema in Collins Street, seriously taking stock, a young man with his girlfriend took advantage of the R Certificate language and proclaim for all and sundry, "what the fuck was that?". And, I suppose, well might he ask.

Over thirty years later, British film critic, Mark Kermode, worked on your restored version, inserting some nakedly hysterical (literally) previously cut sequences. He asked a number of friends to contribute some talking head comments for a documentary for Channel 4. I can't remember what I said (and must search out the DVD copy) but it gave us the opportunity to reassess the history, the mad spirituality, the political manipulation, and the excessive and caricature characterisations by a number of Russell's acting associates, the leering Max Adrian, the bespectacled and fanatical exorcist of Michael Gothard, the pipsqueak pomposity of Murray Melvin.

But I have kept the best to last. I want to remind you that the central character, the Jesuit Father Urban Grandier, was played by Oliver Reed in one of his best, controlled performances. He was the object of hostility, persecution, torture, he and Gemma Jones as the young woman he was in love with. In the midst of the chaos, they have beautifully quiet scenes which offer us some hope in reality rather than be overwhelmed by the discouraging excess. It raises the question of priests in love, marriage, humanity – scenes of a journey, the quiet and contemplation of mountain scenery, a pause in the madness.

And the theology classes? Screening you opened up the young students to a history of the church which was not edifying, was mad, some realities that they might not have been expected to face, and facing them while watching you in an academic situation, helping them to cope, helping them to learn. Delirious as you are, you did some good deeds in those days.

Dear

LES MISERABLES

An amicable question as an opener. Would you be pleased when I tell you that your central character, Jean Valjean, is an "omnivert"? I hope so.

Speaking of Jean Valjean, estimation of him as a significant character probably depends on the initial encounter, whether reading Victor Hugo, whether seeing one of your film versions, or whether going to the theatre and experiencing Claude-Michel Schoenberg and Alain Boubil's musical theatre version (and the marvellous English translation by Herbert Kratzmer).

Since the 1950s, at least, you have had a version every decade: the sombre film of 1952, the Italian television series with Gaston Moschin in the 1960s, television bringing us the classic version with Frederick March and Charles Laughton from the 1930s, the musical in the 1980s, Geoffrey Rush confronting Liam Neeson in the 1990s, the film version of the musical in 2012, and, at this moment, anticipation of another television series where, with interesting casting, David Oyelolo confronts Dominic West. Perennial!

With such a range, I have to confess that I was overwhelmed at the age of 13 by seeing the tall and gaunt Michael Rennie as Jean Valjean. He seemed a majestic hero, a truly noble man. And there was Robert Newton (and I don't remember whether he used his eye-rolling technique as he did with Bill Sykes and Long John Silver) as the sinister Inspector Javert. And, despite seeing the final confrontation many times, it is still frightening to remember Javert's suicide from that time. Strong stuff for a 13-year-old in the early 1950s.

But, the you I am writing to in this letter is the 2012 version of the music theatre. In fact, I've seen the theatrical version three times and could easily go again today or tomorrow. From the initial drumbeats in the galleys, through Jean Valjean's escape and encounter with Fantine (and I'm hearing Anne Hathaway singing 'I dreamed a dream') via the Thenardiers (actually, they are a bit much!), or the pathos of empty chairs and empty tables, to the stirring of revolution, 'Do you hear the people sing', to the beauty of 'God on high, hear my prayer'... There is so much tragedy, so much beauty, and sublime is a word that comes to mind.

In parenthesis – Hugh Jackman seemed the part but his singing range was not as great and beautiful as that of Colm Wilkinson (whom I still hear), the earliest theatre Jean Valjean, and, thankfully, appearing in your film as the

Bishop. And Russell Crowe, good actor as he is and looking the part, did not have the range for Javert.

Perhaps you are still wondering about the "omnivert". No problem in using the words introvert and extrovert to illustrate our behaviour, where we get our energy from, so to speak, from in here or out there. But a character (from literature or drama, not so many in real life) who seems a grounded, authentic person, with inner integrity as well as a capacity for the fullest of interactions, how can you describe that person? And so, those who explore personality have come up with the all-rounded description, omnivert.

Here is an aside. Those of a religious bent often ask whether Jesus was an extrovert or an introvert. An omnivert? Certainly – but, not always in each of the four Gospels as such. You could say that in Mark's Gospel he is rather extroverted while in John's Gospel he is rather introverted. But, 1900 years or more before Carl Jung and his *Personality Types*, Christianity got to grips with his psychology without realising it and offered four Gospels for a complete picture of an omnivert!

As I glance back at this letter, it seems rather adulatory, which is not my usual style. Once upon a time, I was advised "everything in moderation". But, you have a great story and great characters, you show tragedy and the transcending of tragedy. I'm sure commentators are right when they describe you as a classic of the human spirit.

Would you be pleased if I finish this letter, still rather adulatory I'm afraid, with praising you as an "omnifilm"?

DEAD POETS SOCIETY

You have stayed in my memory quite vividly. You are still alive in my memory.

I can often feel the power of that wonderful sequence where Robin Williams as teacher, John Keating, is standing in front of the class, a picture of Walt Whitman above, writing his name, Uncle Walt, on the blackboard, urging the boys to think, to imagine, poetically. He has also written the quote, 'a barbaric yawp'. And there, near the front, is the young Ethan Hawke as Todd Anderson, looking miserable, dragged reluctantly onto the dais.

And it is Robin Williams, urging, pressurising, cajoling him to yell a yawp, tantalising and tormenting, rejecting the tentative choice of rather mundane words ('crazy madman') delighted instead with the unexpectedly poetic ('sweaty-toothed madman'), exhorting him to close his eyes, to blurt out anything that comes to his mind, even if it is nonsense, shouts at him and, suddenly, feelings, words, unexpected images, personal rage and energy erupt from Todd, 'the madman mumbling... truth', pouring out with increasing momentum (and Peter Weir has used a camera swirling in circles around teacher and pupil): "Truth is like, like a blanket that always leaves your feet cold. You push it, stretch it, it'll never be enough. You kick at it, beat it, it'll never cover any of us. From the moment we enter crying to the moment we leave dying, it will just cover your face as you wail and cry and scream."

The class applauds as John Keating whispers to Todd "don't you forget this".

Obviously, you are a film that speaks to teachers and, one hopes, to students (and, even more, to education administrators).

Your setting is 1959 in a rather prim and proper school, many students yet to break out. John Keating is a teacher of vision, believing that words and ideas can change the world, valuing poetry, rekindling the episodes of his own school past where students gathered quietly for poetry, a dead poets society. The 1960s didn't quite turn out as might have been anticipated in 1959 – there was far more change, far more freedoms, John F. Kennedy becoming president, offering some vision, his assassination, the Civil Rights movement, the consequences, the Vietnam war.

For those of us who taught secondary school in the 1960s (my memories are of teaching English literature at high school in Canberra in 1966-7 as well as in 1970), students by this time were rather restless, school and family discipline beginning to alter, sometimes fade, definitely a day-after-day challenge. I'm sure I never said "Carpe diem" to any class but I think we were imbued at that time with something of that message. Many of us had become idealists. Some of your scenes would have resonated with us, John Keating urging the students to tear out the pages of a textbook, his standing on the desk and getting the students to get onto the desks to get, to see, a different perspective on the classroom, to 'suck the marrow out of life: make your lives extraordinary'.

I would like to think back and say that some of my teaching methods were creative (especially in more recent decades with the possibility of illustrating classes and seminars with movie clips). I do remember that at a tertiary institution where I was teaching (creatively), at an institute for sabbaticals for teachers, we were being reviewed in 1987. The delegate responsible for interviews cheered me immensely when he said that students commented favourably about my classes and methods. And then added (and it could have been straight out of your screenplay) that authorities liked tried-and-true methods better!

In this letter to you, I have been concentrating on Ethan Hawke's character, Todd Anderson – I'm sorry that I don't have time to follow through the strand of the plot concerning Robert Sean Leonard's character, Neil Perry, his love of drama and, particularly, the conflict with his dictatorial father. And that would lead us into the other strand – American school traditions and authorities.

You are both exhilarating and inspiring. It's not my quotation but you might appreciate it, that you are the kind of film that gets under your skin and won't come out.

Dear

EVIL ANGELS

You have been, and are, a conscience film.

In fact, this was your initial role when you were released in Australia in 1988. We needed a conscience jolt. I certainly needed a conscience jolt – and, the jolt was so powerful when I first saw you that I had to go immediately to watch you again. The first viewing was not enough for review, at least not for me. So, a second viewing, trying to put you into a truthful perspective.

You might be wondering what I mean. You were the story of the disappearance of Azariah Chamberlain at Uluru in 1980. You were the story of the accusations against her parents, Lindy and Michael Chamberlain, the subsequent trials, the extraordinary media circuses, the speculations, the gossip, the pre-verdict judgments, contrasting with those who felt, and then demonstrated and protested, that justice was not being done, that there was bigotry, deep-seated, in the vast Australian public. Conscience and consciousness needed to be challenged.

You made me realise that I was part of that judgmental approach towards Lindy Chamberlain. Your storytelling and conscientious passion, on the part of the writer, Robert Caswell, adapting the powerful book by John Bryson, as well as of director, Fred Schepisi, made me reconsider what I had taken granted for almost 8 years.

And I think you were successful with me and with so many of the Australian public.

You had the advantage of the first class cast. Yes, there were a lot of jokes about Meryl Streep and her accent for Lindy Chamberlain (also unjust because Lindy Chamberlain was from New Zealand and actually had some flat Australian tones in the New Zealand original). Her comment of the time, "the dingo took my baby" was repeated and mocked, later spoofing it with Meryl's accent. Sam Neill, as Michael Chamberlain, was a model of dignity.

(Worldwide audiences, especially the Americans, were not familiar with the story and so your title was changed to *A Cry in the Dark* (Meryl Streep winning the Best Actress award at the Cannes Film Festival and receiving one of her many Oscar nominations) – apparently, the title of the film and the original book, while having some significance in Australia because of the Chamberlain's membership of the Seventh-Day Adventists and all the speculation about Azariah's name, the alleged biblical overtones of a sacrifice in the desert associated with her death and, therefore, murder, sounded to American ears like an exploitation B-budget bikie actioner!)

Your first impact was to make me look in more detail at the situation at Uluru in 1980, some of the mystique about Ayers Rock, soon to lose that 19th century name and for local indigenous people to manage the site. It had ancient religious atmosphere, was seen later as "the Heart of Australia". It was easy to impose suspicions about the family (your screenplay early on has a very significant line in Mt Isa as truckies drive past the Adventist church and ridicule the congregation). Remembering this line makes me realise how easy it is to be condemnatory of groups that we suspect, dislike, the stories and rumours about, Scientology, especially, and the Jehovah Witnesses when they forbid blood transfusions.

The disappearance of the dingo and the matinee jacket added to these suspicions.

Meryl Streep's performance brought home to us how people judge from appearances. Lindy Chamberlain looked severe, was not approachable, her demeanour taken up with hostile intent, news stories and photos, by the media. And not just photos, of course: television footage. As I write this, I was reminded of it by a speech that Christian Bale made at the Golden Globe awards for 2018 when he won for portraying American Vice President, Dick Cheney in *Vice* –

joking (seriously) that he received an award for portraying a charisma-less personality. In her appearances, Lindy Chamberlain gave the impression that she was charisma-less and all the more suspicious for that.

The other significant impact you had for me in 1988 was the portrayal of everybody in Australia gossiping, everybody having an opinion, rumours galore, the friend of a brother of a sister-in-law's neighbour said... Trial by gossip, condemnation by rumour, often scant regard for evidence, prejudiced interpretation.

I think you are one of Australia's great films, directed by one of Australia's great directors, Fred Schepisi who did an enormous service to Australian conscience by bringing you to the screen. Viewings took on even more ominous tones with Lindy Chamberlain's imprisonment, 1982-1986, with the further appeals denied, with different evidence, with release from prison and the Chamberlain's pardon and extensive payment of compensation, 1992.

You should be on the syllabus in Australian high schools for courses on values, civil society, legal issues, and the need for appreciation for human dignity and rights as well as justice.

DOUBLE INDEMNITY

Technical name for an insurance policy? Your title? I'm not sure whether I could give an accurate explanation of what double indemnity actually means. I did know once – but that was more than 60 years ago when I first saw you!

You made a big impact on me long before I knew the term "film noir". I found that you had an enormous reputation as this kind of thriller, one of the earliest examples, I gather, emerging towards the end of World War II in the United States and really taking off from 1945 to the 1950s. I think I appreciate you more because in recent years I have been enjoying, looking at a lot of old films on You Tube, dramas and thrillers from the 1930s, especially, then the succeeding years, all of which are now referred to as film noir. Most of them are brief. Most of them pack quite a punch. Many of them have dramatic twists. And they were all in black and white (taking advantage of chiaroscuro photography, so to speak).

So, what is particularly special about you that you should have made such an impact on the public and on critics? You were based on a novel by James M. Cain, even more popular in the next two years with *Mildred Pierce* and *The Postman Always Rings Twice* – plenty of noir there. And, of course, your screenplay was written by Raymond Chandler, his first screenplay, I think, his character, Philip Marlowe, about to become a dominating screen presence over the next 60 years and more. You certainly had the credentials.

But, it was your intriguing plot that got me in. I do remember that we did have some dramas which could be classified as film noir while we were at school – *Cornered*, with Dick Powell, who was the first screen Marlowe, but it didn't elicit the noir reaction from a 14 or 15-year-old. But you I saw during midwinter holidays in my first year in the seminary, just turning 19, a much better age to be impressed with more adult themes and issues.

And they were.

I don't think I knew the phrase, femme fatale, at this stage, but here she was, an archetypal femme fatale. And it was Barbara Stanwyck, an embodiment of the smooth and seductive (at the same time ruthlessly relentless). Blonde, slinky dresses, more than a come-hither look. And, poor old Fred MacMurray succumbed, even willing himself to be trapped, believing her despite his disbelief.

As I looked at you in those young days, all I saw was Barbara Stanwyck. She was Phyllis Dietrichson. What a name for a femme fatale! But, as I listened to you, I mainly heard Fred MacMurray, his recording his confession, seduced, humiliated, bewildered that he could have been deceived and fall so low. And there was something in the sound of his name, Walter Neff. And I haven't forgotten Edward G. Robinson as the investigator, smoothly persevering in his quest.

I wasn't quite aware of the Oscars in those days, knew about them of course, could tell you some of the more recent nominees (and still use the chronological lists in the main categories to make sure my memory is still functioning). It was a great pity that Barbara Stanwyck didn't get an Oscar for her femme fatale role (she did win an honorary Oscar in 1982 with an excellent citation: For superlative creativity and unique contribution to the art of screen acting.). The award actually went to Ingrid Bergman as the terrified and traumatised wife in *Gaslight* – and she won two more so she could have conceded one to Barbara Stanwyck! Academy members preferring the victim to a victimiser? (In fact, you were nominated for seven Oscars, including Chandler, director Billy Wilder who was moving from screenwriting to an exceptional career in directing, photography and musical score by Miklos Rosza). And you lost out Best Film to the genial *Going My Way*.

You might be interested to know that our seeing films in the late 1950s in the seminary was something of an innovation, a doctor bringing out 16mm prints as well as a projector. A sign of those times in religious circles was that many of the students, seeing *Seven Brides for Seven Brothers* were more than a touch scandalised. Fortunately, Dad had taken Philip and myself to see it some years earlier during the holidays and had enjoyed it. So, films like you, were significant in the early part of our personal formation, an opening to a world that certainly wasn't perfect, that was definitely intriguing, but called for a sharpening of moral sensibilities. So, I'm rather thankful to you.

BABETTE'S FEAST

You might be quite surprised that I'm beginning this letter to you with some travelogue. It is 1990. Winter. And I am blessed with a Eurail pass. And some time to travel to Scandinavia. My point is that travelling from Gothenburg to Copenhagen, I took one of those enormous ferries, some luxury hours between Sweden and Denmark and where we landed in Denmark was Jutland. *Babette's Feast* territory. (The home of Karen Blixen. Isak Dinesen – and did she actually look like Meryl Streep as her in *Out of Africa!*)

It was only two years or so since I had seen you, been greatly moved, glad to hear that you had won the Oscar for Best Foreign Language Film. Jutland had become alive, its 19th century certainly, so a land to reflect on as the train sped through the countryside.

Your screenplay opened up a world quite unfamiliar to me. This was Protestant country. This was territory geographically and religiously far removed, echoes of Lutheranism, strict devotion, dominant clergy, almost making their parishes their own sect. You brought this to life with the Minister, his church and his congregation, imposing his interpretation of God and God's will (imposing his whims) on them. His was a severe God who prevented the minister's daughters from marriage, happy and fulfilling lives, relegating them to long years of spinsterish religious practice.

Time passes. The sisters get older. The congregation gets older, old squabbles surfacing more and more, touches of bitterness, personal crotchiness.

And then Babette arrives, a mysterious woman from France. Stephane Audran's performance as Babette is one of the joys of cinema. Here she is in Jutland, far away from her elegant restaurant in Paris where she created exquisite menus and delighted in her cooking, a master chef. If ever there was a female character in films who could be identified as a Christ-figure, it is Babette.

She is generosity and service personified. What did she do when she wins the lottery? Go shopping! But her shopping is lavish, creative, a wide range of food for a feast, a masterpiece of culinary art.

There is no real reason for Babette to prepare such a feast. But she delights in her talent, innately generous, making it available for the elderly sisters and the members of the parish. In fact, an old beau of one of the sisters, now a general, comes to visit, and is delighted to reminisce about his visits to the Paris restaurant and his delight in the food.

The parishioners all do arrive for the dinner, even get dressed up, approaching it in some ways as a sacred event, but are captive to restrictive religious bonds that make them determine they will be courteous in accepting Babette's gift but will really not taste the food and drink, just go through the motions.

In many ways, the decision of the community powerfully highlights the puritanical elements that have pervaded religious practice. You may have heard the story about the Puritans and bear-baiting in 17th century England, the Puritans not concerned about the pain to the bear but alarm that some of the participants might be enjoying the sport! Catholics have not been immune to these puritanical influences and asceticism, its name being Jansenism from France in the 17th and 18th centuries. Gloom and doom religion, denominational wowserism.

A gospel distraction – Jesus mentions that people criticised John the Baptist for his grim asceticism but condemned Jesus for being a drunkard and a glutton (and the unsavoury company that he kept at meals). But, when you think of it, Jesus was often at meals, enjoying them. A commentator even referred to his dining ministry. Jesus would have been delighted to be at Babette's feast.

Babette takes no credit. She quietly savours some of the food and drink out in the kitchen with the boy and the old man who helped her.

But the point is what happens to the guests. Perhaps they shouldn't have relished the wine so much – but it has an extraordinarily pervading effect, loosens them up, helps them to taste course by course of the meal, breaks down puritanical inhibitions, helps them to renew the religious spirit and the bonds that previously connected them.

If there was ever a parable for Eucharist and reconciliation, it is *Babette's Feast*. Past sins and enmity are acknowledged, forgiveness is manifest – and, delightfully, they go out into the town square, a dance of joy in the circle of life. One of the sisters remarks that the angels are singing.

You might enjoy two stories about you. When Pope Francis was elected, it is said that he had chosen *Babette's Feast* as his favourite film. *The Catholic Herald* in London decided on a follow-up story and asked me to speculate why. Some of the reasons, of course, are there in this letter to you. The other story took place in Hong Kong. I was invited to be present at the 25th anniversary of the Communications Centre. One of the celebrations was your screening. I introduced you and then sat next to the Cardinal, a genial elderly gentleman. Halfway through, he bent over to me and whispered appreciatively, "Makes you hungry, doesn't it?".

THE COURT JESTER

You would have to be one of my most happy film-watching experiences. One of my funniest films - certainly when I first saw you in 1956 in my last year at school, and certainly in subsequent repeats, and, delighted to tell you that lately Foxtel included you in its Movie Classics, a chance to enjoy you once again.

The first thing is to name Danny Kaye. He made a great impression when I was 10 or so, seeing his clowning, his rapid wordplay in *The Inspector General*. He was genial as *Hans Christian Anderson*. He joined Bing Crosby, Rosemary Clooney and Vera Ellen for Yuletide sentiment in *White Christmas*. There was great pathos in *Me and the Colonel*. It was much later in my life that I caught up with one of his breakthrough comedies, *The Secret Life of Walter Mitty*. And there are some scenes in the hilarious *Knock on Wood*.

Naming Danny Kaye and praising him makes me realise how comedy tastes change! Looking back, in school days, we really enjoyed Marjorie Main and Percy Kilbride as Ma and Pa Kettle. There was Donald O'Connor with Francis the talking mule. There was Abbott and Costello.

And, scratching my head as I look back, we went to all the Dean Martin and Jerry Lewis comedies, Dean Martin with his condescending and smug slinging off at Jerry Lewis and Jerry Lewis, over-zany, facial tics and twists, childish voice and tantrums. Makes you wonder!

Yes, Danny Kaye could be childish in many ways, but, with his timing, with his innocence and naivety, and his clever and tantalising way with words, he is still well worth watching.

You had marvellous ingredients for entertainment in the mid-1950s. There was the magic of a mediaeval setting, castles and knights. Cecil Parker was always entertaining with his dithering exclamations, a sly usurper King. And, by that time, Basil Rathbone had been an arch-villain, with arch verbal delivery, for 20 years or so. Glynis Johns, petite and husky voice, and Angela Lansbury, tall with the touch of villainy, were always worth watching. And there was Mildred Natwick, as the witch.

In many ways, you have become immortal in the realm of comedy. What about Danny Kaye and his duel, finger snapping, hypnotised to heroism, finger snapping and recurring dread. The comedy of his moving from *The Black Fox*, master spy and avenger, to the meek Court Jester – and Danny Kaye doing some smart duelling with Basil Rathbone, drinking nonchalantly from one hand while parrying with the other. And the same with his wooing of the Princess. Great timing. And, speaking of timing, the forever amusing scene where Danny Kaye is knighted, all the pomp and circumstance, the drum rolls, the military march, the solemn and slow intonations, "Yea, verily, yea". Even that has become something of a classic quotation. Then the hilarious speeding up.

But, what we all remember you best for is the build-up to the duel, and the machinations of the witch, her advice to Danny Kaye, the underlings supplying the information to his opponent, and both of them marching forward, repeating the words – and, of course, Danny Kaye in his marvellous way mixing them up completely and tonguetwistingly.

Who would have thought that more than 60 years later, so many people would be able to refer to the Flagon with the Dragon, the Vessel with the Pestle – and the accident, breaking one of them and the substitution, the Chalice from the Palace? And what was in them? The Pellet with the Poison and, of course, the Brew that was True. One can't help smiling, broadly, at the memory of this great cinematic moment!

Each decade or so has its movie comedian. You are very fortunate to have had Danny Kaye. And, as he tunefully sang during the credits, "Life could not better be".

Dear

JESUS CHRIST SUPERSTAR

That might sound something like a prayer opening – but it certainly didn't sound like one to many people back in 1969 when the first songs from the LP began to be played on radio. Jesus? A superstar? For many, this sounded pretty blasphemous – equating Jesus with Elvis or the Beatles! It is interesting how from that time, on the word Superstar has been absorbed into our language and nobody bats an eyelid about Jesus Christ Superstar, taking it for granted (well, not necessarily in reality, but as a legitimate title).

I knew I had to get round to you at some stage for a letter. You have been one of my favourite films for 45 years and more. In fact, before your appearance in theatre, there would be songs gradually released from the LP, our getting used to them, liking them, liking them even more, hearing them again – and again. And then there was the Australian stage version, all excitement going to the *Palais* at St Kilda, a dramatic spectacle and, of course, Herod (played by Reg Livermore) with his showstopping moment, "walk across my swimming pool...".

Which means then that we were pretty primed by 1973 to welcome you, film version. I'm going to mention something rather embarrassing. I have watched you many times and use some clips in workshops, especially that wonderful Agony in the Garden sequence where Jesus climbs the cliff, powerful agony lyrics, the agonising questioning of God and, at the top of the cliff, a great primal scream of despair (rock music version of Munch) before gentle tones of acceptance and resignation. In the 1980s, I was asked onto a Catholic Hour program of *Desert Island Discs*. High on my list and high in my enthusiasm was this agony song – Tim Rice's incisive lyrics, Andrew Lloyd Webber's passionate melodies and rhythms (and amazement that they were in their 20s when they wrote *Superstar*).

Actually, that's not the embarrassing story. This is. I was living in London when I turned 60. It was a hot summer's day, August (a contrast with my usual birthdays in midwinter), well 'London-hot', fairly mild. It was a Sunday. There was nobody around. A little celebration in the morning and then I stayed in. What to do in the afternoon of a 60th birthday? You're right. I watched you yet again – and felt all the better for being older after I finished.

Over the years, I have conducted many seminars on Jesus-figures in films. I do have two "realistic" favourites, Zeffirelli's *Jesus of Nazareth* from 1978, originally made for television, and another film made for television in 1999, directed by Roger Young, simply called *Jesus*, made for millennium screenings by CBS. Robert Powell is powerful in the former film. Jeremy Sisto is extremely engaging in the latter.

This highlights how you are a stylised Jesus-figure film. You are a film about the putting on of a Passion play, the troop travelling into the Judaean desert (and wonderful use of scenery and locations), the cast putting on their costumes, going into action, the buzz and the rhythmic music beginning, heralding a re-imagining of the familiar gospel narratives. Some commentators were negative about Ted Neely and his height (well, Max von Sydow was far too tall in *The Greatest Story Ever Told!*). But, he sang well, every word clear.

Then there was the political/racial question of Judas, played by an African-American actor and interpreted by some as a demonising! But, the cast was intense, so were many of the songs, the crowds pressing on Jesus for miracles, "you can heal me, Christ", the zealots and the rabble-rousing, the imperious Pilate, the high priests in their extraordinary black mitre-like headgear.

I was recently surprised while watching Alfonso Cuaron's autobiographical film, *Roma*, set in the early 1970s in Mexico. There were some contemporary references and then, suddenly, some of the characters were listening to

Yvonne Elliman singing 'I Don't Know how to Love Him'. One of the great tenderness songs. And then she sang 'Everything's All Right'. One song I didn't remember from the stage version is one that I happily watch again and again. There are Peter and Mary Magdalene looking at Jesus walking off in the distance, captive, and each of them plaintively asking 'Could we start again please?'.

The dramatic conflict between Judas and Jesus is most powerful, Judas and his ultimate despair, Jesus and his epiphany as the Superstar. There was some criticism of the play at the time, that it focused so specifically on the Passion that there was no hint of the theology or spirituality of the Resurrection. Did those who made this accusation go to sleep during the glamour and glitz of the Superstar manifestation? Well, we weren't expecting glitzy resurrection in the 1970s but, here we are.

Before I finish this letter to you, happy as I am to write, I wanted to make a comment about the music and sound engineering of the 39 lashes, a powerful scourging piece, not so graphic as Mel Gibson's *Passion of the Christ* scourging, but a reminder of the Roman brutality all the same.

Finally, back to that criticism about no resurrection, I noticed that with you the cast, back in ordinary clothes (well at least as ordinary as they were in the early 70s!), all get back into the buses to go home, with the exception of Ted Neely. Gone to resurrection? And, underneath the final credits, there is a glimpse of a shepherd with sheep, wandering the countryside, the sun at early morning or, perhaps, late evening. Intimation of Resurrection, shall we say.

And, for those who are sharing this letter with you in reading it, yes, I know that your response to my 60th birthday viewing was "Get a life!". I have and you are still a big part of it.

Dear

APOCALYPSE NOW

Something to offer you in confidence. Over the years when I have been asked what my favourite film is, I have said *2001: A Space Odyssey*. But, in moments when I felt I needed to change (and, especially, in 2001 which did not look at all as it did in Kubrick's film), I reply, *Apocalypse Now*. And I need to add hurriedly that I would say, "not the *Redux* edition". In fact, I had looked forward to the *Redux*, hoping that it might expand your already visionary perspectives of war and its consequences. But the material gathered up from the cutting room floor, amplifying the scenes with the colonial French family in Vietnam, seemed to me too much of an extra, distracting from your main core. The cutting room floor turns out to be the right place – or, for the historical record, an extra on the DVD edition.

With that out of the way, I would like to explain to you why I hold you in such high regard.

It is accurate to describe you as a "war film", but that does not do you justice. Most war films are re-creations of particular battles, particular arenas of conflict, *Saving Private Ryan* or *Dunkirk*, at their spectacular best. But, there were heartrending World War I stories during the silent era and then *All Quiet on the Western Front* – and then all those war movies, effective propaganda most of them, during World War II.

Yes, you are a war film, but your quality is that you dramatise and explore what I would highlight as the *meaning* of war. Perhaps 21st century moviegoers, taking for granted all the apocalyptic and post-apocalyptic science fiction around in later decades, do not realise it but 'Apocalypse' was not a frequently used word in 1979. Those who knew the biblical references were aware that it was a word for the last times, the last battles between good and evil, hopes for the triumph of good, of resurrection. That made your title more impactful, that these were the last times, that Vietnam was apocalyptic but was also a symbol of all that is apocalyptic in wars – but, you still asked the question whether they could be, would be, resurrection.

Two of the key images that stay in my memory are close-ups. Early in the film, there is Martin Sheen's Willard, the ominous rumbles of The Doors, given the deadly mission to journey up river to assassinate Kurtz. I see him in the water, bandanna around his head, grim, moving slowly and steadily upstream, intent on his deadly quest. He was the character we were asked to identify with, not the range of GIs trying to deal with war and friendship in a strangely exotic terrain, not the various military authority figures.

The second image is that of Kurtz himself, a hyper-intense bald Marlon Brando, in the shadow and dark, contemplating his journey, his war, his violence, "the horror".

Apocalypse Now might be seen as a 1979 title equivalent of Joseph Conrad's archetypal novel, *The Heart of Darkness.* It is Willard's deadly journey into the darkness. It is the journey of those who don't realise the nature of the darkness, the girls in the gaudy entertainment troupe and the yelling, applauding audience, Dennis Hopper as the mad photojournalist revelling, drugged, standing in tableau in the presence of the painted indigenous people.

But your director, Francis Ford Coppola, seems to be asking at the end of the 1970s whether the experience of the Vietnam war and its consequences were one of the United States' journeys into its own heart of darkness.

You also offer a visual and musical metaphor of this journey, Wagner's *Ride of the Valkyries,* the incessant drone of the helicopters, their high-menacing flights, the ocean and the beach, the threat of the bombings – and out of this hellish scenario, completely unaware of his own heart of darkness, Robert Duvall's Kilgore's immortal bellicose enthusiasm, "I love the smell of napalm in the morning".

I do acknowledge that in 1978, Michael Cimino had released his Vietnam war masterpiece, *The Deer Hunter*

(Oscars and all), a blend of Pittsburgh American life as background and the heart of darkness, symbolic Russian roulette, games of death. I do admire *The Deer Hunter* but you are my Vietnam film, my war conscience film, and a reminder that we need to venture, even if unwillingly, into the inner journey to our own heart of darkness.

Dear

SISTER ACT

Incongruous is an apt word that springs to mind. But, more of that later...

I will enjoy saying this, a touch of place-dropping, that my first time seeing you was in Guam, 1992. Fr Fred Chamberlin, Director of the Australian Catholic Film Office, and I had flown in from Brisbane to Guam, arriving in the early hours, greeted in the airport by a huge bank of television screens with images and song, blaring out "Guam begins America's day!)"... That afternoon, we found ourselves in a local cinema, crowded, remembering that 95% of the population of Guam was Catholic. Was that the reason they were all going to see a movie about nuns? Or was it Whoopi Goldberg? Or both?

You are near the top of the list as one of my most enjoyable films. No trouble in watching you again (although, a year later, telling people that I could not sleep on planes, I closed my eyes when you began because I'd seen you already – and then opened them again, but halfway through *Batman Returns!* Sometimes we deceive ourselves.)

There is always something engaging about Whoopi Goldberg, a confident and casual offhand manner, the glow of humour in her repartee, genial nonchalance. No wonder she won an Oscar, two years earlier, embodying all of this as the medium in *Ghost*!

Whoopi Goldberg as a nun? Where else but in a convent could a Las Vegas showgirl hide as part of a witness protection program? So Delores becomes Sister Clarence and, wearing the habit – exhibiting a whole different way of 'inhabiting', movement and body language within religious garb.

Your whole setup is actually very funny – Damon Runyon might be quite envious of your plot and characters. And one of your great advantages for comedy is your supporting cast. How on earth did the rather starchy Maggie Smith (in her superior *Downton Abbey* mode), arrive from England to California? And while it is very hard to steal the show from Whoopi Goldberg, Kathy Najimi made a hilarious attempt as the busy, bustling, ever-cheerful Sister Patrick (who confides that her mother told her she would either be a stewardess or a nun). And, over the decades, Mary Wickes had always been a stalwart for deadpan comments and observations. As Sister Lazarus, she has yet another successful gig.

So, different perspectives on community life – although, memories of nuns' community life, pre-Vatican II style, are becoming things of the historic past.

And there is all the musical enjoyment throughout the film, Sister Clarence in charge of the choir, Sister Patrick all eye-bulging joy in the front, Sister Lazarus standing by as if on guard at the side, Wendy Makkenna as Sister Robert, the novice sings some charming solos. And the sanctification of some of the lyrics, turning a love song into an ode for God, "I will follow him...". And what about 'My Guy' becoming God-oriented, "My God"!

And for some more incongruity, what about the nuns, in habits, mingling, attempting incognito, with the customers at the casinos!

But, there is a touch of the heart-swell in the finale. Having the Pope come to a recital in the local church is not quite an original idea as might have been thought. One of my favourite comedies is *Foul Play* with Goldie Hawn and Chevy Chase from 1978, a crime thriller with a host of entertaining villains, and a plan to assassinate the Pope during a performance of *The Mikado* in San Francisco. The film was actually released at the time of the election of Pope John Paul II (October 1978) so within a couple of years crowds around the world would be more familiar with the exhilaration of an arm-waving, toe-tapping Pope. In that sense, your ending had become more topical, the exuberant singing of the nuns, Whoopi and her cheeky conducting, the Pope enjoying it – and the cover of *Time Magazine* with Sister Clarence/Delores sharing with the Pope.

The makers of *Going My Way* and *The Bells of St Mary's* were probably delighted that nuns, music and comedy entertainment could still top the box office almost half a century later! So, congratulations, your incongruity worked very well and most amusingly.

Dear

A NIGHT OF THE OPERA

After 70 years or so, you still remain vividly in my memory, most hilariously through the famous stateroom scene, one of the best in American comedies. Actually, I read somewhere that you were nominated for the National Film Registry in 1993 by the Library of Congress, their criteria being "culturally, historically, aesthetically significant". I wonder what Groucho Marx would have made of that last criterion. I also read that on the American Film Institute list, *100 Years... 100 Movies*, you were number 85. For a madcap 1935 comedy, that's not bad, not bad at all.

Glancing back at that paragraph, it looks and sounds a little adulatory! However, all praise to the Marx Brothers, their offbeat films at Paramount, *Duck Soup* and the others, their five classics at MGM beginning with you, then at the races, the circus, the big store and going West! But all praise to Groucho, his gliding and lurching walk, his energetic body language, the moustache and suggestive-raising eyebrows, repartee and innuendo, to Chico and his simplicity, sitting at the piano, his ambidexterity and performance, the forlorn but clever Italian, and to Harpo, blond mop hair, ragged clothes, bright grin, honking horn, silent except for his beautiful fingers-strumming harp.

I suppose I needed to write that to you to express how much the Marx Brothers comedies meant to me when I was young, and an affirmation that the world could be a funny place.

When considering why you are number 85 on that AFI list, it is most obvious to those who have seen you that your highlight is 'The Stateroom Scene'. And, of course, I mean the grand climax of the stateroom scene. Actually, your plot is fairly complicated up till then, Groucho as Otis P. Driftwood (always the comic names), a rather chiselling entrepreneur who has set his sights on Hollywood's perennial dowager, Margaret Dumont as Mrs Claypool (is it true what they say, that Margaret Dumont really didn't get Groucho Marx's jokes?). There is also a pleasant young romantic couple, Alan Jones and Kitty Carlyle, very popular at the time, some villainous entrepreneurs and conductors, mixups and mistakes about contracts. And there is Chico, same look, same coat and trousers, same hat, the Italian Fiorello, and the same piano virtuosity that we always looked forward to. And there is Harpo as Tomasso, the silent but not unobtrusive dresser.

Why the stateroom scene appeals is that the cabin is very small, not what Driftwood was expecting, and neither was he expecting the singer, Fiorello and Tomasso to have stowed away in his trunk which has been deposited in the stateroom alongside the bed. Not much room to swing a cat – although, fortunately, that was not required by the screenplay. All kinds of staff also turn up and squeeze into the room. I hope you don't mind, but I'm going to cheat for a moment, having discovered that Wikipedia actually lists everybody who was in the cabin, 15 in all, "Crammed into this little space at the end of the scene are Driftwood, Fiorello, Tomasso, Ricardo, two cleaning ladies who make up the bed, a manicurist, a ship's engineer and his fat assistant, a girl passenger looking for her aunt, a maid and four waiters with trays of food".

Mrs Claypool has an appointment with Driftwood and she is being set up once again, standing ready, then opening the door, Wikipedia uses the word "Tumble" to describe them all pouring out on top of her. I prefer the word "tumbleburst". But, however one describes it, it has been immortalised as a classic.

I don't know about you, but I feel much better having made that excursion into my past, my relishing of Marx Brothers comedy. And I hope it helps to make you feel all that much better. Many thanks.

Dear

UNDER THE MOONLIGHT
ZIR-E NOOR-E MAAH

From Iran? Yes. And was that a complimentary question? Let me explain a little.

If you were to ask which national film industry has received the most Catholic awards and Ecumenical awards at worldwide film festivals over the last four or five decades, which country would be named? Well, you guessed it. Iran. Did you? Even during the time of the Shah, in the decades of Ayatollah Khomeni, and continuing in recent decades, our Catholic and Ecumenical Juries have agreed that Iranian films have dramatised basic human values more often than films from other countries. I suppose congratulations are in order.

And you are one of those, taking your place with films by such directors as Majidi, Kierostami, and more recently, Panahi. Farhadi...

And I know what I am writing to you because it comes from experience. I first saw you in Cannes, Critics

Week, 2001, and we gave you a special award. Then came 9/11and the US war on terror. At the end of 2001, the Vatican received a Cinema delegation from Iran and in a courteous quid pro quo, the Catholic Church was invited to the Fajr festival in Teheran. When I received a message to go to the Iranian Embassy in London for a visa, I thought it was a hoax. But, no. Off I went, more than a touch of trepidation and uncertainty, five months only after 9/11, a week after President Bush referred to Iran as part of the axis of evil. But I was reassured by having seen so many Iranian films, the warm welcome by the hosts, by a discussion which took only 15 minutes or so to agree that we set up a joint Muslim-Catholic award at the festival, an Interfaith Award. And we have continued that to this day – and I feel myself very fortunate to have had seven visits to Teheran, always receiving the utmost hospitality and delighted to have the opportunity to appreciate so many fine local films.

But, back to yourself as an example of this kind of human values film making.

When I note that your central character is a young man from the countryside studying in the city to become an imam, scenes of college life, classes, study, horseplay, any Christians reading this letter will realise that I was already noting parallels between Islamic training and Christian training – already, the inter-faith antennae were up. (And, amusingly and satirically, at times the Rector seemed more preoccupied in having a mobile phone and playing with it than Koranic studies!)

But your plot became even better. The trainee was having doubts, questioning his vocation, conscious of what was expected of him. Despite his uncertainty, he goes into the city to buy material for his robes only for a young boy sitting next to him on the train to steal them and run away. What does a good and proper trainee do in these circumstances? He decides to go to find the boy, to recover the material... But, what happens to him are the first steps on what surely will be a profound life journey.

He does find the boy but he discovers a whole lot more, a kind of underbelly of the city of Teheran, the poor living under bridges (and his staying with them and sharing their experiences), a man with mental problems who is very kind, the boy himself, a little rogue, chewing gum, and introducing his sister who turns out to be a prostitute. Not quite the best image of a Koranic city. In my further visits, there was the discovery that some of the best films from Iran were honest in showing these images, but also the prevalence of drugs, even amongst the wealthy, brought in from the United States, sexual misbehaviour and, shocking in its way, the discarding of a wife and easy processes of divorce.

But, back in 2001, you made quite an impression in telling this story, in creating this character, a better look at the Koranic traditions, ministry, and a young man discovering for himself, by being with the "poor", with the victimised, discovering what his pastoral ministry must be as an imam, going back to visit his new friends, visiting the young boy in prison.

I was lucky to meet your director, Reza Mir Karimi at that screening and again later. A very friendly man, an interfaith man, reinforced by his next film, *Here, a Shining Light* (2003) about an imam going on holidays and leaving the care of the shrine to a lay caretaker – who gives all the shrine's money to the poor. One year, I did miss out on meeting Reza. He was to receive some awards at Fajr but it was announced that he and his son were away in Saudi Arabia, in Mecca, making the Hajj.

Which reminds me of a meeting we arranged during the market at the Cannes Film Festival 2002, we, the directors of SIGNIS (the World Catholic Association for Communication) with the Minister for Cinema and the Fajr directors. We wanted to discuss our criteria for awards – after a while I was embarrassed to realise that we were listening to see whether we approved their criteria, (taking a somewhat superior stance?), when I realised that the Iranians were doing the same concerning their approval of our criteria!

Personally, I feel very indebted to you as a fine film, to the Iranian film industry, the many films that Christians and Muslims could agree were excellent dramatisations of basic human values.

THE THIRD MAN

You are one of the great post-war thrillers, a film noir, British style. For many years, we had only to hear the opening strains of Anton Karas' zither theme, for you to come to mind, and stir some memories.

We saw you at school, so an important film when we were rather young. You introduced us into a shadowy world of racketeering, exploiting black market for drugs with the desperately ill who had survived the war, as well as police investigations in a very black and white Vienna, an extraordinary use of noir and sudden shocks of white, like the light coming on and a smirking Harry Lime glimpsed at the drain entry before the light went off again.

John Hanrahan, one of my friends when we were studying English at University, wrote a sentence about Graham Greene that I have always remembered and quoted: "Graham Greene tasted life through rotten teeth". I don't know whether John had you in mind but your screenplay and treatment are certainly a Greenish exemplar of providing a foul taste in the mouth, which cinematically, we relish.

This zither music was named 'The Harry Lime Theme'. Not that Harry Lime was the main character. That belonged to his friend, the American novelist played by Joseph Cotton, Holly Martins, invited to Austria by Harry for a job. Holly is an example of those Americans, innocents abroad, and his search for Harry, and his finding Harry, is an extraordinary disillusionment. At the age when we saw you at school, we had no idea that the Harry Limes of this world could be so morally bankrupt. I suppose that meant that, while we were being educated, we were also being led into being disillusioned about real life.

It is impossible to forget Orson Welles as Harry Lime. He is a smilingly corrupt character, any scruple long since crushed. We remember not only that scene of revelation, of his literally emerging from a gutter, the sewer, but also the sardonic comments he made about the Swiss and all their inventiveness for centuries simply going into the cuckoo clock. There he was, Harry Lime, on the top of the Ferris Wheel, looking down on his fellow humans. Harry Lime is a powerfully disturbing incarnation of human evil.

Which is a bit of a worry about Graham Greene and his own rotten teeth with the characters he created. When writing to *Bad Lieutenant*, I said one of the ways of understanding the title character is to appreciate that he had fallen to moral depths and, as the psalm said, 'De Profundis, out of the depths I call to you, God'. Many of

Graham Greene's characters, especially Pinky and his hell-bent malevolence in *Brighton Rock*, have no awareness that they should cry out from the depths. In the title of the film by provocative Brazilian director, Gaspar Noe, for them, it is "Enter the Void". Or as Sartre said about the human condition, "No Exit".

Well, Graham Greene wrote your screenplay so he knew what he was creating, he knew what he was saying. You were very lucky to have Carol Reed as your director, Robert Krasker as your Oscar-winning director of photography, British character favourites like Trevor Howard, Bernard Lee, Wilfrid Hyde White as the fussy host of the book club meeting.

It is certainly about time that I saw you again. But, when I had the opportunity to visit Vienna and I wanted to see the Cathedral where Cardinal Innitzer spoke at the time of the Anschluss, 1938 (featured in the film *The Cardinal*), I also wanted to see Freud's house, the blue of the Danube (it wasn't), the Vienna woods and echoes of Strauss – and a special trip to look at the Ferris Wheel and realise that Harry Lime was not only memorable but was unforgettable.

Dear

THE LIFE OF BRIAN

"... I went down to the Russell Centre last Saturday morning and laughed unashamedly." That was the reply of Fred Chamberlin, Director of the Australian Catholic Film Office, back at the end of 1979. He had been away that month at a meeting overseas, missing out on a batch of complaining letters, both clerical and lay, as they landed on his desk – denunciations of what they called a blasphemous film. What were the Monty Python Team up to!

Well, most of us laughed uproariously, certainly not unashamedly, in 1979 and long since. But, as indicated, not everyone found you so funny.

In fact, you were the opportunity and occasion for discovering or appreciating more discerningly, differing religious sensibilities. For many, especially those who took a very literal approach to interpreting the Bible, there was no connection between the funny and the sacred. Which was to miss a great deal of subtlety in the Scriptures, the satire on prophetic superiority in the tale of Jonah, Jesus and his exaggerated metaphors in his sermons and parables, and some stand-up comic repartee in his interchanges with those listening to his teachings (check out the Sermon on the Mount or Luke 11, about father's giving their sons serpents instead of eggs!).

In North America, even some Catholic classification indicated that you were blasphemous, and your receiving a morally objectionable rating. Meanwhile, in the UK, a number of local councils banned your screening, something which stayed in place for almost twenty years. I was rather surprised when I went to England in 1999 and found myself being interviewed on Channel 5 when the ban was lifted and you were able to be screened on television. I think the interview was somewhat scandalised when I was able to reveal that we had been enjoying your company for two decades, quite freely.

And, as regards Fred Chamberlin's being unashamed, I included that in an article for the *Catholic Herald*, with a light ironic touch only to find an irate lady writing in to say that that priest certainly should be ashamed of himself for laughing!

Yes, I do have to admit that the Pythons were skating on thin ice with the crucifixion scene, Eric Idle in the line-up for crosses suggesting that he wanted freedom rather than crucifixion but finally admitting he was joking and that he did want a cross, Michael Palin as the centurion, greatly relieved. And, of course, Eric Idle again and the lyrics of "Always look on the bright side of life" and all that toe-tapping of the victims on the crosses. Many asked at the time, would Jesus laugh? I think so. I hope so. (Melbourne's top cartoonist of those decades, Ron Tandberg, responded to the respectability criticisms by doing a small sketch of Jesus on the cross in a suit and tie.)

Well, laugh we did. In Australia, we tend to be more at home in the British ironic sense of humour rather than in the broader, often less than subtle, American sense. The Pythons were very popular in Australia.

So, a moment for some pleasant reminders. The women all disguised as bearded men shouting and approval of stonings (women being forbidden to attend, and then having to deepen their voices as they shouted). Michael Palin as the beggar who was cured and so complaining about having lost his livelihood. John Cleese giving Graham Chapman Latin lessons about his graffiti in that John Cleese headmasterish way. The bands of followers who decided that Brian was the Messiah, some hanging onto his gourd, others clinging to his shoe, each group wanting to prove that they were authentic disciples – with Terry Jones's mother rousing on them to go away because Brian was not the Messiah just a naughty boy. Actually, there was the very funny joke about the Magi arriving in Bethlehem and giving their gifts of gold, frankincense and myrrh to baby Brian and then suddenly glimpsing the light and glow up the street, the real manger, swiftly gathering up their gifts and hurrying up to the right location.

There were many, many more – and who can resist the Sermon on the Mount and 'blessed are the cheesemakers' (and the aristocrat explaining that Jesus was referring not to a particular craft but to industry in general).

One is tempted to go on with laughter and reminiscence – but, of course, why not put you in the DVD player yet again!

MIDNIGHT COWBOY

You remember Harry Nelson singing this,

> Everybody's talkin' at me
> I don't hear a word they're sayin'
> Only the echoes of my mind.

> People stoppin' starin'
> I can't see the faces
> only the shadows of their eyes.

And the image that immediately comes to mind is Jon Voight, Joe Buck in his pseudo-buckskin getup, long shot, his being isolated on the New York sidewalk, crowds indifferently walking past. And then comes the image of Dustin Hoffman, 'Ratso' Rizzo, and looking a bedraggled rat, standing dishevelled and forlorn. Two images of isolation, aloneness, loneliness.

I think this was theme that appealed to me most when I first saw you in late 1969. Already, you were a controversial film. And, of course, there was always that story about the innocents who went and bought their tickets thinking that you were a Western! Speaking of 1969, did you know that there were cuts to you authorised by the Customs and Excise Department in Australia, the office which had the responsibility for censoring films. In many ways, Australia had the laxest approach to availability of films, even for children, strictest for adults, relying on snipping unsuitable scenes so that the film could pass customs.

At the time, there was a parliamentary discussion (over three years) to reconsider regulations for the entry of films into the country. In January 1, 1972, new legislation came into effect as well as new classifications. Your snips and cuts were, in fact, restored, with a Restricted Certificate meaning that anyone under 18 could not see you legally. The consequence of this legislation was that more films could come into the country complete rather than having to be re-edited so the children might be able to sit through them, whether the film was suitable or not.

So that was how we were at the end of the 1960s. On the one hand, you won a number of Oscars (including Best Film and Best Director, John Schlesinger, Best Adapted Screenplay, Waldo Salt) and your two leads both had nominations (and the youngsters lost out to the veteran, Oscar at last, John Wayne as Rooster Cogburn in *True Grit*). The same time, at the Berlin Film Festival, the International Catholic Cinema Organisation gave you its award. This was hailed in some circles, hail-stones in other circles, especially more official Catholic circles.

In many ways, you were something of a shock. There had not been too many mainstream films about sex hustlers, the Joe Bucks of that world, naive young men coming to the big city, thinking that they were God's gift to women, putting on the moccasin outfit, New York sexual cowboy – and Joe's initial shock after his encounter with the prostitute, her asking him for money. And, the sleazy Ratso Rizzo, sneak, fraud, sick, but befriending Joe.

So, a film dealing with aloneness, you became a film dealing with both friendship and dependence. There were many of your characters who were down in the depths. Joe and Ratso are did not realise that they were crying out of these depths, dreams beyond depravity, but, somehow or other, their voices were heard. A bus to Miami may not have been the greatest symbol of salvation but, in the world of midnight cowboys and their clients, in the rough underbelly of the American metropolis, it worked.

But let me tell you about your screenings for religious sisters. In Sydney and Melbourne at the time, the nuns did not normally go out to see films, except for those that the public would have considered suitable for them (really seriously underestimating their maturity and moral sensitivities). So there were special screenings and you were one of them. A story comes to mind told to me by a group of novices, just beginning their religious formation, and discussing you with some of the older sisters. The novices wanted to make a point, discovering that the older sisters relied on words and dialogue to gauge the moral worth of the film. The younger ones argued with the sisters about a scene on that bus to Miami. The bus stopped, Joe and Ratso went into a shop, Joe buying a colourful Hawaiian shirt, popular at the time, taking off his midnight cowboy outfit and emerging back onto the bus, "normal". For the novices, this was a visual symbol of a dramatic moral choice which the older sisters hadn't picked up in that way because not a word had been said.

That certainly reminds me that at the end of the 60s; we were really doing a lot of work on appreciating how morality operated in films, moving us beyond moral naivety and inexperience. You did us a service.

Dear

LAWRENCE OF ARABIA

Overwhelming is what comes to mind, overwhelming back in 1962, participating in a Cineforum in Rome as a student, overwhelming ever since (even when you appeared on commercial television punctuated by ad breaks, and even with the famous transition editing of the close-up of the match lit to the immensity and beauty of the desert, someone at channel 7 deciding that this was the perfect cut for an ad!).

The thing about you is that everything was big. Director David Lean had embarked on his journey of making big and bold films, *The Bridge on the River Kwai,* then *Dr Zhivago, Ryan's Daughter* and *A Passage to India.* They all had beauty and grandeur but, for me, you are still the greatest. Everything about you was big. T. E. Lawrence thought he was the biggest of World War I heroes. Perhaps his reputation in real life doesn't stand up to the treatment that you gave him, but in 1962 and always after, you presented him in epic dimensions.

Isn't there something in human nature that delights in the epic? Before stories were written down, there were oral histories that were larger than life (which, of course, is a way into interpreting biblical stories, small in historical reality, large as sagas). And then writers were inspired to epic poems, legends, Homer and his successors. Come to think of it, with printing, there was scope to go beyond the written and illuminated manuscripts of mediaeval times so that more epic novels, from, say, *Don Quixote* to *War and Peace* became part of cultural achievement. Not to forget the theatre, the old Greeks, mystery plays and morality plays, Shakespeare and the dramatists. Which could all be gathered together, so to speak, with images and sound into what the 20th century named as the seventh art, cinema. That's what you inherited and David Lean magnified.

At the moment I'm trying to recall the wondrous impact you had over half a century ago. Maybe we all have a passion for looking at extraordinary desert landscapes, the dunes, the wind and sand, the sun – and moments of oasis. Actually, what comes into my mind immediately is Maurice Jarre's score. Somehow or other, he composed rhythms and melodies that brought the desert to life, the sweep of the sands, the rhythm of camels and riders, yes, an epic score. Which was then the background for the actor who had been around for some years but who was, searing eyes, inner intensity, to become unforgettable Lawrence, Peter O'Toole.

The World War I films that we were used to were generally stories of the Western front. The Australian industry had its own story of the charge at Beersheba, the Palestine story, *40,000 Horsemen* released at the beginning of World War II and then, a spectacular 1988 version, *The Lighthorsemen.* But, the desert war, the warrior tribes, the hostile Turks, the superior British, the trains through the sands – and, once again the word big, for the cast from Alec Guinness to Anthony Quinn, and the introduction, shimmering silhouette in the distance, for the entry of Omar Sharif.

There are the scenes of military strategy. There are battle scenes and quiet in Cairo. There are grim sequences of prison and torture. There are the meetings of the tribal leaders. Close-up touches of intimacy and torment. And, all the time, the vast sweep of all-encompassing 70 mm cameras.

And, in amusing distraction, the scene where Lawrence admires himself, shadows on the sand, his new robes, swirling and twirling – and *Mad Magazine* doing a spoof sketch with Lawrence taking his cue from *West Side Story*, "I feel pretty...". (Now that's an odd memory but it is strongly in there along with the vastness and the epic.)

I suppose the main thing I wanted to say to you is that you were an extraordinary cinematic experience, over three hours of immersion in visual beauty, in that moving soundtrack, of experiencing towering performances, of a dramatic past period re-created with detail and grandeur, an opportunity to go back into history, for history to be present, for a stimulus to the emotions concerning war, heroism, violence and destruction, for the opportunity to reflect on the meaning of war and, after coming out of the cinema, reading reviews, commentaries on the history, to try to interpret what all this meant for Allied victory in World War I – and, so many of the dire consequences of the Western creation of artificial countries in the Middle East and the continuing 20th century struggles for oil, forcing 21st century invasions and continuing wars, and the internal tribal and religious conflicts that plague the people still.

Epic, majestic – and grim.

Dear

SALO OR THE 120 DAYS OF SODOM

You are probably not expecting a letter from me. And, when I started writing my letters, I was not expecting to communicate with you. But, you came into my awareness, a significant film, the finale for the career of Pier Paolo Pasolini, and a sign of contradiction in many countries, especially where you were banned.

In the 1970s, our classifications board in Australia vetoed your release. We certainly didn't expect to be able to see you. However, during a sabbatical in Berkeley, California, 1978, you were screening just down the street one night and so off I went. Disturbing, certainly, shockingly graphic for audiences even during the 70s. But, I went back to my apartment, wrote my notes as usual, wrote my discussion questions, just as I would for any other film. I drew the conclusion that you shouldn't have been censored, that your themes and treatment were quite significant, and that audiences should have access to you.

Then, nothing until the 1990s, 1993 in Australia when the classifications board reversed the ban. It was fifteen years since I had seen you so I thought I should go again. The *Trak* cinema was packed, as might be expected. But it dawned on me very early that audience anticipation of whatever was not being fulfilled, that the audience was bored and restless, and not everybody stayed until the end.

Because I was working in film seminars for students, and some for parents, at the time, and the chief censor, John Dickie, came to Melbourne to participate in our seminars, I was invited to join a government workshop on censorship and my topic was the reception of you, an opportunity to draw on the distinction that has served and saved me over the decades, the distinction between what is presented and how it is presented, that there is no limit on what can be presented in terms of all human experience, the challenge comes in the how, the exercise of sensitivities in making a film which is challengingly controversial.

You are the kind of film which makes us realise how naive we frequently are, that I had no knowledge of the Republic of Salo during World War II – and not too much knowledge at that time of the Marquis De Sade (except an American feature with Keir Dullea in the title role, *De Sade*, Geoffrey Rush's *Quills* was to come much later,).

The discussion problems about your release tended to centre on nudity and sexuality, gross behaviour, disgusting behaviour, by adults towards adolescents. While the impact of the film came from the shocking sequences and behaviour but also from the portrait of the adults who perpetrated these acts, the representatives of the law, of the judiciary, of the church, exploitative depravity. We have learnt in more explicit recent times that sexual aggression is basically an exercise of power, a cruel way of domination.

And, that is what you showed – with most commentators not noticing Pasolini's compassion for those who suffered, at one stage, the screenplay likening their sufferings to the passion and death of Jesus.

Perhaps some critics were tangling Pasolini's films with his personal life (and can I make a suggestion to you that you track down Abel Ferrara's portrait of *Pasolini* with Willem Dafoe). You were his last film before his murder with the sexual and political overtones and undertones that emerged.

I prefer to think about you in connection with the achievement of so many of his other films, *Accatone* and focusing on Roman thugs, on his versions of Greek tragedies like *Oedipus*, the complexities of the seductive stranger in relating to members of a household, *Teorema*, and the fact that he made what many critics, who object to saccharine portraits of Jesus, Hollywood treatment of Jesus, say is the best Jesus film, starkly black-and-white, *The Gospel according to Matthew* (which Pasolini decided to make when he was stuck in a hotel during Pope John XXIII's visit to Assisi, and was looking through the Gideon Bible, struck by Matthew's Gospel and its social concern, his dedicating the film to the Pope.

Obviously, you are not a film that audiences eagerly or even willingly sit through, often not lasting the distance. But, still, you are a film which dramatises themes that have emerged so much more explicitly in recent decades, the sexual abuse of the young and the unmasking of powerful perpetrators.

And, you know, times have so changed that you merely have to Google Youtube and there you are in clips or, in some cases fully available, uncut. Yes, times change. But, I hope you have opened audience eyes, as you did mine, to the atrocities of abuse.

Dear

WHAT'S UP DOC

Enthusiastic greetings to you. You may be wondering about your place amongst these letters. I had written my letter to *Salo,* tough material so thought I would watch you again, after all these years. Foxtel is screening you amongst its Movie Greats. They were not wrong. And, you were certainly a tonic after *Salo*, which means a differently-toned letter to you. During the opening credits, Barbra Streisand sings Cole Porter's "You're the top". And, she is exactly right. Amongst American comedies, you are the top.

Almost fifty years ago, when I first saw you and now again, I began to smile during the opening credits, even the jokes with the page turning fingertips, and, continued smiles, some laughs building up to the hilarity of the chase through the hilly streets of San Francisco. I remember thinking that with the comic car chase instead of a police chase, you were trying to outdo *Bullitt*. And you did (even outdoing the exciting car chase six years on in *Foul Play*).

Peter Bogdanovich had an encyclopedic knowledge of the movies and draws on this all the way through, capitalising on Barbra Streisand's Judy with her impetuous cheekiness,

Ryan O'Neal's ability and timing to play a charmingly distracted nerd, Howard Bannister, introducing Madeline Kahn before she went into those comedies with Mel Brooks and Gene Wilder, and an excellent array of character actors doing some of the best caricatures, especially Kenneth Mars and his arrogant toss of the head and hair, Austin Pendleton as the enthusiastic entrepreneur, Liam Dunn as the perpetually-harassed judge, and the characters who played concierges, house detectives (both eager to rob jewels), the government spy and the thieving spy, and those who made the most of the few minutes and small lines of dialogue, generally funny and/or sparkling.

However, watching you again when I am now older and, I hope, wiser, I have been constantly in admiration of the screenplay, from Buck Henry who had written *The Graduate* and David Newman and Robert Benton who were to write *Superman: The Movie* although Robert Brenton moved from comedy to many successful serious films, *Kramer versus Kramer* and *Places in the Heart.* I really hope they enjoyed their work as they collaborated because the results are truly clever and funny.

In fact, from the opening with the plaid travelling bag (Hitchcock would be envious of this McGuffin) and even more plaid travelling bags, there are sight gags, often very swift, one after the other, relying on the audience noticing them, then funny dialogues, quips and puns, deadpan reactions, and what seems like improvised dialogue but was probably expertly crafted.

And, you play gleefully with the conventions of spy stories, jewel thieves, eccentric musicologists, fast-talking women, harridan fiancées, arrogant music frauds, mixing them all up, one corridor, many rooms and an elevator, people going in and out either hiding or wanting to steal the bags. You have complications with Barbra Streisand in the bath leading to her being stranded high on a window ledge then the room going up in flames. You have a banquet which she gatecrashes, incessant patter, Ryan O'Neal desperately exasperated.

And the car chase, not just with cars but with a pizza delivery bike, hills and crashes, the big pane of glass and the unanticipated way in which it broke, the man laying cement eventually stomping on it in frustration, the garbage bins rolling down the sidewalk the man avoiding them by leaping over the wall and landing on restaurant tables, the Chinese dragon – how to climax this escapade – of course, everyone crashing into San Francisco Bay.

The thing is, how to top this? It might have seemed dubious on paper, after so much action, a whole lot of talk. But, you have perfect talk, the crotchety judge, the confusion of the accused, the even further confusion by Ryan O'Neal's attempted explanation, and the funny line to climax the scene when the judge asks the person under the blanket to give an explanation, "Hello, daddy".

Of course, it is a remake-update of Howard Hawks' *Bringing up Baby* (Katherine Hepburn a Barbra Streisand, Cary Grant a Ryan O'Neal?) all a play on Bugs Bunny and Doc, Barbra Streisand's scene early munching carrots, eyeing off Dr Bannister, even asking What's up Doc! And then Bugs and Doc are again on screen in the plane. It was funny at the time with its reference to Ryan O'Neal's romantic pathos in *Love Story*, and the famous quote and advertising tagline, "Love means never having to say you're sorry...". Judy repeats it with an eye flutter and he retorts that this is the dumbest thing he had ever heard. Interestingly, Dr Bannister has the last word. "You're the top". Definitely.

Dear

RICHARD III

'Now is the winter of our discontent...'

Our cinema introduction to Shakespeare, 1956. Yes, we had already studied *The Merchant of Venice* for the Intermediate certificate, had struggled our way through *Hamlet* the year after, and were now caught up with *Henry IV, Part I*, revelling in the world of Falstaff and his besotted companions, amazed to be told that Prince Hal, leading a larrikin life, had transformed into Laurence Olivier and would become Kenneth Branagh in the versions of *Henry V*, once more into the breach, dear friends!

And then, the school excursion to see you. Who can forget your opening, Olivier himself, skulking hunchbacked, lurking down the corridors, absolutely articulate, sinister rhetoric, introducing us to the War of the Roses? We could not help but be caught up in the intrigue, our first time listening to John Gielgud as Clarence, caught, imprisoned, drowned. Not the first time for Ralph Richardson (*The Sound Barrier*, for instance) as political Buckingham, nor for Cedric Hardwicke (hiss the villain in *The Hunchback of Notre Dame*), as the king himself. Claire Bloom, Pamela Brown,

Alec Clunes, a whole range of British stars, culminating with Stanley Baker as Henry VII.

I have to confess to being fixed in the hostile attitude towards Richard III himself, the princes in the tower, his harshness to Anne, and Olivier's passionate rhetoric on Bosworth Field, "my kingdom for a horse". I also have to confess that my brother is a passionate defender of Richard, Shakespeare's victim, not as evil as handed down, and thwarted by the odious Henry VII – and at least, some intimations of resurrection, from his burial under the car park in Leicester to some kind of recognition and honourable restoration.

You see how influential you were as a film, immersing us in Shakespeare, all in wonderful pageantry, late mediaeval colour, costumes and decor, and betrayals and murder. I'm sure you helped me persevere with Shakespeare for some years, even helping me to receive a British Library scholarship in 1965, six wonderful weeks at the Shakespeare Institute in Stratford-upon-Avon, exhilarating lectures, the performance of that year's repertoire, *A Midsummer Night's Dream* in the hotel grounds where it may have been first performed, excursions to Tintern Abbey... Marvellous just to dwell on it briefly.

One of the principal qualities of Laurence Olivier was his clear diction. We understood every word. He gave

Shakespeare's verse and language a dignity that we assumed was how Shakespeare would have wanted it. Of course, we discovered that there could be many interpretations, many readings, many tones – and in the 90s, quite a contrast with you in seeing Ian McKellen as Richard in the fascist 1930s-style version. (Actually, Ian McKellen in the National Theatres version of *King Lear*, not only was he articulate, we could all hear with absolute clarity each final plosive consonant, the sound, dramatic pause, on to the next word.)

Staying for a moment in the same listening vein, I always hear again Peter Sellers' recitation of the lyrics of the Beatles' *A Hard Day's Night*, imitating Olivier's Richard III-style, a very funny clipped parody of the winter of discontent.

In many ways, your interpretation of Richard belongs for me to a style of dramatising Shakespeare that has departed. Olivier was not trying to experiment. He was fashioning the play to communicate its drama, relying on his so-strong opening, confiding to camera to capture his audience. And he did. Looking back, his *Henry V* is theatrically rhetorical. His *Hamlet* a dignified exercise in dramatic heroism, even omitting the usual restoration of authority and order by cutting Fortinbras at the end which the more faithful Brannagh included. I took a group of fifth formers in Canberra to see him in *Othello* – strong recommendation not to take a group of schoolboys, a mixture of restlessness and giggles!

But, for us at this stage at school in the mid-1950s, at this stage of our Shakespeare experience, you were breathtakingly marvellous.

Dear

JACK REACHER

I'll bet you were never expecting a letter from me. In fact, I wonder whether you receive many letters at all, probably no Love-letters, but I do hope some Like-letters. This is one of those – but, of course, I will have to tackle the Tom Cruise controversy.

The reason you came into my epistolary consciousness is that for the last 20 years or more, my recreational reading has been crime thrillers. (Of course, Agatha Christie was a passion at school.) And now, in older age, a passion for Lee Child. But, there is Jeffrey Deaver with Lincoln Rhyme and Amelia Sachs, extending to California with Kathryn Dance; reading all over the East Coast with Kay Scarpetta and Benton Wesley (and even Pete Marino); John Sandford's Lucas Davenport in Minnesota; Michael Connelly's Hieronymus Bosch and Mickey Haller in Los Angeles; and with thanks to UK writers such as Val McDermid, Mark Billingham, Peter James, and back to the US to Carl Hiassen, Robert Crais, Tess Gerritson, John Grisham... (This sounds not only like a profound confession but also like a list of candidates for a Litany of the Saints! But, certainly, thanks to them all.)

There have been quite a number of film versions, especially of Grisham novels, Denzel Washington and Angelina Jolie in *The Bone Collector*, and there are press releases about a Lincoln Rhyme series for television, Bosch was also successful on television. But, as an avid fan of Jack Reacher, I was very happy to hear that his name was the very title of your first film version of his fisticuffic but intelligent crime solving.

And then Tom Cruise! According to back cover information, Child himself is 6'5", so he knows what the tall, big and muscly Reacher is like. Like himself. But, Tom Cruise? At least one foot shorter – who did the casting? I would have preferred Gerard Butler (Scottish, so originally from Britain like Child himself in his real identity as James D. (Jim) Grant). Butler looks physically right and proved his credentials in that series "... *Has Fallen (Olympus, London, Angel...)* And proved his worth in the submarine thriller, *Hunter Killer*. Actually, had the Reacher films been made earlier, Liam Neeson would have been a good contender (also British – from Northern Ireland), with his experience of *Taken, Taken 2, Taken 3...*

But, and here is the compliment, the "like" aspect of this letter: I didn't mind Tom Cruise at all. I found I was able to accept him, did the right thing concerning dramatic theory and suspended disbelief, appreciated that your director and fight choreographer could create credible cinema versions of all those relentlessly all-in tough fights that permeate the books.

Perhaps one thing that made me very agreeable was that your first 10 to 15 minutes were very close to the book on which you were based, *One Shot*, bringing it to exciting life before my eyes – and, though some characters were compressed, staying pretty faithful to the novel's plot and developments, who would ever have guessed that director, Werner Herzog, would turn up as the arch-villain? Or that that nice British actor, David Oyelowo, would be revealed as Reacher's betrayer!.

For anyone who hasn't seen you or the sequel, *Never Go Back* (which, I thought, wasn't bad either though you were much better) but has read all the 20 novels or more, Reacher himself is the embodiment of a kind of 21st century action hero. He has an interesting background (and those who haven't caught up with later books certainly need to with an unexpected story about his father), very patriotic American, Army service, military police, bond with his brother, angry at his murder, but changing his life after discharge. He is the loner, always alert, resourceful, money in the bank but not in his pocket unless necessary, on the road, traversing the whole of the United States through the books, buying clothes as needed, discarding those used in the rubbish, seeing where life would take him. There have been various liaisons on the way, some important, some not.

He has encountered many villains, experienced all kinds of crimes. And, while he can give as good as he gets, he has experienced torture, and has used his wits and his brawn to survive. Well, maybe. well definitely, unless we are having ourselves on, we can't exactly identify with him, but Lee Child tells his tales, drawing us in.

So, you have provided an opportunity to see a Jack Reacher novel on the screen and I really appreciate it. As we now let Tom Cruise recede into memories of the past, perhaps there could be a new franchise. I nominate Gerard Butler...

Dear

ON THE WATERFRONT

You are certainly one of the movie greats of the 1950s and, since I used to choose the film program each year at secondary school, you definitely had to be booked in for 1955. Not sure how ready we were as teenage boys to see you or appreciate you. We saw the picture of the New York docks. We saw Lee J. Cobb as the corrupt union boss. And there was Rod Steiger in the taxi with his brother, Marlon Brando's Terry Malloy – 'I could have been a contender' (which we have heard so many times since). There was Eva Marie Saint's Edie, with Terry and the pigeons up on the roof. And there were fights and bashings, Terry Malloy bloodied, on the waterfront.

Actually, one of the biggest memories, reinforced by continued watching (and it has been readily available on Youtube), is the sequence of the sermon, pretty tough, delivered by Karl Malden in the basement after Edie had told him to get out of the church and mix with the real people. Writer, the Jewish Budd Schulberg, assured interviewers that the sermon was authentic, that he had gone out and listened to the Jesuit Fr Corrigan on many an occasion and that this was definitely the thrust of his words and his message - before the Second Vatican Council was thought of, and relying on the social teaching of Pope Leo XIII at the end of the 19th century, so influential around the world in Catholic participation in Labour movements – but a bit more of that in a few minutes.

I just want to relish some of his powerful words:

"Boys, this is my church! And if you don't think Christ is down here on the waterfront, you've got another guess coming!

"Some people think the Crucifixion only took place on Calvary. They better wise up! Taking Joey Doyle's life to stop him from testifying is a crucifixion. And dropping a sling on Kayo Dugan because he was ready to spill his guts tomorrow, that's a crucifixion. And every time the Mob puts the pressure on a good man, tries to stop him from doing his duty as a citizen, it's a crucifixion. And anybody who sits around and lets it happen, keeps silent about something he knows that happened, shares the guilt of it just as much as the Roman soldier who pierced the flesh of our Lord to see if he was dead.

"Christ is saying with all of you: if you do it to the least of mine, you do it to me!"

I really wonder what we made of all that back in 1955. It was the post war era, the era of anti-communism. Our Prime Minister had initiated a national referendum in 1951 to condemn Communism (and the slogan, "Reds under the beds") – but it failed (and we had our own film covering these issues, *Newsfront*). When I look at an essay I wrote in third year, 1954, I see it was very pro-anti-Communism. At Easter, we had experienced the Petrov Affair, the dragging of the wife of a Soviet official out of a plane in Darwin so that she and her husband could stay in Australia. Very patriotic stuff.

Yet, at the same time, while the opposition Labor Party was being denounced as sympathetic to communism, while the Catholic Movement was combating cells in the unions, the archbishops of Sydney and Melbourne were taking different sides, the Labor Party actually splitting. We came from Sydney and Sydney remained pro-Australian Labor Party, not following the predominantly Catholic Democratic Labor Party. (In recent decades, the DLP has declined and there have been so many Catholics in the ALP.)

But the discovery in later years was the atmosphere in the United States, the hostility towards the Soviet Union, the descent of the Iron Curtain while the US and the Soviet Union had been allies in World War II, suspicions, accusations, the House of un-American activities, Senator Joe McCarthy and the witchhunts, representatives of the movie industry naming Communist names, the blacklisting of so many directors and actors. So, it was also a surprise to hear criticisms of your director, Elia Kazan, and his collaboration with the investigations, actors taking a stance against him at Academy Award ceremonies, denunciations, and comments that you were a film to justify these collaborative stances. Maybe, maybe not.

You remain an outstanding film. But, your later history and that of your director are a reminder of times of fascist-type loyalties, ruining of reputations – in fact, Lillian Hellman rightly referred to "Scoundrel Times".

Nevertheless, you rightly live on in cinema history.

Dear

A CLOCKWORK ORANGE

Some readers of my reviews in 1972 looked sideways, even beyond, when they saw that I was a great fan of yours. How could this possibly be? Such a violent film, banned in some areas of the UK, disreputable. I had to ask myself a lot of questions back then, but the answers were always in your favour.

1972 was the year when the new classifications came in in Australia. You could be screened, uncut. And you were. I don't think I was too influenced by my response to Stanley Kubrick, to *Dr Strangelove* or *2001*. I appreciated you in your own right.

One of the factors that broke through any hesitations I had was the fact that you were a fantasy – a touch of the apocalyptic even before we used that word for cinema futures. This was certainly a future society, a UK with young thugs, streetgroups which reminded audiences of the Mods and Rockers of the 1960s, threatening society, passive parents who did not know what was going on, the wealthy class whose lavish homes could be invaded and those who lived there brutalised. Actually, those sentences don't make you an attractive film, do they?

Fantasy is the word, the idea, that came to my rescue. You are a fantasy, you are a "what if...?". You are a fable, a cautionary tale. Maybe that is what Western society needed after all the breakthroughs of the 1960s, the new freedoms, liberation of expression, protest and demonstration, some disillusionment with government and leadership.

So, for those who were able, it was an invitation to enter this imaginary world, to get close to Alex, the leader of the Droogs, with Malcolm McDowell playing him as truly sinister, despite his shrewd and knowing smile, seemingly carefree, with his hat, cheeky clothes, eye make-up, his domination of his fellow-Droogs, his love for a bit of the old "ultra-violence", empathy-free, conscience-free.

Stanley Kubrick was extraordinarily creative in imagining this world created by Anthony Burgess. The obvious, and now classic, sequence of Alex bashing the author in his house, the tone of Gene Kelly's voice and *Singin' in the Rain*, Alex putting the boot in to the rhythms of the song, and the mimicry of the dance, alarmingly memorable.

But, one of the striking things for an audience, especially for reviewers who watch so many films, good and bad, playful and violent, asexual and sexual, was the theme of aversion therapy. Not only were the sequences fascinating in terms of explorations of psychology, hopes for cures, hopes for rehabilitation, and the device of clamping eyelids, eyes wide open (but, maybe, simultaneously, in the mind and imagination, to coin a phrase, "eyes wide shut").

What was happening to us as reviewers, what was happening to the general public as they, willingly, perhaps with some unwillingness, forced themselves to watch you. Was there some aversion? Was there some reinforcement? Or was this part of a maturing process, enabling audiences to have a more robust sensitivity towards what they watched, towards what they were forced to watch, and the enabling of us all to face the realities of life and try to deal with them maturely? Is this reading too much into you or do you agree? Was this something of what was behind the condemnations, the bannings, the unwillingness to face your realities – and for authorities cowering in the face of public opinion or determining that this was material that should not be seen?

Whatever the case, I was immediately your admirer and have been a supporter ever since. We need films like you, not just films of brutal violence in the name of realism, but provocations to the moral imagination and mature abilities to face reality.

This is something of PS. In recent years, I heard this story about Paul Byrnes, for some years Director of the

Sydney Film Festival, continuing reviewer and commentator for the Fairfax Press. He confirmed the story later when I met him. He attended Chevalier College (where I went to school). Because my religious order's magazine, *The Annals*, circulated in its schools of which Chevalier was one, he used to read my reviews. He told me that the fact that a priest could review *A Clockwork Orange* so favourably, could inspire him to go on the path that led him to his own career. (Many thanks for the affirmation – but I take no responsibility for his subsequent reviews and opinions!!)

Dear

SORRY TO BOTHER YOU

I wasn't really expecting to be writing a letter to you. You were very much a surprise at the end of 2018, going to watch you at a press preview, no knowledge of you or your filmmakers. To that extent, you more than crept up on me as your plot unfolded. And providing many more surprises before the final credits. I did put you on the list of my striking films of the year. And since then, you have continued to be eerily present.

I have just been writing to *A Clockwork Orange*, explaining that my involvement there, despite the ultra-violence of the themes, was due to the fact that this was not realism but fantasy, an appeal to the moral imagination. What I want to tell you is that I would use the same argument in your regard. On the one hand, you have a great many sequences which are "realistic", life in an American city, going daily to the routine of the workplace, social protests, personal relationships. But, you are forever undercutting, so to speak, this realism with fantasy – and sometimes, beyond! You could be described as fascinating/intriguing.

Your writer-director, Boots (Raymond Lawrence) Riley, is a veteran rapper but, interestingly, in terms of your social concerns, he was born into a family of social justice organisers in Chicago 1971. Let's say it shows (tellingly) in this screenplay for his directorial debut.

I enjoyed the company of your hero, Cassius Green, with the ironic nickname of Cash (and US notes are green!). I thought Lakeith Stanfield was very effective. On the one hand, you send an ordinary character, African-American, looking for a job, going for an interview, being employed by one of those phone-sales companies, a telemarketer, ringing targeted men and women for their investments, offhand "sorry to bother you". I especially appreciated the spoof sense of humour where Cash is advised by Danny Glover that he needs a white voice to convince his potential clients – great moments of absurdity as David Cross's voice, intonations and modulations emerge from Lakeith Stanfield's mouth ... But, where can a plot go from there?

On the one hand, you offer a realistic picture of oppression in the workplace, high and mighty bosses, inconsistent in their behaviour, but offering an opportunity of promotion for Cash. On the other hand, there are injustices in the workplace (I saw somebody referred to you as a "workplace satire"). This leads to meetings, protests, and anti-boss conspiracies and demonstrations. That has its own dynamic, especially as Cash received offers that he considers too good to refuse, alienating himself from friends and his girlfriend.

If you're just that, you would be one of many. However, you show a number of arresting commercials, glowing testimonials for an industrial company, Worry Free, which turns out to be a system of indenture where the workers sign away their lives for minimum food and lodging. The smarmy CEO, Armie Hammer, is all smiles and platitudes, trying to swindle Cash into temptation.

And this is where you really come into your own – well, perhaps not exclusively your own, because you seem to be drawing very effectively, terrifyingly, on HG Wells' story, *The Island of Dr Moreau* and the various film versions, weird experimentation on humans and animals.

This is very apt symbolism for capitalist exploitation of the masses, visually provocative, emotionally disturbing, intellectually challenging – as it does become for Cash when it is revealed to him – and he is trapped.

For a while there, I thought you were going to come to a very conventional happy ending, exposure, protests and campaigns against Worry Free, a final hug and kiss. But no, my compliments to your shock ending. Is this the way the world ends, no apocalyptic bangs, but shocking exploitative animal/ human whimpers? No need to apologise, I'm very glad you bothered us.

THE CASTLE

If someone from the future had visited the team at Working Dog productions in Melbourne, 1996, and told them that the project they were working on would become one of the most beloved of Australian films, Rob Sitch might have said "Yerdreamin'!". But, in fact, you definitely have.

The press preview in Melbourne was at the Jam Factory, Prahran, a very hot evening in February and, in the spirit of the film we were about to watch, *Village Roadshow* gave everyone a complimentary ice cream. Then, you more than matched the ice cream on a hot night!

A lot of people have speculated about how you communicated with the Australian audience. Up there on the screen was the family, ordinary enough for most Australians to identify with although they could have done with a bit more polish and aplomb. But, as you went on, the social issues about land, compulsory acquisition, ownership and title, legal implications, the Kerrigans showed that they could, in an Aussie accent way, and Aussie with vocabulary, achieve their goals. Actually, Tiriel Mora is the lawyer was the one who got tongue-tied and losing his bargaining aplomb, trying to give his rationale because of "the vibes".

There was a caution. I remember writing at the time "The danger is that the film can be patronising to the Kerrigans and their real-life counterparts. But the film-makers really like their characters, and so do we. So that when it comes time for them to go to the courts, we are definitely on their side".

For an Australian, his home was his castle. Here was a family, being imposed on by business, the threat of being ousted from their home (and, ironically, the actual house later being purchased and set up as a homage museum), standing by their rights, making their appeal through common sense and the law, "on just terms" as the judge advised – and winning.

The phrase, from Depression times, "the Aussie Battler", proved to be more than relevant in the 1990s. The Kerrigans were battlers of the nicest kind.

But, the quality of the screenplay was in the humour. Already Working Dog had had television and radio success. Rob Sitch as the newsreader, full of himself, on the series, *Frontline*, was hilarious in its sendup of the pompous Australian while the screenplay dealt with serious current problems. (Even more television success was to come 20 years later with *Utopia*.)

"You must be dreamin'" became part of the Australian vocabulary, often quoted to describe ambitions for the impossible. And again, the Kerrigans poring over the ads in *The Trading Post* showed the Aussie love of the bargain. They were strongly a bonded family, Michael Caton becoming the image of everyone's dad, Anne Tenney the cheerfully devoted wife able to name the meal that her husband was enjoying, "rissoles". Sophie Lee and Stephen Curry had good roles as the children.

But, for me, your funniest joke was spoken by Eric Bana as the son-in-law, having taken his wife on their honeymoon to Thailand to see the kickboxing. You remember the meal when the couple returned, they were discussing in-flight meals, beef with some pastry on it, Mum coming to the rescue and naming it Beef Wellington. And then a line which Qantas (obviously the right company to fly with) would never have thought of. Eric Bana declares with more than a hint of satisfied approval, "and it was a credit to them". The best tribute to meals on planes ever!

Dear

THE CHANT OF JIMMY BLACKSMITH

An audience watching you overseas might become very involved with your characters and the racial situations, the rage and the violence, all in a beautiful Australian bush setting. But they might be observing at a distance – something like an Australian audience watching an equivalent film about Native Americans and the United States.

For us at home, it is different. Or, it should be.

I have already written to *Evil Angels* and have declared that it was a conscience film. However, 10 years earlier, Fred Schepisi had directed you, a profound examination of the Australian conscience and consciousness, an experience for all Australians, for Aboriginal Australians here for more than 60,000 years, for the newcomers to the land after 1788, and for more recent arrivals, especially after World War II, after the defeat in Vietnam, from the 21st century migrations from the Middle East. You contain Australian issues that everyone should be aware of, that challenge everyone.

I should mention to you that for years, in an introduction theology course for men and women beginning a formation program for life in religious orders, you were the film to alert them to the culture in which they would be ministering.

First of all, a compliment. Ian Baker's cinematography is, as some critics declare, struggling for the appropriate word, "breathtaking". You offer a vision of the Australian bush, the flora, fauna, the unique eucalyptic atmosphere of the bush.

But, what takes place, is not so beautiful.

One of your impressive features is that you are based on a celebrated novel by one of our most celebrated writers, Thomas Keneally, adapted by your director, Fred Schepisi. Over more than half a century of his writing, Keneally has shown many profound insights into human nature (thinking *Schindler's Ark/Schindler's List*), but also provocative insights into more recent Australian history, the inherent racism of the foundation of modern Australia – the "invasion" of the colonial British exploiting a foreign and distant land as a dumping prison ground, the lack of understanding for local culture and the lack of desire to understand it, the experience of the Federation of the colonies to become states of the Commonwealth of Australia in 1901, the White Australia policy of the Constitution, excluding an admission of non-white races, and not even acknowledgment of the original inhabitants of the land. We are still the inheritors of this violent and racist beginning.

Tommy Lewis, who was to have a career in Australian cinema, creates a memorable Jimmie Blacksmith (ironically, the actual name of the character on whom he is based, was Jimmie Governor). Jimmie and his friend Mort are caught in the consequences of the white settlement and occupation of the bush, know some of their own traditions and sacred places (seen vandalised by white tourists), are under the influence of well-meaning Christian ministers and their families, are employed in manual labour by families, have a genial presence, communicate with some charm, even if it is with great reserve, but, eventually, the inner rage will erupt in violence and massacre.

On your release, many Australians found you too much to watch. You were not really commercially successful (and it led your director to the United States for 10 years before his return for *Evil Angels*). There was criticism of one scene, Jimmie shooting the older woman played by Ruth Cracknell, descriptions of the bullet cutting through her. In fact, this is an example of skilful editing, a shot of the gun and Jimmie aiming, the sound of firing, the woman collapsing – and people so affected that they thought they really saw the shot and the bullet and the actual winding.

So, while your screenplay offers a disturbing exploration of Australian racism, it is also a reminder that history not only needs revisiting but continual re-examining, and, with Keneally's religious background and interest in the churches, you offer a challenge to the relationship between Aboriginal religious traditions and the tenets of Christianity, of the dangers of imposition of creed and practice, the danger of subconscious white supremacist presuppositions even in about people who want to contribute to racial peace, reconciliation and betterment.

In case you did not realise it, I now have to tell you that you are the answer when anyone asks me what is my favourite Australian film.

Dear

PRIDE AND PREJUDICE

I feel something of an obligation in writing to you, not an obligation to Jane Austen (though this is the Austen novel that I have read twice!), but to Fr John Burford who was the rector of Chevalier College for the five years I was at school there. He had a devotion (passion and commitment) to Greer Garson. I had to book as many Greer Garson films as I could each year, and I realise I could write a really lengthy letter to Miss Garson herself: the introduction through *Goodbye Mr Chips*, the archetypal *Mrs Miniver*, suburban maybe, but so dignified in manner, regal in voice, mellifluously elegant.

But, when it came time to write a letter to a Greer Garson film, you were the choice. You were my introduction to Jane Austen's world – at the age of 13! I found you thoroughly entertaining, a really enjoyable experience, an entry into a Regency England very remote from me, and very remote from the world of the convicts being transported to the other side of the world, my side, from a port not very far from the Austen home. Nothing rough here, good manners, mainly genteel – but, later realising that under the surface respectability, the same passions of human nature would be in turmoil, that Lydia could run off with Wickham, that it was the period of the Napoleonic wars. (I'm wondering whether you have come across *Pride and Prejudice and Zombies* – not on the top of the movie list for an Austin purist, but I actually very much enjoyed it, entering the subterranean, subconscious vein of the original, acknowledging that the early 1800s were not as serene as Miss Austen's novels suggested.)

It was only much later, reinforced by television's Jennifer Ehle and Colin Firth (25 and 24 while filming) and later, Keira Knightley and Matthew McFadyen (19 and 30) on the big screen, it dawned on me that Greer Garson and Laurence Olivier (35 and 32 at the time of filming) were actually far too old for the roles! But that did not deter us. In our day, 20 was old! Olivier's Mr Darcy was starchy and constricted (embodiment of prejudice) but spoke beautifully! But, there was absolutely nothing wrong with Greer Garson especially in the stately conclusion to romantic episodes, "that chapter is definitely closed". She had every right to be Pride!

Your photography was in black and white. The costumes and decor were of the period. The dialogue was smart, catchy (and why not with Aldous Huxley as one of the writers)? But, it is the principal supporting characters who linger in my memory most distinctively. Who could surpass Mary Boland as the loudly fussing, impossibly obtuse, Mrs Bennett, preoccupied with marrying off her daughters (also a strong group, Maureen O'Sullivan, Ann

Rutherford, Marsha Hunt)? And, by contrast, the quietly patient bookishness of Edmund Gwenn as Mr Bennett and his wise conversations with the astute Elizabeth.

But, I look back with great pleasure, especially when I see these character actors in other films, Melville Cooper as the most unsuitable fiancé, Mr Collins, pomposity personified, and his extreme deferential regard for his patron, Lady Catherine De Burgh. Judi Dench later played a strong-minded Lady Catherine, but who could compare with the imperious manner, glinting eyes, tight mouth, the haughty sweep of Edna May Oliver? Presumptuously demanding, infallibly unquestioning in her judgments. (She had been Miss Pross in *A Tale of Two Cities* where she could do the same performance in an entirely different context.)

You had all the MGM high production values of the time, you appealed to a wide, generally well-read, audience had who had learned to admire Olivier (*Wuthering Heights, Rebecca*) and who, like Fr Burford, were well on the way to enthroning Greer Garson on their Hollywood pedestal.

Dear

GRAN TORINO

and

THE MULE

I am doing something that I have not done before: writing a joint letter. Of course, you are wondering why.

I just got the tram back from Camberwell, the 10.50 session at the *Rivoli* of *The Mule*. I found you an unexpectedly moving experience, Clint Eastwood directing and, especially, acting at 88. You seem to be quite an elegiac film (despite the drug-running and the cartels) probably right for Eastward's last acting role.

But, in fact, I experienced something of the same watching you, *Gran Torino*, ten years ago. I had thought of his performance as Walt as a fine final opportunity for him as an actor. (Actually, he threw a curved ball three years later by acting again in *The Trouble with the Curve!*). Walt and his love for his Gran Torino offered something of a reversal of his making his day as Dirty Harry Callahan. He buries his wife, is retired in suburbia, discovers the Hmong neighbours that he does not understand but becoming involved in their troubles, takes a stand against thugs (well, that has more than a glimpse of Dirty Harry), defends these new friends with more than tolerance, giving his life for their safety. One remembers that in the Westerns that Clint Eastwood directed himself, there is a great deal of Christ-like self-giving in death.

I should add that I think you, *Gran Torino*, should be a must-see for every seminarian or pastoral worker of any Christian tradition, of any faith at all. You have a Catholic focus and some marvellous interaction scenes between Walt and the recently ordained young priest. Walt's late wife had asked the priest to get Walt to confession. That is certainly not on Walt's agenda but the two meet, have lots of discussions, Walt doing a bit of relenting, the priest acquiring some worldly wisdom for his religious ministry.

One can't help liking you, a variation on the American dream, the crusty old man mellowing (but not absolutely), embracing a broader world than he was used to.

I have to mention one of my favourite scenes, the opening with the funeral in the Church, Walt at the front observing his family arriving, then the deepest of Eastwood growls as his granddaughter in the pew goes for her mobile phone – instant empathy all round from clergy and preachers. He doesn't growl about modern use of technology in you, *The Mule*, but he does growl at internet sales which put him out of business as a specialist flower gardener and he makes many accusatory comments on how people forever hold their phone and their attention in their hand. But he does promise to text, even getting a lesson or two.

What made me want to write this joint letter is that his role as Earl Stone in you, *The Mule*, seems an end of life, appropriate end-of-career role. Earl is no better than he should be. He has devoted his life to work, to flowers (and your opening and closing sequences with close-ups of flowers are really beautiful). He reminisces with his ex-wife, Mary, that they had had ten good years. But he has avoided, then abandoned, his family for work (he says he *loved* the flowers), happy with buddies and workers, missing anniversaries, his daughter's wedding. As we learn more about Earl (who is an immediately genial character), he has been carelessly self-centred, a womaniser, and continuing, eyes wide open, as a driver, a mule for the cartels, the police pursuing him.

In many ways, you could be a fable on the Gospel text of gaining the world and losing one's life. Your screenplay believes that there is a basic goodness in human nature, that we can be redeemed, if providence, situation, family love, or a challenge to conscience, present themselves – and are accepted, even welcomed.

Clint Eastwood has had something of a colourful personal life in terms of marriage and relationships. He has cast his own daughter, Alison Eastwood, in the role of Earl's angry and alienated daughter. When he goes to his dying wife's bedside and her funeral, they are reconciled and he is welcomed again into his family. An old man's peace with his family.

Which means that the end of you, *Gran Torino*, would have had Clint Eastwood, screen hero, the complete self-sacrifice, death with a heroic note. Great.

But you, *The Mule*, have an ordinary man, a man who has made selfish mistakes and hurt his family, acknowledging the wrong he has done and accepting the consequences – which bring him love and redemption. Now, that's a finale. Earl Stone doesn't die. He serves his sentence in prison, once again growing the flowers. He lives on – so, if Clint Eastwood does act again, it will be like a pleasing postscript because you two films have already provided him with perfect acting career-endings.

Dear

THE IMPORTANCE OF BEING EARNEST

If you don't mind, a rather important clarification before I begin this letter in earnest, so to speak. This is a letter to you, the version of 1952, the classic version. I hasten to say that it is not a letter to the version of 2002 – that would be a rather uncomplimentary letter. I presume writer-director, Oliver Parker, was trying to make Oscar Wilde of 1895 sound relevant to the 21st-century. Apart from omitting some of my favourite lines (practically unforgiveable), he made Algernon and Ernest too much men about town (they are dilettantes in their way), devotees of the music halls and – perish the thought – despite Judi Dench having the role, making the young Lady Bracknell a gold-digging chorus girl! And when it was revealed that Gwendoline had a tattoo of the name Earnest on her posterior, that reached the bottom (or beyond!).

So back to 1952 and elegance and the more subtle wit, humour and satire. You are very much a staged film, reminding us of the origins of the play and theatrical performance. Your sets are, city and country, beginning and ending on stage, framed by the proscenium. The costumes and decor, the technicolour, are all very pretty. You look and sound like a late Victorian play – as you should.

We saw you at school and so an introduction to Oscar Wilde at an early age, 13. I enjoyed your language, the repartee, the wit and paradoxes, "the truth is never pure and rarely simple". On the one hand, the dialogue sounded frivolous, at times even trite. And it was frequently waspish! Yet, on the other hand, as we were delighted with the words, nuances of phrasing often beautifully enunciated by the cast, some of the depth of meaning stayed with us, in terms of relationships, in terms of honesty and truth, in the portrait of human nature.

Would you believe that some of the entertaining interactions between Gwendoline and Cecily were omitted by Oliver Parker (couldn't he see that they were essential!). In the afternoon tea sequence when Gwendoline asks for bread and butter because cake is not fashionable, Cecily serves her up quite a slice. With Joan Greenwood and her deep cast of voice and intonation, her response is a profound lament with her phraseology, "I have asked for bread and butter and you gave me... cake). And he omitted Cecily's down-to-earth comment that she calls a spade a spade. And Joan Greenwood again with quiet superior disdain, "I am glad to say I have never seen a spade". (I'm glad I've got that off my chest at last.)

The cast is wonderful, Michael Redgrave and Michael Denison – but, come to think of it, the deceptions with Bunburying (later speculations about whether that was a cover for gay rendezvous), might mean that they were more men about town than a 13-year-old might have thought or known. Joan Greenwood and Dorothy Tutin were a perfect contrast as Gwendoline and Cecily. Miles Malleson embodied the doddering clergyman and there was Margaret Rutherford, all bumbling (as she did from Madame Arcati to Miss Marple, even getting an Oscar for it with *The VIPs*) humbled about her loss of the baby but so relieved at the recovery of her manuscript. (And Wilde having digs at the popularity of the over-voluminous novels of the period.)

Which, of course, leaves Lady Bracknell to last. Over the decades, at any mention of the word "handbag", Edith Evans' voice looms in many memories. No one has really delivered the word with such bombast and condescension. A truly memorable cinema and drama moment. (I have seen an amateur production in Melbourne where both the performers as Lady Bracknell and Miss Prism delivered all these lines in subdued monotone!). Did you see the giggly handbag scene with David Suchet in drag as Lady Bracknell!

In so many ways, Wilde has created the perfect comedy, delightful, entertaining, insightful, sounding like a soufflé but, in reality, far more substantial. If anyone wants to be introduced to the work of Wilde for the theatre, despite the excellence of *An Ideal Husband, Lady Windermere's Fan* or *A Woman of No Importance*, you and your version are at the top of the list.

Dear

MODERN TIMES

A cog in a wheel!

Let's leave that image to later. The word I really wanted to begin with is "smile". That is your last word, your last message to an audience which has been laughing at the antics of Charlie Chaplin (really his last performance in that old silent comedy vein, his then moving on to the Hitler parody in *The Great Dictator* and then becoming older and more serious in *Limelight*). A distraction: who could forget his elegant supper, the little tramp, eating (with proper cutlery) his boots and laces in *The Gold Rush*! But 'Smile' is also your last message to an audience which has been saddened at this picture of the industrial world of the 1930s, of management, of production, of exploitation of workers. Smile.

Chaplin wrote songs and music to accompany his films. 'Smile', for me, is his best and most moving. It is plaintive. It is sad. Many may call it sentimental (I always like to quote Somerset Maugham's dictum at moments like this that sentimentality is really sentiment that one doesn't approve of!). Well, however "Smile' may be described, it is one of my favourite songs, the music playing, the words heard as The Factory Worker and The Gamin (their names in the credits) walk into the distance, into an uncertain future.

Some of the lyrics:

Smile through your fear and sorrow
Smile and maybe tomorrow
You'll see the sun come shining thru for you.
Light up your face with gladness
Hide ev'ry trace of sadness

What's the use of crying
You'll find that life is still worthwhile
If you'll just…
Smile.

`I feel all the better for that even though I had to supply the melody in my imagination.

Back to the cog in the wheel.

I find it interesting to note that Fritz Lang in 1927 in *Metropolis* had the workers marching up in procession to be devoured by a giant face and mouth of the cruel deity, Moloch, a stylised and symbolic critique of industrialisation. Seriously destructive. Chaplin, on the other hand, in the aftermath of the Depression, chooses a comic mode to comment on industrialisation, on the behaviour of the CEOs of the company (jigsaw puzzles, reading their papers) and the labour of the factory workers, Chaplin keeping this title, *The Factory Worker*, anonymity rather than any personal name, just one of the many cogs in the wheel.

And, as I write to you, there is that image of Chaplin, his spanner, going around the wheel as a cog. (Was that one of the reasons – as well as a scene with a social protest demonstration – that the Americans began to denounce him as a Communist!). And, the quaint name for the leading lady, Paulette Goddard, Chaplin's wife at the time, The Gamin, the image of the female victim of this kind of society?

So, you have Chaplin as seriously comic as well as comically serious.

Dear

HAPPY DEATHDAY 2 U

Anyone looking over my shoulder at the moment might well be surprised that I'm sending this letter to you. It means that, in the collection, you will be found along with *2001, A Space Odyssey, Apocalypse Now, Silence* and many other favourite films.

It's just over an hour since I watched your final credits – and, always remaining for them, meant that I liked your funny culminating episode and the final joke while most of the (young) audience had already rushed from the back of the *Vue Cinema 2*, Shepherd's Bush, to the exit and missed what they really would have enjoyed.

Would you believe that the other day my good friend and film critic, Alan, gave me exasperated warnings against seeing you. He certainly won't be writing you a letter! But, I enjoyed *Happy Deathday* and was looking forward to seeing you, even if it was just to be a passing hour and a half's entertainment. But, you provided much more – and that anyone looking over my shoulder now will be tempted to be judgmental, that my taste is very lowbrow. In some ways it is, but I want to commend you for not being as lowbrow

(as gorily and swearingly self-indulgent as audiences might have expected!)

I notice that Christopher Landon, who directed the first film, has written the screenplay as well as directing you. He must have enjoyed doing the original and let his imagination really run almost-riot while writing you (of course, he had lots of previous horror-touch speculation with the *Paranormal Activity* series). And what about his use of the Flower Song from *Lakme* as background to the central characters being hurled through the air in slow motion and the jauntiness of the Bee Gees' 'Stayin' Alive' for the final credits as your heroine, Tree, finally stayed alive!)

Technically, I suppose you are to be described as a sequel. However, with all the déjà vu and with all the déjà vu all over again, you are more of what we might call at a meal, seconds, a second helping, the same course but with extra garnishings. Again, you could be called an exercise in recycling, all the key plot elements, the central characters, the murder mystery and the ever-suffering and frequently-dying heroine. One of the jokes I enjoyed was that in the first film, she had never heard of *Groundhog Day* and this time is bewildered when *Back to the Future* is quoted!

At first, I thought you were going to have an alternate character having the nightmares and being continually killed, quite an entertaining lead-on. But, after getting interested in Ryan, the scientist and inventor, we discover that he was part of Tree's recurring nightmares. She again was the target. I did enjoy, déjà vu, seeing her initial birthday scene from the first film as she walked through the university grounds, our being reminded of those characters she met. And then, there was her waking up in Carter's room, yet again, same dialogue, the enjoyable repetitions.

One of the aspects that I enjoyed very much was the whole tongue-in-cheek approach to the dialogue, sometimes very corny, at other times witty, the cast playing it for laughs as well as fright, the creative variations on the being murdered every day theme.

I also like the twist in the plot, the murderer in the first film still alive and not guilty, nor the criminally insane man – but an enjoyable shooting denouement.

And, for the young audience, the creation of the time machine with all its logarithms (and your device of having Tree memorise what she learned every day and communicate that to the inventors who are getting it every day for the first time, cumulative effect for a solution). As regards the multiverse possibilities, I rather enjoyed the quick demonstration of folding a serviette, poking a pen through it, opening it up and finding six identical pieces with holes. There were other scientific jargon explanations which I wouldn't try to understand!

This all added up to a pleasing re-visit, enjoyment of the twists in the plot, something akin to those ways of storytelling where the audience has the option of pressing one button, a "what if...?: and going in that direction or pressing an alternate button and finding a different plot development, a different "what if...?". So, some sentiment with Tree meeting her mother again, some romance with Carter who was involved with the insufferable Danielle. But the screenplay did capitalise ironically on the character, her pretentious pontificating, but then utilising her acting practice as a blind person so to distract the Dean (with his knitting as an antidote to smoking), get the Dean's keys to steal back their machine which he had angrily confiscated many times at the zero moment.

But, you know that you are an entertainment for a younger audience who enjoy various horror tropes while not wanting too much gore. Which means that you are an entertainment for some older audiences like me as well!

Dear

WIT

You are a fine film, a profound film. You won an Ecumenical award at the Berlin Film Festival as well as two American Catholic awards, The Christopher Award and The Humanitas Prize.

Your portrait of a teacher, of a woman who looks at life objectively fascinated the teacher in me. And, with Emma Thompson's moving presence and performance as Vivian (not all sweetness and light), and her articulation of poetry, you are a sad joy to watch. mainly Vivian's experience of terminal illness, care and dying.

Margaret Edson's play and this adaptation speak a great deal about knowledge, about knowing and knowing more (rather less on understanding). Vivian has been an academic, a senior scholar, a researcher who lectured (and, perhaps, sometimes taught). She values truth, 'uncompromising scholarly standards making a significant contribution to knowledge'. Words she uses about herself include disciplined, uncompromising, steadfast and 'resolute in the extreme'. In the eight months of her chemotherapy, she keeps asking questions, wanting to know what is going on.

So, a close-up of an English poetry professor with incurable ovarian cancer who has agreed to undergo the strongest chemotherapy available as a resource for research rather than for any real hope of remission or cure. As played by Emma Thompson, Vivian Bearing bares her soul to the audience and we share intimately the process of dying by a brave and tough woman. Professor Bearing has taught Metaphysical Poetry. Your screenplay uses several of John Donne's Holy Sonnets, especially 'Death be not Proud', as a philosophical and religious grounding for the experience of death.

But Vivian's childhood, especially with her father, is glimpsed in flashback. Her working life is shown in some flashbacks, interviews with her tutor and in her own lectures. But you are a profound film which both delights in and has respect for words, for grammar and for articulating words.

I am in danger of going off on a lecture on these poets so I will restrict myself to saying that the metaphysical poets, while noted for their love poetry (though this is not mentioned in the film), are concerned about mortality, about immortality, about sin, God's mercy, forgiveness and God forgetting our transgressions. For them, the barrier ('which is not insuperable') between mortality and immortality is a paradox. They explore it as a puzzle but do not 'solve' it.

Wit is a portrait of a life in death.

You are beautifully written: 'Both published and perished!', Vivian says. Other polished phrases are delightful - and psychologically sound and insightful. Vivian loves knowledge and has a great respect for words. Her illness is insidious, which means treacherous; it is pernicious; she mulls over 'ratiocination', 'coruscation'. However, she ironically has to lapse into American quickspeak in hospital, 'How are you today?', 'Fine.' 'That's great.'

During her career, she had preferred research to humanity. Her course is described as bootcamp where the brain had to be in knots. But, In facing the reality of her illness and acknowledging how humiliating the poking and prodding of her body by doctors and students, the interminable questionnaires and tests, the agony of a colonoscopy, how degrading it felt to experience a pelvic examination by a former student, Vivian moves towards some kind of inner peace – and learning empathy.

At the end, Vivian tells the audience, 'We are discussing life and death, not in the abstract, but my life, my death. There would be nothing worse than a scholarly analysis with erudition. Now is the time for simplicity, time for, dare

I say it, kindness... I thought that being extremely smart would take care of it, but now I am found out.'

By this time, you were a film that completely moved me. Her mentor and friend, Evelyn (Eileen Atkins also wonderful), visits Vivian, quietly takes off her shoes and lies beside her, offering to read. She says she will not read Donne but reads the children's story, *The Runaway Bunny* (including the publishing and copyright details!). 'A little allegory of the soul: wherever you hide, God will find you.'

Evelyn had told Vivian that in the last line of 'Death be not Proud', there should only be a comma, a simple pause between this life and the next, life separated from eternal life by a pause, overcoming the seemingly insuperable barrier between life and death and eternal life...

'And death shall be no more, comma, death thou shalt die.'

Well, this has been a rather metaphysical letter to you. What more can I write to you except to say that writing this letter makes me want to watch you again?

Dear

PRIEST

You were ahead of your time and when released in 1995 or were you right on time? Whatever the answer, you certainly caused quite an amount of controversy. While Bishops Conferences in Europe arranged for screenings for clergy, New York's Cardinal O'Connor described you as the worst film that had ever 'rotted on the silver screen', then shots were fired in a New Jersey cinema.

My introduction to you was far more calm and positive. You were part of the Panorama section of the 1995 Berlinale and the Ecumenical Jury went to see you. The president of the International Catholic organisation for cinema, a Dutch Carmelite priest, Henk Hoekstra, organised that he and I write an official statement on you. Not only did we write the statement, but the media bishop for the German Bishops Conference read it aloud at a public and ecumenical gathering. And, soon afterwards, there was an eight-page supplement with articles and reviews on you published in Brussels by the Secretariat of the Catholic cinema organisation. So, this was a positive approach before any 'rotting...' headlines were issued.

One of the best things for me was that I had the opportunity to interview your director, Antonia Bird. She mentioned that Derek Worlock, the Archbishop of Liverpool, had forbidden the use of any Catholic Church for filming so she had to use Anglican churches in London. However, she did comment on the welcome that Catholic priests gave her in Liverpool, inviting her and the congregation to stand around the altar during the celebration.

The other great advantage you had was that your screenwriter was Jimmy McGovern, writing from experience of the church and clergy as he did later with *Liam* and, for the screenplay of his excellent television series about a Liverpool priest, played by Sean Bean, *Broken*. So, excellent credentials.

I remember thinking, as you opened, that any film which began with an upset priest grabbing a large cross and charging towards the windows of the Bishop's house was definitely a challenge – even exciting! Your picture of the priests in the parish was very complex. Tom Wilkinson, before he became an international star, was the parish priest who had worked in the missions, returned home, but was living in his presbytery with his housekeeper. So, immediate questions about priestly celibacy, fidelity to vows and commitment, emotional and sexual needs, the issue of married clergy, used women. With that, a substantial agenda.

Then there was the issue of the curate, Fr Greg (Linus Roache) and the realisation of his homosexual orientation, something which was acknowledged in those years but not always explicitly and not always with help to the seminarian or the priest. So, an added agenda, the priest dealing with his sexuality, emotional needs, sexual liaison and the consequences, not only for himself but, when this became known in the parish, his being shunned, his being removed and having to live with a senior priest (who was prone to speaking in Latin and not the most empathetic).

I am adding a distraction, the main parishioner hostile to Fr Greg was played by Tony Booth, father of Cherie and soon to be the father-in-law of the Prime Minister of the UK, Tony Blair!

It is no wonder that some bishops were upset, that others thought clergy should view the film and discuss it. There is a Melbourne story that Archbishop Frank Little suggested the local priests not go to see the film but on the Queen's Birthday holiday afternoon, when the lights went up at the *Rivoli*, not only were there lots of clergy but the Archbishop himself!

When there was the shooting in New Jersey, it seemed to me in my job in the Australian Catholic Office, that it was best to publish the statement from Berlin even though it was two months until the film was to be released in Australia.

This was wise, led to a lot of radio discussions, a television interview, and Australian Catholics dealing with you in an adult response.

But there was also another most significant theme that you covered, child sexual abuse, but not by the clergy but within the family. A young girl goes to Fr Greg to confession and reveals the situation. Her father also comes to confession but is smugly defiant towards Fr Greg. Yet, Jimmy McGovern's screenplay creates a providential situation. A parish meeting breaks up early with some disputes, the members going home, Greg going to his room, kneeling before the crucifix, praying desperately about the absolute seal, his being bound not to reveal or act on the young girl's confession. This is a great scene of priestly prayer and anguish. But, ironically, the mother arrives home early from the meeting and discovers her husband and his behaviour with her daughter. Now out in the open.

I want to mention two key scenes that have stayed with me over the decades, two concerning the receiving of communion. One of the scenes concerns Fr Greg, distributing communion and the man with whom he had the relationship comes up to receive – and Greg refuses, a self-condemning act and harsh to the man in line. The other scene occurs at the end of the film when Fr Greg is back in ministry and he and the parish priest are both distributing communion. No one comes up to Fr. Greg until the little girl who was the object of her father's sexual abuse comes to him. He is tearful (and we) – and in the background is the song from *Carousel* (significant for Liverpool football), 'You'll Never Walk Alone'.

In many ways, you were ahead of the times, considering what has happened in the lives of Catholic clergy since the 1990s and the shocking revelations about clerical sexual abuse and the need for compassion and justice for survivors. While you offer no definitive solutions, you ask significant questions and show us emotional sequences to challenge us.

Dear

THE YEAR OF LIVING DANGEROUSLY

You have been on my letter-list for some time, happy memories of you in the early 1980s, again Peter Weir directing. And, for me, one of the most arresting screen characters, Billy Kwan. So, delighted when the opportunity came to watch you again on a Qantas flight!

Something personal which made me interested in Indonesia. In fact, the first country I visited outside Australia was Indonesia, from a boat on a trip to Europe, September 1962 (three years before the dangerous year). I had no expectations, just eager anticipation. The first thing was that we were prevented for several hours from disembarking in Djakarta. So, in the afternoon we were driven around the city, a blend of interest and shock, out to the newly built sports stadium, lots of impressions. It was actually the first time I'd seen police carrying guns. And, the superior of the mission, Andreas, had to slip cash to the guards so that we could go back onto the wharf to re-board. Although you were released almost 20 years later, those memories were still vivid in my mind.

As I mentioned, Billy Kwan is the fascinating character. You are really Billy Kwan's story even though Mel Gibson's eager and then disillusioned journalist has top billing, as does Sigourney Weaver, highlighting the romance as well as making you a film about journalism and working-journalists. But the immediately fascinating thing about Billy Kwan is that he is played by Linda Hunt who earned the Best Supporting Actress Oscar for her performance. Actually, rather disconcerting to see Linda Hunt in other films, so different from Billy Kwan.

After the opening credits, Billy explains the Indonesian puppets, the Wayang, to his new friend, Guy Hamilton – heroic puppets, some sinister puppets, preparing us for our appreciation of the journalist as hero, the journalist as prince, the journalist fallible and capable of betrayal. Billy himself then emerges as a puppeteer, controlling Hamilton, matchmaking (with an overtone even of pimping), promoting Jilly who is a spy at the British Embassy. At the end, with regrets and some disillusionment, Billy tells Hamilton that he created him.

And watching Billy in his processes of creation, there is an intriguing portrait. Billy as an idealist. He has enthroned President Sukarno on a pedestal. As Hamilton goes out into the crowds of Indonesia, declaring that there is little he could do in the face of such poverty, Billy quotes the Gospel of St Luke to him, 3:10, "what then must we do?" Billy later declares that we must help those that God puts in our way. He is quietly supportive of a mother, with a sick baby, forced to work on the streets. The death of the baby is the key to Billy's disillusionment.

The Jesus' imagery, from novelist Christopher Koch's Catholicism, applies to Billy himself, some of the journalists mocking him, talking about putting him on the cross and suffering. And, ultimately, he is killed for his witnessing, the banner denouncing Sukarno from the hotel window, quickly removed before the president, driving by in his cavalcade, can glimpse it.

Billy Kwan is certainly a flawed character, looking up at life and at other people from his dwarf short height, being taken for granted, underestimated, or sometimes the butt for mockery. Like God, whom he sometimes tries to imitate, he tries to provide situations where people can better themselves, creating (but unlike God, manipulating), full of hope, prone, of course, to idealistic disappointment. And this leads to his death – and something of a Jesus-like martyr.

You certainly create the atmosphere of uncertainty in Indonesia in 1965, the president's dictatorship, the murmurings and the Communist uprising, the defeat of the Communists. I'm sure you would be a good visual reference to students of Indonesian history and of the period.

Don't you think it is ironic that you could not be filmed in Indonesia in the early 1980s because of the political situation – but, cast and crew could go to the Philippines: and it was in the Marcos era! But, five years later, those years of living dangerously came to an end.

Dear

THE HOUSE THAT JACK BUILT

You would probably not be expecting to read 'Dear...', especially if you are conscious of the controversies you have raised, audiences walking out in disgust, critical insults about your director, his ambitions – and pretensions – Lars von Trier. I can tell you that I've seen most of his films, found *Dancing in the Dark* and Bjork rather unbearable, found *Melancholia* too melancholic, but was intrigued by *Dogville, Mandalay*, and the two *Nymphomania* films. So, I was certainly ready to give you a go!

Of course, I sympathise with audiences who have an aversion to watching serial killer films. The killings here are grisly, sometimes long, images repeated – although they are not as gory as some contemporary horror films. And, in your running time of 2 ½ hours, there are many other elements to counterbalance the killings.

What I was not expecting was to like you so much or, rather, to find so much in you to appreciate, to reflect on.

I suppose that you would agree with me in stating that Jack, the engineer and would-be architect who wanted to build a house, who created a model, went on site and built but then continually demolished, can be described as an evil Everyman character. And Matt Dillon embodied him skilfully, looking neat at the beginning, obsessively compulsive, more killings and feeling freer, letting himself go, more and more unkempt. He is trapped in his own ever-increasing urges but destiny and retribution take over.

In fact, your structure is very straightforward, five incidents of killing and an epilogue which brings revelation and justice. You show Jack in his ordinary life. You also show some flashbacks of the troubled child Jack who has no family, who hides in reeds, perhaps always eluding pursuit.

Before I tell you my appreciation of the voice offscreen, Verge, with the exciting revelation of who he really is, Vergil himself, I want to take a moment to reflect on how much philosophy there is in your screenplay and how extensive a range of the arts, architecture, painting, animation, music, poetry... (I wonder if the audience who walked out were not so much disturbed by the gruesome images of death but found it difficult to cope with all this reflection, even thinking it pretentious or irrelevant and/or boring.)

But, very early, there are images of architectural frames, Gothic cathedrals, Glenn Gould playing the piano.

You have an animation allegory about streetlights and shadows before and behind the character walking the night, symbolising a movement from pleasure to pain. There are more paintings, classical paintings. And William Blake has a rather important role for reflection, his sketches, images of God, the Lamb and the Tiger, symbols of innocence and evil. Quite exhilarating!

And then there are all the verbal references to history and to world events, suggestions of hunting and culling as ethnic cleansing, a reflection on icons with footage of Stukas dropping bombs, the engineered whining sound of death, and images of the 20th century iconic dictators. Vergil will reference Buchenwald and the oak tree there during the Holocaust, the tree under which Goethe sat and wrote. (A momentary mean thought – what if those escaping the film were interviewed as they left the cinema about the meaning of all these images. What would they, what could they say?)

Verge (heard off-screen with Bruno Ganz's voice) eventually mentions *The Aeneid* and we realise that this is *the* Vergil. And, when he finally appears, in an epilogue, *Katabasis*, descent and downfall, we remember that Dante chose him to be the guide to *The Inferno*. He has accompanied Jack on his journey, commenting, challenging, condemning, and here he takes Jack into the depths, visually red depths, climbing down ladders, Jack being given the chance to choose, wanting an escape route which he cannot manage, falling into hell. And Vergil has the classic quotation, hubris leads to nemesis.

I just paused, remembering that immediately, instead of something solemn, up come your credits and the song, 'Hit the road, Jack', popular and jaunty, but whose lyrics do form a commentary on what we have watched.

So, an experience of realism, experience of surrealism, touches of theatre of the absurd, allegories and metaphors, discussions about the nature of art, philosophical ruminations about the nature of good and evil and of human nature. You always have something arresting for the senses, stimulating for the mind, to counterbalance the grim. You're right, not the expected perspectives in a serial killer film.

Even while I was watching you, you were becoming an ever more interesting choice for a *Dear Movie*.

HIGHER GROUND

I came across you at an important moment in my life, doing some work on the possibility for using films for programs in spiritual direction training. I had just written a paper on this theme and was outlining a program for a course – and there you were. Unfortunately, when the time came for the course to start, you were not available on DVD! (And I had to fall back on a worthy successor for testing spiritual directors and their approach, Neil Jordan's version of Graham Greene's *The End of the Affair*.)

You might be wondering about the term spiritual direction and how it relates to your narrative. Towards the end, Corrine, the central character, is experiencing a faith crisis. She visits the church advisor and he gives her some plain advice, suggesting what she should do, even telling her what to do. With spiritual direction, it is important for the director to be able to keep quiet, to listen, to help the directee appreciate God's presence, the role of prayer, to discover ways of discerning what decisions should be made, what is called the language of the Spirit. The advice session was certainly not spiritual direction and not particularly helpful to Corrine even as counselling.

You are based on a memoir by Carolyn S. Briggs who co-wrote your screenplay. Which means that there is an authenticity and urgency. The setting is an evangelical church in the American South, a church and community of God's Word, to be interpreted literally without historical or literary nuance. It is a church of pastors who exercise strong, even dominating, leadership. There are prayer meetings, some members experiencing the gift of tongues. There are strict moral codes. And, as you show, young children relish being in special groups in the church, absorbing the spirit and fellowship of the church, enabled to grow up faithful.

So, you are an interesting example of a film that shows the faith journey of a woman from childhood, through moments of rebellion, to marriage, to the almost loss of her child and a re-discovery of faith. You are full of a great deal of enjoyable moments, especially in music, composing and performance, the contribution of Corinne's husband, who shares in her recovery of faith. Lots of detail as well, bringing the characters and the community to life.

But, as the years go on, doubts arise, questions are asked, the possibility of leaving the church, despite the warm encouragement of Pastor Bud, the religious experience of husband and friends: where is the life of faith leading?

I want to compliment you on your director and star, Vera Farmiga, an actress I admire and who has shown a great talent for versatility in many roles. She is the perfect embodiment of Corrine, enabling the audience to share her life with her, move into her difficulties, puzzled about her future.

When I was reviewing you on your commercial release, I came across a number of quotations from Vera Farmiga herself, brought up as Ukrainian Catholic. 'You've got fundamentalism, and you've got relativism. I wanted to push both ways and try to come at it from a middle ground. Doubt is the middle position between knowledge and ignorance. It encompasses cynicism but also genuine questioning.'

And commenting on the difficulties she encountered in casting *Higher Ground,* she noted: I'd say, 'It's about a woman enmeshed in this very particular spiritual community who's trying to conceptualise and define God for herself'. And you use the word 'God' and people quake with fear. That's when I started to realise what a touchy, bizarre, sensitive, combative subject matter it is.

I hope that explains something of why I appreciated you and how you would be of great help to those working in courses on spiritual direction.

Dear

RAINING STONES

The title sounds a bit biblical! Retribution? Well, not exactly.

You have the great advantage of being directed by Ken Loach, especially at the beginning of his recent decades of critical and commercial success. (We appreciated his 60s drama about poverty and family and, of course, *Cathy Come Home, Kes* and *Family Life*. And while there were many films for the next 20 plus years, they did not have the success that he has enjoyed since making you and *Riffraff* in the earlier 1990s.)

Your writer was Jim Allen who had strong Catholic sense (and a bit to the left with his next film, *Land and Freedom* about the Spanish Civil War) which won an Ecumenical Award at Cannes, 1995, surprising Loach when he received a call from the churches and assumed that he was being condemned – but he had the good grace to praise his subsequent writer for more than twenty years, former seminarian, Scot Paul Laverty, declaring that he discovered that the Catholic Church was not monolithic!.

Actually, the picture of Catholicism that you offer is both heart-warming and gritty, a fine parish priest in Manchester, played by Tom Hickey, who knows his parishioners and shares their life, hearing confessions but also turning somewhat of a blind eye to misdemeanours and troubles. I find it interesting that you were released at the same time as *Priest*, written by Jimmy McGovern, set not far away in Liverpool, priests with problems, issues of sexuality, issues of abuse by parents, the role of the seal of confession. You offer a decent priest, a pastorally concerned priest.

The family at the centre of the film has an unemployed father, played by Bruce Jones, doing a bit of stealing of meat on the side, selling it at pubs, trying to get work, clearing drains – but, ambitious that his little daughter will have a First Communion dress that matches any bought by a family with more income. He is even prepared to go to a loan shark and gets into more trouble, especially when the drunken loan shark crashes his car and dies. But he can always go to the priest who can encourage him and offer practical advice.

But one of the aspects of Catholicism that I particularly enjoyed, and happily show it to catechists or groups of parents, is the preparation for Communion, the scenes in the church and the little daughter reciting her catechism, commended by the priest but, then at home, puzzled a lot about the meanings of Communion and the story of the Last

Supper, and her dad, at the evening meal, trying to explain –
increasingly desperately.

Jim Allen wrote you some very entertaining dialogue
and Ken Loach brought it to life. it is a very-funny-for-
Catholics meal scene where the father tries to explain what
tradition calls the doctrine of Transubstantiation concerning
Jesus' presence in the bread and wine. His wife is cooking
and he sits at the table, telling his daughter about Jesus and
his mates at the Last Supper. He takes bread and tells his
daughter that this is him, that Jesus told them that 'this is
me'. She looks at her father, quite uncomprehending. He
asks her whether she understands. 'No.' He still perseveres
but has a memory lapse and has to call out to his wife in the
kitchen, asking her what comes after the bread. She calls
out 'the wine'. And, again, asked by her father whether she
knows what he's talking about, she replies, 'No'.

Looking back at that description, I find it still funny,
but it might be rather 'in' for wider audiences.

No need to remind you that Ken Loach is a great promoter
of social justice and social care – for more than fifty years.
You may not be surprised that of all the directors who have
been given awards by Catholic and Protestant film juries at
international festivals, Ken Loach has won the most. You
will appreciate this Loach story. The churches invited him
to Cannes in 2004 for a special medal commemorating his

record of awards (and I have to tell you he has won several more since). Not only did he come and make a speech. There was a strike of entertainment industry workers during the festival. Loach brought two young strikers into the ceremony with him, reinforcing his speech about society, work and rights.

Thanks for offering me the opportunity to enthuse about you and write some congratulatory words about Ken Loach.

Dear

LA STRADA

Even as I begin this letter to you, the strains of Nino Rota's melodies are playing in my imagination. The plaintive strains, with their melancholy, the jaunty tunes on the roads, the circus-like performances, echoes of the *Nutcracker Suite*, they all bring to mind the face of Giulietta Masina, and the deep pathos of her character, Gelsomina. It makes me reflect on what pathos (and its root in suffering) does to an audience when it is encountered in real life, let alone on-screen. Perhaps pathos could be described as sympathy/empathy and understanding for life's victims/survivors.

And there is something of the sound in your title, *La Strada*, which does not go so well in the Anglo-Saxon, *The Road* (and Cormac Murphy's post-Apocalyptic novel and John Hillcoat's powerful film have appropriated it). But, the title is archetypal, symbolic, all of those, all of us, on life's road.

You are early Fellini, drawing on so many of his favourite themes, circus and clowns, harshness and love, the world of the poor in spirit. And, here is Giulietta Masina, his wife, portraying Gelsomina, waif-like, a beautifully simple soul we might say, being directed by her husband to whom she was devoted for a half-century's marriage. (And, you must admit that she was a fine actress given her other Fellini roles – the prostitute, Cabiria, the religious matron as *Juliet of the Spirits*, lighthearted dancer in *Ginger and Fred*.)

One way that I have responded to your portrait of Gelsomina is to consider her a 'Beatitudes Person'. Just going through Jesus' list in Matthew's Gospel, she embodies most of them. In her simplicity, limited brainpower but with her delightful as well as sad emotional intelligence, she can be called "poor in spirit", a way of describing humility, remembering the Latin origins of the word "humus/ground", truly grounded in herself, her eagerness in working with the strongman, Zampano (remembering Anthony Quinn's powerful performance, rough and angry, abandoning Gelsomina, lying grief stricken on the shore), befriending the clown, Motto (mischievously provocative and with simple wisdom, Richard Basehart).

There is no doubt that Gelsomina is meek, 'blessed are the meek' not assertive, that in her instinctive response to Zampano, she is innately kind and compassionate, 'blessed are the merciful'. And, in her suffering, she grieves, 'blessed are they who mourn'. There is no doubt, of course, that she is pure of heart. They are certainly blessed. Given her lowly status in her society and even in the circus, she cannot be seen as a warrior for justice, but the need for respect for human rights is significant in her life. In her life, in the circus, in her small way, she is a peacemaker. They too are certainly blessed. The last Beatitudes focuses on the experience of suffering and persecution, as one translation puts it "because they do what God requires". Gelsomina suffers violence, she dies.

Do you think that this makes Gelsomina a perfect human being in terms of being true to herself, her self, and the way that she lived her life? I think so.

To get in the mood for writing this letter to you, I was not able to watch you again, but decided to Google Wikipedia and its entry on Giulietta Masina. I recommend it, in many ways, homage to a beautiful life, a consistent life. She died only a few months after Fellini and they are buried together in Rimini. There is also a wonderful indication in the entry – she asked that at her funeral, trumpeter, Mauro Maur, play Nino Rota's music that pervades (and I rather like the word) to describe that pervading 'leitmotiv'.

And then I Googled Youtube and relived you with a five-minute collage, *Gelsomina from La Strada, by Federico Fellini*, the music, Gelsomina playing the trumpet, five minutes of such wonderful memories of Giulietta Masina, funny, clown make-up, make-up, sad, joyful, devout, such a beautifully expressive face.

Which means, that as I finish this letter to you, the musical strains, especially the plaintive, are playing again in my imagination.

Dear

THE GODFATHER

This letter is just for you, not for your two sequels – although *Godfather II* won a Best Film Oscar, as you did, and one for your director, Francis Ford Coppola, and *Godfather III* had great deal of melodrama, Vatican financial scandals and the resolution of Michael Corleone's life.

I wonder how many others, as I do, think of a particular scene when your title is mentioned. I see, once again, still in disbelief, that severed horse's head in the bed, its size, the blood, John Marley terrified, the horror that anyone could carry out the slaughter let alone put that head in the bed. Of course, that was not the only horror, but I felt that I need to mention it first.

I remember at the time that some of the critics, some of the commentators, thought that that you were something of a glorification of The Mafia. I can see why they might say that because you are a very solemn film, a vast portrait of a Mafioso family, the extended family, associates, criminal connections, a family of codes, rituals, considered Honourable, Cosa Nostra. In a sense, you were Mafia myth-making, not merely a gangster show set amongst Italian-

Americans, Sicilian in origin, and their crimes in the 1930s and 40s. There have been plenty of this kind of film, both before and after you. But, in your solemnity, strong cast, Mario Puzo's dialogue, your assured director, another memorable Nino Rota score, *The Godfather* theme, you were and still are, special.

And this was enhanced, of course, by the portrait of Don Vito – immortalised by Marlon Brando's performance, a quietly sinister presence, a highly demanding presence, the very embodiment of the Mafia code, illustrating once and for all the nature of an offer one cannot refuse. It was the way Brando was filmed, light and shadow, at his desk – but, in some ways, perhaps a little romantically, shown outside his office, with children, gardens, a seemingly benevolent grandfather figure. And, on reflection, all the more frightening.

The other aspect of your drama is the reliance on family rituals, religious rituals, Catholic sacraments. So much time is spent at the opening with the marriage sequence, all the fuss, all the fanfare, all the preparations, the lavish style, the Sicilian traditions, the religious ceremony, the aftermath, eating and drinking, music and dancing – and its being background to sinister meetings and reverence for the Don.

And, of course, with the play on your name, Godfather, the culminating baptism sequence and the question of how such men (often with the tacit, even fearful, complicity of the women) could be so murderous, ostensibly religious, the intercutting of the ceremony with the massacres.

So, as a gangster film, you could be called archetypal. More than the activities of the gangsters, the killings, discriminant and indiscriminate, the deceptions and betrayals, the bookkeeping, the pragmatic issues of whether to go beyond the numbers racket into drug business, you are a film that looks as if you are enshrining the Mafiosi. This makes for both intriguing and repellent drama.

But, apart from the horse's head, the main horror feature which struck me at the time was the portrait of Michael Corleone. Al Pacino gives an extraordinary performance, a seemingly ingenuous young man, military service, marriage to Kay, faced with the realities of his father's role and influence, opting for absolute loyalty to his family, brought more and more into the ethos as well as the murderous activities, a fully-fledged Mafia don by the end of the film. I was very taken with the comment by Pauline Kael that we watched the corruption of Michael Corleone before our very eyes, immoral disintegration combined with such exercises of power. At the time, I watched with a certain amount of disbelief, how could this young man become...

It was with a certain relief (and faith and hope) that I watched *Godfather III* and the ageing Michael with the cardinal – a sacrament at the end of his life, confession and penance.

As I write, memories of your solemn treatment of the Mafia, the religious dimensions, the family rituals, and, yes, the vicious and brutal violence, mean that you opened up this gangster world and changed (well, maybe, modified) our perspectives on it.

Dear

DES HOMMES ET DES DIEUX/ OF GODS AND MEN

You are one of the finest religious films, and one of the best Catholic films in years. No controversy here. You won the Ecumenical Prize at Cannes 2010. You also won the Grand Prix du Jury from the festival itself (with, of all directors, Tim Burton presiding).

You take on an important story, the Trappist community of Mt Atlas, Algeria, in the 1990s. Living their monastic life amongst the local people and ministering to them, especially with medical services, they were viewed more and more with suspicion in the country, especially because they were French expatriates, by government troops who were becoming more active against the increasing terrorist attacks, and by the terrorists themselves. Seven of the monks were killed in the latter part of May, 1996. Your centre is the life of the monks and their preparation for death.

And, with Moroccan location photography, you are both beautiful and austere in landscapes and in the interiors of the monastery – and in the interior lives of the monks. Your cast looks, moves, speaks and acts as if they were authentic monks. Lambert Wilson shows the complexity of a man elected to be superior but who has a tendency to make decisions himself but is ultimately willing to be guided in discernment by the whole community. Veteran Michel Lonsdale as the ageing doctor who offers practical wisdom in his medical skills and down-to-earth counsel.

I don't want this to sound too much like a talk on religious orders but you are able to cover all aspects of the religious routine of the monastery in accurate detail. In fact, you communicate the life and spirit, the prayer, Eucharist, sung liturgy, silence and contemplation, the detachment of the vow of poverty, the taken-for-granted sacrifices of the vow of chastity, the work, the meals and the readings, the community meetings, the outreach. You show this in episodes throughout the film which are as effective, even more effective, than a documentary. You could well serve as a recruitment vehicle because you show the life as both credible and authentic.

All the time, you challenge the audience to wonder what they would do in such dangerous circumstances, especially after official advice from the area is given, recommending the monks leave and return to France. At a community gathering, the superior asks them all to give voice to whether each wanted to stay or leave. Some speak in favour of leaving and explain why: family, illness, the opportunity to continue their work elsewhere. Some are still uncertain. Others wish to stay, intuitively knowing that this is where God wanted them to be.

After this, each of the monks has to discern his path in terms of his commitment and understanding of God's will. One of the monks experiences dark night in his prayer and the sequence where the superior listens, allows him to voice his doubts, is moving, and enables him to find some peace of soul.

After the advice to leave, the monks listen to the opinions of the local people, especially those who come to the monastery for medical help. Their argument is that the monks remain in solidarity with the people. At the final discernment meeting, this argument is given great attention, with Gospel backing and the spirituality of Jesus who stayed faithful until his death. But death seems inevitable.

For an audience wanting to know and understand something deeper about Christian spirituality, something deeper underlying, despite the sins and failures of the church and of church people, these scenes offer a great deal to ponder.

So does the letter that the superior writes before the monks are abducted in vans, audio-taped for their identity, knowing that they are hostages, and led into the snow and the mountains to their deaths. He goes over the decisions and the motivation but also acknowledges that the monks have lived in a Muslim country with its Quranic ideals and spirituality and its God, far from the fanaticism of those who do not really read their scriptures fully or are caught up in bellicose righteousness. The superior develops the theme that they will go to death in the same way that Jesus did.

One of my favourite sequences: the community sits to enjoy something of a last supper together, the camera focusing on each, their smiles, then their tears, then their deep resignation, drinking a glass of wine together, and all to the powerful rhythms and melodies of Tchaikovsky's ..

These Trappists of Algeria were not considered saints in the ordinariness of their religious lives. They did their best. However, faced with the reality of impending death, like many a religious or a secular hero, they found their depths, despite any fear, and discovered a martyr's saintliness in giving a life for others.

Did you know that they were all declared 'Blessed' in 2018, a step towards being officially declared saints?

Dear

CALVARY

Difficult years for priests these days. And, your title focuses on suffering – and possibilities in redemptive suffering.

I think you are one of the best films on priests in recent years. John Michael McDonagh in your screenplay reveals quite detailed knowledge of the church in Ireland and which brings the plot to contemporary life – even though, one hopes, that the principal events of the film would not happen in real life.

In the mid-20th century, a key film on the life of a parish priest was Robert Bresson's version (he of Transcendental Cinema) Georges Bernanos' novel, *Diary of a Country Priest.* You are the diary of an Irish country priest of the 21st century. Brendan Gleeson gives a totally persuasive performance as the priest. And your setting is on the Irish Atlantic coast, 38 km from Sligo, according to a road sign.

With the focus of the title, it is clear that you will be a film about suffering, or that the priest will be a significant

Christ-figure, a victim of his own Calvary, an innocent victim, atoning for the sins of others.

This is made very clear from your alarming opening sequence, the priest sitting in the confessional, a man coming into the box and declaring that he has been a victim of a priest's sexual abuse, that it happened over many years, that it has ruined his life. And then the also-alarming threat that he will kill the parish priest on the following Sunday, not because he is a guilty man, but because he is innocent and that will make his death more significant.

Since your initial theme is that of clerical sexual abuse, you have to be viewed and valued in the context of the revelations of recent decades, of government enquiries, Royal Commissions, of sentences for guilty clergy, and the criticism of church officials (including Cardinals) for not understanding the crisis and for not acting on it well. This gives a powerful framework for this week in the life of the parish priest, considering what he has been told, preparing for his possible death. The accuser could be anyone in the village, although the priest has recognised his voice.

So, within your framework, we watch the priest going about his ordinary ministry in this parish. Significantly for his life experience, he is a 'late vocation', a widower who decided on priesthood after his wife's death. We are introduced to his daughter, who has attempted suicide, but has come to visit her father and talk things over with him. Which means he is a priest of some life experience, of family life, even though he reflects that he was something of a failure – and a drinker.

You take us with the priest, his visiting different people in the parish, a woman who does his washing, is separated from her husband, the local butcher, is having an affair with the local garage man. She is not averse to other relationships, especially to the atheist and mocking doctor in the local hospital. But, as with the other characters, she is able to speak frankly to the priest and he is able to speak frankly with her. It is the same with her husband, the butcher.

Then there is the young man, rather prim and proper, awkward in his manner, who comes to the priest to discuss his ambitions, his personality, his sexual problems, his future. Other visits include the man from the garage, the local policeman and his rather exhibitionist son, a local landowner who is alienated from his family, drinks a great deal, and confesses that he cares for nothing and no one. On the lighter side, there is an old American author who welcomes the priest, getting food from him, but wanting a gun just in case he gets ill and needs to leave this world. We watch a busy priest.

You offer a significant scene, an accident with the death of a foreign visitor. The priest anoints the dead man, comforts his widow, encounters her at the airport when he is inclined to leave the village and avoid his imminent death. It is the words of the widow as well as his watching two workers slouching over the dead man's coffin, that indicate that he should go back to face whatever will come.

Mounting tension as the Sunday draws nearer. The priest is very fond of his pet dog and is devastated when he finds the dog's throat slit. And this follows his church being burnt down by the accuser. It is clear that the priest is moving towards Calvary. In moments of agony, he takes to drinking, returning alone to his spartan room. In some way it is not so important whether the priest is killed or not. It is the priest's preparation and readiness which is more important than what might happen. However, one significant question for the priest from his accuser is whether he wept at his dog's death – and whether he wept at the plight of the victims of sex abuse. A key question for the church, hierarchy and laity.

John Michael McDonagh does have a key idea, which you reveal early, when his daughter asks the priest about virtues. He replies that forgiveness has been underrated – something that pervades the ending of the film.

You are well worth seeing, the story of a priest and his own agony and Calvary in a contemporary situation, showing contemporary problems, illustrating the response of contemporary parishioners and non-believers. In fact, you should be seen.

AMADEUS

Sheer total enjoyment. Well, maybe there's a bit of redundancy in that comment but I think I shall stand by it.

I remember thinking at the time of your release that F. Murray Abraham should have received two Best Actor Oscar awards – one for playing Salieri when he was younger, one for playing Salieri when he was older and more sinister. He made Salieri most memorable. Not that Tom Hulce wasn't very good as Mozart, young, silly and giggly, genius, somewhat flippant in his relationships, very little insight into Salieri and his jealousy. I remember being very glad that F. Murray Abraham was gracious to Tom Hulce and his performance in his Oscar acceptance speech. Do you remember that at the Oscar ceremony, Laurence Olivier was to present the award for Best Film but made a mess of it, blurting out your name before the rest of the nominees could be honoured and their lips screened. Olivier was almost 77, and not well. Anyway, you won.

The question for me is how to describe the sheer total enjoyment. Here is an attempt.

How you looked. The word that immediately comes to mind is 'sumptuous'. After all, this was the 18th century, the Austro-Hungarian Empire, life in Vienna. There were the palaces with their magnificent interiors. There were opera houses, beauty on stage, large applauding audiences. Yes, of course, there were the streets and the ordinary homes – and a growing darkness as you continued, especially in Salieri's world and the evocation of Mozart's last days, insinuations of murder, his Requiem.

How you sounded. Well, 'sumptuous' comes to mind again. Your running time was almost 3 hours which gave ample opportunity for audiences to hear, appreciate and relish, the range of Mozart's music, Mozart, young sometimes with the seemingly improvised, Mozart's more mature works and the orchestrations, the excerpts from the operas. The exhilaration of the notes, the phrasings, the cadences, the dramatic effect of the operatic – and that despite the emperor's would-be critic's comment "too many notes"! Poor Salieri – 'sumptuous' is not exactly the words that critics use about his carefully-composed, well-intended exercises in composition.

How you felt. There is something exciting in being immersed in a past world, a very different world, an at times exotic world, an at times sinister world. We feel exuberant most of the time that we are in Mozart's company, his innate joy, his rapid ability to compose and play, his giggling innocence. Which means that a lot of the feeling you communicate was focused on Salieri. There was a feeling of intrigue, curious about the man himself, his position in Vienna and the court, his ambitions for music and composition, his image of himself with touches of complacency. Later, the feeling was – perhaps to mix a metaphor – darker. You felt sinister as we were made party to Salieri's inner feelings, the suppressed envy, the growing jealousy, its flowing over into action, scheming against Mozart, deep animosity.

Which means, then, that you are actually a powerful drama. I should have mentioned the name of Peter Shaffer earlier, playwright of versatility from *The Royal Hunt of the Sun* to *Equus*. After all, you are basically his creation, his creativity and imagination, his insight into Mozart and his character as well as his genius, his creating the character of Salieri, giving him more of a fame than he ever had during his lifetime. While the music is foremost, Peter Shaffer's language is also striking. And a tribute to director, Milos Forman, refugee in the 1960s from Communist Czechoslovakia. (I wanted to mention that I saw a theatre production of *Amadeus* at London's *Old Vic* in 1999, with excellent performances by David Suchet as Salieri and Michael Sheen as Mozart.)

Music and the knowledge and appreciation of music is not my forte, but I welcomed the opportunity to get to know something of Mozart himself as well as be open to the range of his music. So, a word of thanks – for the sheer total enjoyment.

Dear

JESUS

That could sound like a prayer or, perhaps, an expletive. This letter is more aligned to the former rather than the latter!

Have you experienced much comparison with other Jesus films? And that could be going back to 1916 with *Intolerance*, to 1927 with Cecil B. DeMille's *King of Kings*, then a huge leap over the decades without Jesus films, to *The King of Kings* in Panavision and colour, the range of films during the 1960s, 1970s and up to the present time. That situates you in the latter part of the development of the Jesus film, 1999. And, you were produced for television and for the celebration of the millennium.

I'm writing this letter to you because not only have I appreciated your approach to Jesus in the Gospels but because, for over almost 15 years, you have been a staple for seminars on Jesus-figures, some of the sequences very impressive and I will remind you of them later.

But, I did want to mention that in 2007 in Manila, during breaks in a seminar on Jesus films over a three day period, those attending wanted to keep watching you, section by section. And, at the end, with your very nice finale of Jesus in the 20th century and the children, they burst into enthusiastic applause. I have to tell you that showing the sequences in London, they were appreciated but only by respectful and reticent silence!

One of the things I like about you is that Jeremy Sisto's performance as Jesus (and he was only 24 at the time of filming), avoids any of the declaiming of so many of the previous films. Since you were made for television, his style of speaking is quiet, sometimes seemingly offhand, gently as, kneeling and looking up at the woman taken in adultery, he almost whispers, "Go, and sin no more". This certainly makes him more approachable. And, speaking of approachable, many audiences get a surprise when, after arriving in Jerusalem, Jesus and the apostles are approached by a cheerful beggar who invites them to dance, Jesus dancing happily, but trying to drag a solemnly recalcitrant Thomas into the dancing group. Jesus then suggests a drink of water. They go to the fountain and, surprisingly, Jesus splashes the others and they get into a water splashing fight. (This is an aside, but some serious viewers thought this was a bit too flippant until they saw Mel Gibson's *The Passion of the Christ's* where there is a flashback to Nazareth and Jesus with Mary, washing his hands, and flicking her with the water – everybody remembers the intensity of the scourging but they tend to forget more personal and personable moments like this!)

Your screenplay was written by Canadian, Suzanne Couture, who has not written any other biblical films – it is quite a creative achievement. But, your director, Roger Young, did direct a number of the Old Testament movies.

I mentioned earlier some scenes that I particularly appreciate and like showing to groups. An early one is the temptations in the desert, mountainous desert scenery, a number of women appearing in flowing red dresses, temptresses, but then Satan himself appearing in the form of Jeroen Krabbe, black suit, short back and sides haircut, the picture of a gentleman – and with a subtly enticing, tempting voice. One striking thing is that there are visions of the future, of the poor and hungry of our times. And these themes are quite amplified during the agony in the garden of Gethsemane, Satan reappearing, quite a long discussion with his dominating the agonising Jesus, showing him visions of the futility of his crucifixion, scenes of the Crusades and massacres in Jesus' name, the burning of a witch in the Middle Ages, again in his name, and then a powerful scene of Satan and Jesus walking through the trenches of World War I. In fact, they also have quite a serious philosophical/theological discussion about human nature, sinfulness, God not intervening to prevent evil, and the significance of human free will.

I assure you these two sequences work well for prayer evenings and reflection in Lent.

I just had a distraction of about the Protestant-financed film of 1979, *Jesus*, with Brian Deacon, a film that has been subtitled and dubbed into many languages making it, probably, the most widely seen Jesus film. The distraction is this: that, in the temptations in the desert, they show a literal snake slithering in front of Jesus and tempting him with posh-sounding Valentine Dyall-like intonations. No wonder he resisted these temptations!

The South African *Son of Man* , a contemporary, post-Apartheid interpretation in the Xhosa language, opens on sandy hills on the coast with the temptation of Jesus, Satan a sinister-looking figure. The two sit together. And, when Jesus cannot bear him any more, he shoves him, Satan rolling down the sand. That's a way of dealing with temptation!

I had better finish with something a bit more serious. The crucifixion scene is grim but not overwhelming. The best part for me is Jesus taken down from the cross, laid in his mother's lap, a visual *Piet*à – and, wonderfully, Andrew Lloyd Webber's *Requiem,* 'Pie Jesu', creating a beautiful sound background. It is followed by the burying of Jesus' body and, arrestingly, his mother, Mary, leading the burial and anointing rituals.

A bit of a PS. In John's Gospel, when Mary Magdalene discovers Jesus and clings to him, the Latin is rather brusque, "Noli me tangere", literally "don't touch me". Here it is rather beautifully translated as "you have to let me go" and then the reference to his going back to the father.

Finally, in the upper room, with a heartfelt farewell to everyone, there is a quite exhilarating transition, reminding us that Jesus promised to be with us until the end time. If anyone else is reading this letter, no spoilers, better for them to see it for themselves (either with British reserve or with Filipino enthusiastic outburst).

Dear

JESUS OF MONTRÉAL

While still in the vein of writing about Jesus, a letter to you.

You came as something of a surprise in 1990, a very welcome surprise as it turned out. In fact, you stayed on screen for a year at the Kino Cinema in Collins Street, here in Melbourne. I also heard that you spent a year in some New York and American cinemas.

I keep wondering why you were and are so popular, what intrigued an audience that was probably more secular than Christian. I do remember standing outside the preview and spending a long time in discussion with some other reviewers, wanting to talk about you, checking some of the scenes with reference to the Gospels. A case in point was a scene in an upper floor of a skyscraper, looking down of the city, at the world, a lawyer echoing Satan tempting Jesus to power.

There was another very striking sequence which people talked about, Jesus going to a television studio. Previously, we had seen some actors working in dubbing pornographic films, meant to be an equivalent of the tradition of Mary

Magdalene's being a prostitute (tradition rather than based on any evidence from any of the Gospels, her being identified wrongly with the "sinful woman in the city" weeping and pouring ointment on Jesus' feet at Simon the Pharisee's dinner, Luke 7). In the striking sequence, Daniel, the Christ-figure of the film, strides into the studio with the equivalent of a whip, turning over the tables, pushing the cameras to the floor, rebuking and hitting the camera crew and director. Yes, that was a 20th century equivalent of Jesus cleansing the temple, overturning the tables of the money changers. (Your Director Denys Arcand obviously loathes TV commercials, sending them up.)

So, the question arose, who is Jesus of Montréal and how does he relate to the biblical Jesus?

In a documentary of the time, *Jesus Christ Moviestar*, a British Anglican production, your director, Denys Arcand, was interviewed about you, making the assertion that we know nothing at all about Jesus, historically, an opinion also incorporated into your dialogue, part of a commentary during a Passion Play. Arcand was brought up as a Catholic, was part of the French-Canadians 1960s reaction against the church and its influence in their lives. Yet, he made you, a film valued by believers and nonbelievers alike. And, curiously, cast himself as a judge in the case against Daniel's violence at the television studio – a Pontius Pilate figure.

He created your character, Daniel (a rather wistful performance by Lothaire Bluteau who, a couple of years later, was so effective as the missionary Jesuit in Bruce Beresford's *Black Robe*). Daniel, who has led a hidden life, returns to Montréal and is commissioned by a Dominican priest (rather disreputable in his personal life) to do a modernising rewrite of the traditional Passion Play performed in the grounds of St Joseph's Oratory on Mount Royal. Lots of provocative differences from the Gospels, including an opinion that Jesus' father was a Roman centurion. Grounds for controversy.

You provide sequences well worthwhile for those who appreciate Jesus films, episodes of Jesus' life enacted, the audience walking along with the actors, even given portions of bread at the re-enactment of the multiplication of the loaves and fishes. And, very enjoyably, when Jesus is naked on the cross, an ardent woman from the West Indies can't restrain herself, prays aloud, goes to the cross with her emotional pleas. Then the policeman on duty moves her back into the crowd and gives the signal to Jesus that the performance can continue!

While you have your moments re-enacting the Gospel, your screenplay is tantalising, effectively so, in the parallels between Daniel and Jesus, even in his injuries and death, the attempts to get him into a hospital, turned away from the crowded Catholic hospital but welcomed at the Jewish hospital. And, there are the speculations about commemorating his memory, re-enacting the play, hIs living on in the drama and minds of his friends.

So, you are what a modern Jesus film could be like.

Dear

THE BROWNING VERSION

It is more than a puzzle for me as to why I am writing to you, why you have come up in my memory, puzzled as to the significance you had in my film-watching. I'm not sure whether I will come to a clear conclusion but thank you for your patience in considering my trying to probe the puzzle rather than solve it.

So, the first question is when did I actually see you and at what age? It was at school at Chevalier College, probably in 1953 or 1954, which means that in those years I was turning 14 or 15. You are definitely not a film for a boy of that age. But, there you were at school, with me projecting you!

Father Gerry Kelly who ran the projection room, quietly and with more than a touch of irony, admired Michael Redgrave. One year we had to screen *The Night My Number Came Up* for him. I realise in looking back I always admired Michael Redgrave (from *Being Earnest* to *The Green Scarf*). A story comes to mind. Years later I met Gerry Kelly and remarked that some of the films that we were seeing in the student house were not so good. His comment, "Now you know what I had to put up with"!

But, I see Michael Redgrave as the teacher in the secondary school, not liked at all by the students, reticent, withdrawn, scholarly, and his name, Crocker-Harris. Your screenplay reveals that he was called the 'Himmler of the Upper Fifth' by the boys.

I have realised that he was opposite of Robert Donat in *Goodbye Mr Chips*. No one could dislike Mr Chips. He was the archetypal amiable teacher. And, of course we had already seen *Mr Chips* at school. Perhaps, I was intrigued by the complete contrast between the two men, Mr Chips being obviously endearing, Crocker-Harris something of a mystery, an enigma. Perhaps I felt sorry for him, trying to understand how he became an unpopular teacher (and, perhaps, I thought such a sad human being).

Come to think of it, although I did not give much thought to it until my final year at school, I think I must have presumed that I would finish up teaching (and, for some time at Daramalan College in Canberra, I did).

The other question that comes to mind, particularly puzzling, is how I actually responded to the situation with Mrs Crocker-Harris. We had loved Greer Garson as Mrs Chips. But, here was Mrs Crocker-Harris and her infidelities, her affair with the teacher, played by the genial Nigel Patrick, a further betrayal and wounding of Crocker-Harris. Jean Kent was so effective as the brittle and seemingly heartless wife, jeering at her husband, that that was the way I saw her in every other film in which she acted. Obviously a powerful performance affecting a young teenage boy! Did I understand what was going on? Obviously, it made me think. I probably understood the basic infidelity but had no realisation of what that actually meant in physical and psychological practice.

The Browning Version, poet Robert Browning's translation of Aeschylus's *Agamemnon,* is more than the fact of the book. It was a classics gift for Crocker-Harris in his retirement by one of the boys, Taplow. Crocker-Harris is bewildered, grateful. Come to think of it, it is a moment of grace in Crocker-Harris's life – and, probably, that is one of the reasons why it appealed and attracted then as it does now. It leads to Crocker-Harris transcending his pathos, starting a speech, hesitating, putting his notes aside and speaking from the heart. The heart can triumph.

I used to know a lot of detail in those years, working in the projection room, reading reviews in the Catholic British magazine, *Focus* (a publication by OCIC, the International Catholic Organisation for Cinema which I was to head up 45 years later!) and introduced to seeking meaning in films through pamphlets, *Films and You, You and the Movies,* by Father Fred Chamberlin who was to draw me into the film ministry of OCIC. So, I was aware that your screenplay was written by Terence Rattigan (and we had seen *The Winslow*

Boy at school as well), the director was Anthony Asquith who collaborated with Rattigan several times including *The VIPs*. In fact, I do remember recommending to a confrere who directed plays in the seminary that he might think about putting on *The Browning Version*. He did.

I don't know whether that helps. *The Browning Version* being significant for me, especially at that age, but still fairly vivid (just had images in my imagination of Michael Redgrave looking sombre and Jean Kent looking as hard as nails).

Yes, I did see the 1994 version with Albert Finney and Greta Scacchi but I was still fixed in seeing you four decades earlier.

Well, that's my letter to you – the presentation of my puzzle. I think I will have to re-read you later and see if anything else surfaces.

Dear

THE CARDINAL

Actually, that's not an address that can so easily used these days, days of clerical abuse, days of disgraced Cardinals, not the appearances of the church that was.

In fact, you are the appearances of the church that was. And, for a film of 1963, you were uncannily prescient. While I enjoyed seeing you at the time, I think you are a film that grows in significance when seen in retrospect. Actually, that's quite a compliment.

I just checked and found that Henry Morton Robinson's novel was actually published in 1950 – no thoughts of the Second Vatican Council at that time. The novel was firmly rooted in a familiar church or the image of a familiar church. But, when you were released, the Second Vatican Council had already completed one session in 1962. The jovial Pope John XXIII had died in June 1963. Paul VI had been elected and had opted to continue the work of the Council. While so many in the church at that time would not have known what was going on, and while so many were apprehensive – change not being a priority – there were many who were feeling exhilaration, hope. After all, this was the 1960s and change was very much in the air, even more so as the decade progressed.

I had made a note to remind me to include some features in this letter. I see I had jotted down "principles", "pageantry" (and in parenthesis I had written "pomp"). Perhaps that's a good place to start.

The church that you initially feature is an American church, the church of Boston, traditional, more than a touch of the Irish, a church of families who were loyal, hard-working priests who could be exiled if they fell out of favour with the bishop, a bishop who was pleased to be in the hierarchy and to be treated as such. I remember thinking that John Huston certainly embodied the proud (you can say arrogant now) and confident Cardinal while poor Fr Burgess Meredith suffered out in the sticks.

So, you offered a picture of a church of principles, which are illustrated in a moral dilemma of those times, moral choices between the life of a child and the life of the mother, the option for the child. At the same time, you offered a picture of the church of pageantry. Your hero, the eventual Cardinal, Stephen Fermoyle (a serious if somewhat stolid Tom Tryon) has an ordination scene, the church of ritual, an Episcopal ordination scene in Rome, a great deal of life in the Vatican with its prevailing pageantry. And, again the temptation to refer to pomp.

But to go back to that idea of your being prescient. While there were priests who had time out or who eventually left the church prior to 1950, who would have thought in 1963 that within the next two decades, so many priests would have chosen to leave the priesthood, opt out, found themselves exhausted, frustrated, severely done by, misunderstood or neglected? But you showed a serious man taking time off, leaving duty, if not devotion, aside, catching up as so many priests had to do (and many being eventually caught) by the poor training in formation they experienced, young men, isolated, in male communities, asked to sacrifice/consecrate their affective life and finding this an unanticipated burden. And that is one reason you are very interesting to see in retrospect, putting into a pre-Vatican II perspective, the reality and consequences of a celibate life.

However, your narrative also has episodes of the church's tradition of social justice concern. There is Stephen Fermoyle's diplomatic mission in Nazi 1938, the experience of Austria and the Anschluss, Cardinal Innitzer and his sermon in Vienna Cathedral (and it was this scene that was foremost in my mind when I eventually did visit the cathedral). And, striking for the American church, there was Stephen Fermoyle's mission to the deep south, his being taken by the Ku Klux Klan, tied to a cross, the prospect of fire...

I just had a distraction – we saw you in the cinema in Rome for a clerical audience. Some weeks later, at another film, the projector broke down and the lights came on. My Australian sensibility had not anticipated such a clerical hullabaloo. Then someone got to a microphone and called out," Non siamo nella Georgia". Which means "we aren't in Georgia", his equating the response to the disruption to the memories of watching your yelling fanaticism of the Ku Klux Klan!

Ultimately, you show Stephen Fermoyle making a choice. Given his experience as a priest in Boston, given his experience in Rome and the Vatican, given his option for taking time out and his experience of meeting a woman whom he could marry, he makes a choice for the priesthood. And, choice is the key. Of course, the vast majority of priests do not have the rather exotic life that Stephen Fermoyle experienced. But the key to their formation, their training, their pastoral experience, the relating well to children, women and men, their priesthood is: choice.

Not sure whether Otto Preminger had all this in mind while he was directing you. But, my memory tells me that he was awarded a Papal Medal during the second session of Vatican II – and, when I went to check years ago, as I just did before writing to you, Googling for a confirmation of this piece of information, there were three references – but they were to something I had written! But I still stand by his getting the medal – and, if my memory has failed me and he did not receive it, he should have!

Dear

CITIZEN KANE

I'm not sure that I would write a letter a Dear letter to William Randolph Hearst who, under the guise of Charles Foster Kane, is your true subject. Not one of my favourite people from American history, particularly unsympathetic in his involvement with the war between Cuba and Spain, not particularly in admiration of his contribution to the development of the "Yellow press" and fickle tabloid imagination and reporting, and not the most edifying life story either. Yet, he was a man of note, a capitalist chief of note, a man who symbolised American Empire making. But, of course, you know that.

I saw you first when I was very young, again a school experience. However, I've had the opportunity to see you several times since, always with great admiration. Of course, the name which springs to mind is Orson Welles, your director, showing what a precocious enfant terrible was artistically capable of. He created in you a classic – perhaps too classic for 1941 and Oscar awards (not)! In recent times, a number of critics have tried to turn the spotlight on to your writer, Herman Mankiewicz, perhaps too often overlooked, not considered important enough in the light of Welles, but a man who actually wrote a dramatically compelling screenplay with astute observations on American society, wealth, power and influence, the press, in the early 20th century. It was he who did win the Oscar.

The collaboration between Orson Welles as director and your accomplished cinematographer, Gregg Toland, created some extraordinary uses of black-and-white, light and darkness, angles and editing which have been frequently praised all these years. Everybody comments on your famous breakfast seen, Kane and his wife sitting, the passing of days, the accumulation of moods, the distance looming as the couple sit facing each other – so why don't I do it as well in this letter?

Perhaps tourists have visited Hearst's Californian castle, San Simeone – but could it ever match the chiaroscuro photography of the camera approaching Xanadu (for San Simeone) - enough to make both Kublai Khan and Coleridge envious!

Could I add an encomium about the cast, a tribute to Welles and his Mercury Theatre ensemble, some making their screen debut here and all going on to stardom for some, Joseph Cotton, an excellent character actor career for others, Agnes Morehead... and a pre-Hitchcock score by Bernard Herrmann (actually I discovered it was his first!).

But, the word that has entered cinema consciousness is "Rosebud", whispered at the beginning as Kane dies, whispered again at the end, close-up of moustachioed lips. For those seeing you for the first time, Rosebud turns out to be just a sled, possibly memories of a happy childhood, out in the sticks and obscurity, long since forgotten. But Rosebud could be translated, "what does it profit someone to gain the whole world and lose their soul". And, while it is an expression of yearning and longing, it could serve as an epitaph for Charles Foster Kane.

And, in connection with you, I did realise one could ask questions about Citizen Trump and Citizen Murdoch (more to the point, of course).

Orson Welles' screen presence (to be magnified considerably during the coming years, a bloated Cardinal Wolsey, a big bouncy Falstaff) makes him bluff, shrewd, devious, exploitative, cannily cunning, and archly arrogant manipulator – and this just a few of the descriptions which might be applied to him! Kane is a supreme example of the self-confident achiever, at others' sacrifice and expense, the personification of American hubris. But, after hubris, nemesis - fate catching up, missions not accomplished, forced letting go in death, and a yearning from the depths, Rosebud.

P.S. After writing this letter to you, I found a wonderful link on Google from the British Film Institute, brief but powerful glimpses, recommended:

https://www.bfi.org.uk/news-opinion/news-bfi/features/20-inspired-visual-moments-citizen-kane.

WHITE PALACE

I encountered you just at the right moment. I had better explain.

In my Dear Movies letter to Woody Allen's *Interiors*, I referred to a focus on personality, the Myers-Briggs Type Indicator, a particular spotlight on some of our traits, exploring themes from the work of Carl Jung. In fact, when I first saw *Interiors* in Hayward, California, I was on sabbatical for a term in Berkeley and had not been introduced to Myers-Briggs. That happened a month later. I found it something of a revelation and have been working with it now for over forty years.

And yourself? I had written some sketch studies on movie characters and Type during the 1980s. An editor in New York made the suggestion that I do longer studies. And it was precisely the right time when you were released in 1991. You did fit the bill excellently. And, you appear in the book titled (with acknowledgment to *Snow White*), *Mirror, Mirror on the Screen*.

I was able to get a VHS copy and use some of your sequences to illustrate aspects of Type. Later, in 1999, you were one of the stars at a conference at Trinity and All Saints, at Horsforth, now the Catholic campus of Leeds University. My friend, Maggie Roux, explored film and characters for those involved in social work and chaplaincy. Bernie Wooder, a psychologist from East London, who, in the 60s, was a union man, played in a band and converted to Buddhism. In his work, with his love for movies, he used the title 'The Movie Therapist'. The three of us spent three days working with participants exploring films according to each of our specialties. For Type, the main feature was you.

Let me tell you something about what appealed to me. In fact, you had me from your version of hello! (With thanks to *Jerry Maguire* for that reference!) We are introduced to a young executive in St Louis, Max, played by James Spader (more weight and less hair in more recent television series), then to a middle-aged woman, Nora, played by Susan Sarandon (who looks much the same as the years go on). You begin with his driving home, a widower, planning to go out with his friends for the evening.

Some of the focal points for Type include asking questions about where we get our energy from, from the outside world or from our inner life. There are questions as to whether we are prone to make decisions or would prefer to take time in getting more data for decisions. Some people are very much in the here and now, observing reality around them, while others tend to act more on intuitions and hunches, editing out the reality that they are not particularly interested in. And then there are the criteria by which we make decisions, objectively and logically, or criteria with nuances, subjectively.

For those interested in Type, the impression that Max makes as he parks his car with precision, enters his immaculately tidy house (except for straightening out small mat tassels, not once, but twice), placing his watch with care, going to his cupboards with the neatest rows of shirts and suits one could see, taking care with his getting dressed (meticulous care), is that he is the embodiment of the person who is completely focused on the detail of here and now.

I'd like to cut to a scene after he has been drinking with friends and finds himself at the apartment of Nora, the burger-outlet waitress (the outlet being the White Palace). Her place is a mess, everything everywhere or, more particularly, on the floor. She finds she is out of coffee but suggests "when you can't drive, you drink"). He feels sick and goes to the bathroom – mess again. Nora is obviously not focused particularly on the here and now.

In many ways, your screenplay offers stereotypes of Types, even with a touch of caricature. But, that is very useful for identifying Type. Max is an inward Type, decisive, focused, clear and logical. Nora is the exact opposite, outward energy, not decisive, not focused, personalised in her approach to everything. Your screenplay is also rather schematic in pitting one responding to the other.

Carl Jung urges a process of life moving towards increasing capacity for exercising our opposite traits. He calls it 'Individuation '. Your plot shows both Max and Nora moving towards their opposites, his becoming a more mellow and relational character, she moving towards more order in her life.

The sequence that goes down very well comes after they have been dating for a while. He buys her a present and she eagerly rips open the lid, rushes out the paper, lifts out the gift. It is a mini vacuum cleaner which, in her American way, she refers to as "cleanin' equipment". Not only is she taken aback, she tells him off, that the gift should be given because he cares for her not because he thinks her house is dirty. Still objective as he is, he bluntly tells her that her house is dirty, ringdings under the furniture. A touch of poignancy follows as she invites him to go into her dining room, he muttering that it is difficult to look at her house, but finding that she has cleaned it, laid the table nicely, candles lit...

So, for almost twenty years, you have been a significant presence in my courses on Type – and you are in my mind for this letter because it is only two days since the last seminar and you featured well.

For which, many thanks.

Dear

LES NEIGES DE KILIMANDJARO/THE SNOWS OF KILIMANJARO

A film about goodness, not an easy accomplishment. But you have achieved it – admirably.

Your director is one of my favourite French directors, Robert Guideguian, and I have seen many of his films. I was alerted to him in the mid-1990s and have looked forward to seeing as many films of his as I could. But, you stand out for me, a most moving experience and, as I mentioned, a film about goodness.

Audiences can identify with your central couple and get a lift from what they think and feel – and do – especially after a challenge to their way of life. And, it has nothing to do with Ernest Hemingway. Mt Kilimanjaro serves as an ideal goal, somewhere exotic but seemingly unattainable. More to the immediate point, it is also in the title of a popular French song that is sung in the film.

I should have mentioned that Robert Guediguian usually works with his wife, Ariane Ascariade, and several close friends. It is the same this time. He lives in Marseilles and usually sets his stories there. He so immerses his characters in the sights and sounds of Marseilles that we really believe we have been there.

We are once again on the Marseilles waterfront. Workers are being laid off. Michel (Jean-Pierre Darroussin) is a union official but has decided to put his name in the hat for the lottery for retrenchment so that someone else can keep his job, against the advice of his close friend, Raoul (Gerard Meylan). He deliberately pulls his name out and goes into retirement – which, after a busy life, he doesn't find easy. However, he is supported by his wife of almost thirty years, Marie-Claire (Ariane Ascaride). She also is an earnest woman who works in care for the homebound. Their married children and grandchildren visit for meals and are concerned about the financial situation of their parents. But their parents are people of generosity, simplicity, concerned for others.

One of your happy sequences is a joyous party for their thirtieth wedding anniversary, with some of the retrenched men as guests, where they are given a gift of money and a ticket for a trip to Tanzania and Mt Kilimanjaro.

Spoiler: they do not get there.

What happens next is a reminder that bad things do happen to good people. Wasn't there a story in the Jewish Scriptures, the tale of Job, the worst of scenarios descending on him, his critical friends who are sometimes called 'comforters ' coming to exhort him to acknowledge that he is being punished for some evil done? Playing cards one night with Raoul and his wife, who is Marie-Claire's sister, the house is invaded by two burglars who steal their money, take the ticket and bind and hurt them.

By chance, later, Michel sees a clue which leads him to one of the thieves. Your screenplay does not follow any expectations; rather the contrary. What follows has an enormous effect on Michel and Marie-Claire. The thief is one of the retrenched men, young, with a chip on his shoulder, highly critical of the older generation, the way they managed union matters, their being stuck in the ways of the past. The young man has two little brothers – and their mother couldn't care less and is away working on a liner.

The goodness in the film is in how the couple deal with their anger, angry certainly, spurred on by the fierce attitude of Raoul, and somewhat bewildered by the sullenness of the young man and his tirades. The goodness concerns the two young brothers and the decision by Michel and by Marie-Claire, both arriving at their goodness decision separately, to come to the support of the boys (despite the hostile response of their own son and daughter who want attention for their children).

Of course, in this portrait of two ordinary people, after their lifetime of experience, concern for others, moved by the plight of others and not concerned with themselves, the audience is challenged to ask whether this kind of day-by-day heroism is what they would do.

So the audience is immersed in the life of this part of Marseilles. The performances are moving. And the picture of kindness in human nature is positive and hopeful. No mean achievement.

Dear

THE WIZARD OF OZ

Sorry to tell you that you were not the first time that I was excited by a transition from black-and-white suddenly moving into colour. That was with Dean Stockwell and Margaret O'Brien opening the door to *The Secret Garden*. You must have come soon enough after, the story of the farm in Kansas, the tornado, everything and everyone flying through the air, even Miss Gulch peddling hard on her bicycle, the house, Toto, Dorothy, and then suddenly the bright colours of Oz and we were not in Kansas anymore.

One thing I would like to tell you is that I am older than you are – looking up the IMDb to check when you were released, 17 days after me or, if you premiered in the US evening, 18 days. Movie historians tell us that it was a very good year for cinema, 1939, with *Dark Victory, Stagecoach, Gunga Din, Goodbye Mr Chips*, but I'm not a fan of the Oscar-winner, *Gone with the Wind*. (I do like the siege of Atlanta sequences, Scarlet O'Hara knowing that tomorrow is another day while Clive Gable couldn't give a damn, frankly, and Hattie McDaniel won the first American-African Oscar for Best Supporting Actress.)

You are a wonderful film for children and I saw you as a young boy still in primary school. Who could not fall in love with Judy Garland as Dorothy (16 when she made you – and with such a strong and powerful voice)? Who could not want to follow the yellow brick road, wherever it led, especially if it was to see the Wizard, the wonderful Wizard of Oz?

It was more than a disappointment to discover that he was a sham, not terrifying at all despite his amplification. But then, we had to learn that a movie is not just an entertainment but, to work well, it has to have a moral!

Actually, the moral that really appealed to me was to discover that Dorothy, competent as she was, courageous, especially with the Wicked Witch of the West, had three alter egos. They symbolised her mind, her heart, her strength. And they appeared in three memorable characters, Ray Bolger as the Straw Man, if I only had a brain, Bert Lahr who would always look like The Cowardly Lion in whatever film he appeared, if I only had the noive, and Jack Haley as The Tin Man, if I only had a heart. And Dorothy embraced the three.

Speaking of actors looking the part, Margaret Hamilton was doomed forever to look like the Wicked Witch of the West and a rather simperingly sweet Billie Burke always sounded like Glinda. And there were always the mysterious little guides, singing and dancing, the Munchkins. (You knew that many of them were from Europe, some refugees from the Nazis. Being a reviewer, I was not able to avoid the disillusionment about some of them so this is fair warning, don't see a film with the ominous title Under the Rainbow.)

And, speaking of the rainbow, there are your songs. Once it is in your head, it's hard to lose 'the wiz, the wiz, the wiz, the wiz, the wonderful Wizard of Oz'. And, Straw, Tin, Lion, plaintive with 'If I only had a... ' But, there is always Over the Rainbow. It is a cry from the heart for idealists.

You might be surprised that in workshops on personality, I play the Mary Poppinsish practical precision of 'A Spoonful of Sugar', especially with the lines

> A robin furthering its nest
> has little time to rest,
> while gathering into bits of twine and twig...
> he knows the song will move the job along...

And then I play the wistful hopefulness with Dorothy's longing, 'Over the Rainbow',

> Somewhere over the rainbow
> bluebirds fly
> and the dreams that you dream of
> dreams really do come true
> ... Oh why, oh why, can't I?

And the other moral of the story: back to reality, back to home, down-to-earth, life with genial family and friends – and fantasy lessons learnt. Dorothy, the wiser, is back from the rainbow.

Dear

DJANGO UNCHAINED

I am succumbing to the temptation to start this letter to you with reference to your director, Quentin Tarantino. Everybody knows Tarantino whether they like his films or not. One of my thoughts was to comment on his films as The Good, The Bad, The Ugly. While there are plenty of bad characters, for my taste, his *Death Proof* is both bad and ugly. And, despite bad characters so many, and situations ugly, so many, we all come to the conclusion that the work of Tarantino is good. After all, what other director very quickly acquired their own adjective to describe their work, Tarantinoesque! After all, Robert Zemeckis whose *Forrest Gump* beat *Pulp Fiction* to the Best Film Oscar, has never been referred to as Zemeckisesque!

Oh, come to think of it, there is Fellini-esque and Bergman-esque.

There are many moments in Tarantino's films which are very good. Who can ever forget (or shudder at the memory) of Michael Madsen as Mr Blonde and the ear-torture sequence, to the rhythms of Stuck in the middle...?

Or John Travolta and Samuel L. Jackson discussing burgers in *Pulp Fiction*? Or the near-perfect short story, that first story in *Inglorious Barsterds*, the tranquillity of the French farm – and the dread hiding beneath it?

But it turns out that the film I am writing to you is you, the very good.

If I were to choose a film about the American West and the American South in 1858, or any time before the Civil War abolition of slavery, it would be you. You immediately plunge us into this West, introduce us to the violent themes, the then-called Negroes, migrants, and out and beyond with the bounty hunters, the Ku Klux Klan, sheriffs and hard riding, and to the plantations, the workers, the decadently cruel owners, the downtrodden and their rising up. Hope that does some justice to the range of your screenplay, Tarantino again.

The thing with Tarantino, born in Tennessee but growing up in California, eccentric movie buff, video store worker and expert, is that he is so vividly aware of all the genres, of all the conventions, can draw on them at a moment's notice – just listen to any of his interviews rising boy's enthusiasm, faster and faster pace, his enthusiasm for both pulp and pop fiction. And, while he is serious, he has an extraordinarily sardonic sense of humour, the gift of the gab (the long conversation sequences in his films are well worth listening to, are sometimes very funny), the gift of beyond-the-gab.

One might consider the Christoph Waltz character, travelling dentist, bounty hunter, with his pedantic devotion to words and pronunciations, not that everybody understood him, a tribute to Tarantino's verbal preoccupations. (Which reminds me, how many actors have been directed to two Oscars by the same director as Waltz was?)

Which means then that you are always interesting, often laughing-funny (Jonah Hill and the Klan discussing the size of the holes they cut out in their sheets), or cruel-funny, the whole character of Samuel L. Jackson's obsequious black servant, Stephen, and the malice of his revenge.

Of course, Tarantino would have lent out many a spaghetti western in his video store days, knowing the films about Django (and inviting Franco Nero to make a guest memorial appearance) and so doing his clever variations on these themes. And, with compliments to Jamie Foxx, he is able to carry the drama, the slavery, the freedom, the riding the range, the bounty hunter, confronting the arrogant whites, searching for his wife.

As regards the number of characters in this West, as I look down the cast list, I can see many allusions to those popular video store Westerns, like a who's-who, memories of the kinds of roles these actors took in their heyday. James Remar, Don Johnson, James Russo, Bruce Dern, Russ Tamblyn, Don Stroud...

Which doesn't explain Leonardo DiCaprio. He must have wanted the opportunity to play a cruel and smarmy villain, quite a contrast to his roles as nice characters (but then he went to Wall Street!).

You do get a bit good, bad, ugly as the drama moves on (particularly bad and ugly is Quentin Tarantino's attempt at an Australian accent, contrasting badly with that of John Jarrett – Tarantino must've really like *Wolf Creek*) and, apocalyptic-like fire and, the two endings which rely on that American icon, the gun.

Apart from *Death Proof* (I can't think of anything redemptive about it at the moment), Tarantino's films are quite striking, the clever *Jackie Brown*, the bloody melodrama of *The Hateful Eight*, the over-the-top almost everything in the *Kill Bill* films.

But, in terms of storytelling, American themes, violent American culture, the blend of the humorous and the serious, critique of history (and of the present), you are my favourite, so very Tarantinoesque.

Dear

THE BOYS ARE BACK

I am very glad I saw you.

The reasons for telling you this are personal and stem from my own life. Since you are concerned with the role of a father for his young sons, I thought it best to indicate why you are so important for me.

We each bring our own experience to the characters of any film and their interactions. Since my mother died when I was seven and my brother five, I was empathising with Artie, the younger boy, but, more importantly, I was finding Clive Owen's portrayal of Joe, the boys' father who was a sports writer (and my father was involved with sport and radio at the time of my mother's death), was helping me to understand and appreciate what my father must have experienced at that time. He was 36, living in Sydney. He changed his life completely, in work and in moving interstate to Melbourne. It is a compliment to you that you have this power to move.

If you were to ask me to say what the film is about, I would answer, 'Parenting'. That may not be the greatest enticement to decide to see you, but it is important to say it. You are based on a memoir by Simon Carr (originally set in New Zealand and my brother and I had a shock in later life to discover that my mother's father was not born in Scotland as we thought, but in New Zealand!) is about a widowed father having to parent his six year old son (without any preparation or any innate ability to do this) and then cope with the arrival of his 14 year old son from a previous marriage. Now, that may not seem the greatest enticement either – but there have not been so many films dealing with a father trying to cope with caring for his children (there was *Kramer vs Kramer* in 1979). This is an important theme and, with a thoughtful screenplay by Alan Cubitt and with the sure hand of director, Scott Hicks (*Shine, Snow Falling on Cedars*), you communicate, and entertain, very well. You also avoid falling into sentimentality and contrived romances.

The father, Joe, seems an ordinary bloke. He is something of a 'man's man'. This may have been part of the reason for his leaving his first wife and marrying his second, Katy. But, the second marriage and his love for his new wife have been transforming for him. His wife and his little son seem to be a catalyst for his showing his feelings with greater ease.

Clive Owen, who has often played dour, unsmiling characters, now gives a wonderfully sympathetic and nuanced performance as the British sports journalist who re-located to South Australia. He left behind his son, Harry, with his mother in England but he and Katy have their own son, Artie. We learn at once that Katy had cancer. We see some brief flashbacks and the suffering and pathos of her death. Joe is distraught. Their six year old son, Artie, understands that his mother has died but cannot, self-consciously, deal with it, so his responses are a mixture of the accepting, the sensible and the bewilderingly emotional. I felt that Nicholas McAnulty's performance as Artie was completely real. In no way does it seem like a performance. And it was often delightful to see how he and Clive Owen play naturally and persuasively off each other.

You raise the issue of what a father is to do in this situation. Joe copes by trying to do the normal things (meals, washing, housekeeping – the latter not well at all) – and show his love at all times for his son, preferring to say yes to his son's wishes and whims rather than say no. He cites this as a principle several times and carries it out with joyful activities. There are some moving and some exhilarating scenes of the two together.

Playing with Artie in holiday mode, reality eventually impinges. Joe has to go back to work.

And then you introduce the further complication, and another step in the theme of parenting arises when 14 year old son, Harry (George Mackay in a just right performance), comes to Australia for the holidays: he is tentative, afraid of his father, wondering why he was abandoned, awkward with other children but bonding with Artie.

This tests Joe and his principle of saying 'yes' at all times. It challenges his strong and matter-of-fact approach to life, bewildering him at times and suggesting alternate possibilities. This leads to a family crisis, when Joe has to go to Melbourne to cover the Australian Tennis Open. Harry is overwhelmed when teenage friends come to the house and party and trash the house. He feels that he has failed in his responsibilities and returns to England.

Now you raise the greatest challenge for Joe. Does he want to have both sons with him, foster greater family bonds? Joe has to move out of his ordinary comfort zone in going to England with Artie and offering Harry the possibility of a new life with them. This means frank discussions with Harry and with his mother which writer, director and actors convey with a persuasive blend of emotion and common sense.

Besides having something worthwhile to show and say about family – and emphasising how important presence, attention and, especially, play are for developing children and for parental relationships – you are a persuasive advertisement for the beauty of South Australia (hills, coast, McLaren Vale) on the Fleury Peninsula where Scott Hicks, in fact, lives!

I really have appreciated the opportunity to write personally about my response to you as well as the family and parenting issues you raise. Many thanks.

GUNGA DIN

'You're a better man than I am, Gunga Din!'.

I'm afraid I can't remember any of the rest of Rudyard Kipling's poem but that is still the line which is always quoted.

You may be wondering why I'm writing a letter to you. Memory has been taking me back to the action adventures that Hollywood produced in the second half of the 1930s – and which we saw at matinees or at boarding school in the late 1940s and early 1950s. The actor that immediately springs to memory is Errol Flynn, Captain Blood, Robin Hood, Essex with Elizabeth, Sea Hawk – and even the Charge of the Light Brigade. All from Warner Brothers and we all enjoyed them thoroughly. Speaking of Rudyard Kipling, Errol Flynn turned up in 1951 in the enjoyable colourful version of Kim.

So, dithering a bit about the letter, you suddenly came to mind – and you are the choice. I don't think RKO made many action shows like you, Paramount had *Beau Geste* which is also a good candidate, but quite a number of your images come to mind – in fact, rather sinister ones come up immediately, I'm afraid, images of the worshippers of the goddess Kali and those frightening and forbidding snakes writhing in the temple. (Actually it's a long time since I saw you, so the memory might not be precisely visual but certainly emotionally disturbing.)

At school, we enjoyed these ra-ra British stories, identifying with these three Brits on campaign in 19th-century India, a kind of Three Musketeers bravado. And we could identify with Cary Grant and his charm, Douglas Fairbanks Jr, so debonair – although, come to think of it, we probably didn't identify with Victor McLaglen and his cheerfully gruff rough-and-tumble. I remember Joan Fontaine as a very subsidiary romantic interest – romantic interest was the least of the interests in your gung-ho show. And I looked up the IMDb to see who was the sinister leader of the group of fanatics who made us shudder back in our early teenage years. It was Eduardo Ciannerlli, sometimes a specialist in this kind of role.

But, of course, there was Sam Jaffe as Gunga Din himself, the faithful water-bearer, loyal to the soldiers three, a subsidiary figure in the plot, although a hero at the end, wounded and struggling, taking the bugle, sounding the warning haltingly, saving the day, dying a hero. (A counter-image just came to mind, Peter Sellers playing an Indian actor in Hollywood in *The Party* - one of the most hilarious of Peter Sellers' comedies, and another chance to do his 'goodness-gracious-me' accent, re-enacting the heroism of Gunga Din, going awry.)

Writing you this letter reminds me of how our Australian mindset was fixed in presuppositions in the early 1950s. There was a lot of Asiaphobia going round, anti-Communist propaganda, stirring fears of the yellow peril hordes who would rush down from China, torture us, bamboo shoots .under our fingernails... How we looked at India and other Asian nations (apart, of course, of coming to terms with the Japanese after World War II), I'm not sure. I think we were, despite the Australian colonial experience, identifying with Britain, empire, the preservation of empire, the heroic battles in India despite mutinies, and I'm not sure whether we were too familiar with Gandhi or Partition in those years.

So you are a reminder of our entertainment days, but a challenge to acknowledge them, to correct past attitudes, re-assessment of what we took for granted, to learning new lessons which could lead to a deepening understanding, universal respect for everyone, deepen our compassion.

The last paragraph has the touch of the sermon, hasn't it? But you do remind us of our living in the past and the importance of coming into the present for a better future.

Dear

EDWARD SCISSORHANDS

You are immediately one of my favourite films, as was Johnny Depp's Edward – and, I remember, people finding it difficult to characterise him. Was he a puppet, marionette, robot, android, punk doll? All suggestions made – and a challenge to the young boy, Kevin, when he took him to school as part of a 'show and tell'. However he could be described, Edward, pallid, mournful, unfinished, the protégé of the creator in his hill-castle, the inimitable Vincent Price, incomplete but with his shears as hands, has to be one of the most arresting characters in films.

Writer, Caroline Thompson, was quoted as saying she imagined a character, intrigued by someone without a capacity for touch.

The other thing that I really liked doing when you were released was talking about your mythological aspects, the variation on the Dr Frankenstein theme and his creature, Edward's encounter with Kim, down in the suburbs, the 'little boxes made a ticky-tacky' of the popular song, and your variation on *Beauty and the Beast*. And, Danny Elfman's, plaintive score was gentle and haunting.

The other thing to talk about was masks, Edward's mysterious face, like a mask, concealing a life inside, moments of revelation from behind the mask, the mask leading to both curiosity and attraction. (And, at one stage, the ladies in the town try make-up on Edward – after all, this was a culture of artifice, with Dianne Wiest not only as the mother but as a very cheerful Avon Lady calling at the castle!).

Edward is the mysterious outsider who has to come down to earth, lives with ordinary people, puzzles them, befriends them, alienates them, eventually turns them against him.

But, you knew that.

What I wanted to tell you was that in the 1990s, there were quite a number of books from religious publishers with chapters linking theological and spiritual themes to cinema themes. And to tell you that I contributed a chapter on you, seeing Edward as something of a Christ-figure, many resemblances to the Jesus of the Gospels. In theological terms, the chapter was on you and Christology. I was very enthusiastic about films and Christ-figures in those days – and, of course, I still am.

Christ-figure likenesses are not exact, of course. Jesus was a first century Jewish man, did not look like Edward at all (who could?). And, his touch was gentle and healing, not cutting or harming. But, he did have a creator father. He did come down from 'on high' and lived amongst ordinary people. He puzzled the people, drew them to himself, as John's Gospel often says, shared the ordinariness of their lives, especially in hair-styling – after all, what other profession can only-Scissorhands take on which is not threatening! The women then want to make him, in a sense, into their own image and likeness.

However, he has a loving foster family, kindly mother, laid-back father, young curious son, and the daughter who befriends him, supports him, defends him against her aggressive boyfriend. Your casting was good, the young Winona Ryder so sympathetic as Kim, and Anthony Michael Hall so obnoxious as the boyfriend, eventually the Judas-figure. (And, eventually and spitefully, Joyce, the leader of the women's posse in the town, becomes the contemporary equivalent of Potiphar's wife denouncing Joseph in Egypt.)

With the townspeople turning against him, Edward becomes a suffering figure, reminiscent of those songs from the Jewish Scriptures, from Isaiah, the character of the beloved servant of God's people who turn against him while he is bearing their sins on his shoulders, eventually a sacrificial lamb from their malice.

Edward has to flee back to the castle, as you know, suggestive of Jesus, persecution and betrayal, leaving this earth and going back home. It is Kim, in her love and devotion, who defends him against the fickle crowd, who tells them that he has gone – is it too much to see her in the light of Mary Magdalene?

At beginning and end of the film, there is Danny Elfman's score again, Kim is continuing to tell the story of Edward to her granddaughter, speaking of who he was, of what he achieved, of what he meant. And there is Edward, using his Scissorhands to create a perfect garden, trimming and shaping the trees, snow gently falling in his garden.

I had better tell you that I try to be very careful in talking about Christ-figures, to ground the parallels with substantial and significant Gospel references as well as the text and texture of the film, reading meaning out of the film rather than reading meaning into it.

I was wondering whether you had received any other letters with these kinds of interpretation, Gospel, mythical, fairytale? I hope so.

Dear

BIG FISH

I was just writing to *Edward Scissorhands* which meant thinking about Tim Burton and his idiosyncratic career, touches of horror (from *Beetlejuice* to *Sweeney Todd!*), his love for eccentrics (Ed Wood or Willie Wonka), and love for fairytales and fantasies (from *Planet of the Apes* to *Alice in Wonderland*). Which meant that, at first glance, you weren't quite what we imagined as a Tim Burton film. But for me, you are – and one that is particularly special. And another Danny Elfman score.

I don't know whether you know that in my letter to *Edward Scissorhands* I explained that I had written a chapter in a book about the film and Gospel themes of Jesus. I'm afraid I didn't have quite the same opportunity to do something similar for you. However, I was commissioned to conduct a Film and Faith seminar on a theological theme, the Catholic Sacraments, their symbolism and their stories. It seemed best to introduce the participants to the cinematic imagination (which, for decades, I have enjoyed referring to as 'visuacy' – a contrast with appreciating the word 'literacy'). That meant some sessions on films and storytelling. *Avatar* was an obvious choice. But my other choice was, in fact, you.

On your first release, I was very surprised how much I had enjoyed watching you, how much I had enjoyed the theme of storytelling which dominates your narrative. You are certainly a film for those who delight in storytelling.

However, there were a few moments at your opening which look rather ordinary, a father talking with his son. But, after we get our bearings, we find we are listening to a story about a larger-than-life fish, Albert Finney as Ed, the father talking to his son, Will, Billy Crudup, at his wedding.

I don't know whether Tim Burton had this in mind that we can use the word 'whopper' to describe a very big fish watching a whopper – and we can use it to describe a very big lie or a very tall story bring a whopper. The trouble is that Will does not appreciate his father, is not on the wavelength of his stories that he has listened to all his life.

What we see in your storytelling is the father inventing his life through these stories – and, their coming alive before our very eyes. After some alienation, Will asking Head for some kind of explanation. In a way, that is the trouble in communication between the highly imaginative, the intuitive person, and the down-to-earth, practical and pragmatic, less than imaginative person. It is enjoyable for me to look at my summary of the kinds of stories Ed told: about a young man who finds he has great talents, leaves towns with a giant and finds himself saving a community, finding and wooing his wife and embarking on a lifetime of adventures from down the street to Vietnam. (And it was Ewan McGregor playing Ed as the young man.) And there was Helena Bonham Carter, so often mysterious, giving one of her calmest performance as a woman who may be a witch.

I just glanced at my text and rather liked this following paragraph which, I hope, also appeals to you:

It is too difficult to communicate in words Burton's ability to create a different and wonderful world full of truly magic moments, a mixture of the mundane and the marvellous, the tragic and the comic, building up to an ending the diehard realists may be annoyed by but illustrates the wonder of storytelling. (I must have been a on a roll when I wrote that!)

While the storyteller is dying, his son wants to understand the mystery, tired of hearing the stories, knowing that they cannot be literally true. He has lost his imagination and, like the journalist he is, desires verifiable facts, which is a worthy task. His exasperation blocks his capacity for true listening. But what does he do at the end? Spin one of the biggest stories of all about his father's death, realising that he now knows and loves his father. His imagination is alive.

I applaud your crusade for storytelling.

Dear

JEAN DE FLORETTE

Do you mind if I ask you a couple of questions to begin with? Do you use the word 'secular saint'? And then, do have secular saints in France? Come to think of it, of course you do. Victor Hugo created Jean Valjean.

So, while watching you and the performance of Gerard Depardieu as Jean, the idea of secular saint came to mind.

However, before I make any more comment on Jean, I want to say something that I'm sure you will agree with: how great is Marcel Pagnol! Before continuing, I decided to glance again at his entry in the IMDb. It took quite a long time to scroll down, just his credits for writing. He created the memorable characters of the Marseillaise trilogy of the 1930s (and so many versions of those stories were produced for film and television). And he directed what are now several classics. But, visually, I go back to you and to your continuation, *Manon des Sources* and the beauty in the photography of the Pagnol Provence countryside. I also go back to the wonder and beauty of his autobiographical stories, *My Father's Glory* and *My Mother's Castle*. But, of course, you know all that.

So, Jean as a secular saint. I have mentioned Jean Valjean and Victor Hugo but there is also a Hugo connection here, isn't there? Jean is a hunchback and, while he might not be a secular saint, he is a martyr-figure, as is Quasimodo of Notre Dame, cruelly done in by self-righteous hypocrites. At one level, Jean is a simple soul, a man who believes in goodness because he is good. Not experienced in country life, he nevertheless brings his wife and daughter to the property he has inherited, with plans to raise rabbits.

I notice that a number of writers comment that he is a dreamer. Maybe that is one of the conditions of being a secular saint. And, secular saints are not perfect. Poor Jean, when he finds that there is a lack of water on his farm, his business beginning to fail, he turns on God. But, at times of testing, what saint doesn't? (What about Jesus and his agony in the garden and life being drained from him on the cross?). But, with diligence, trying to dig a well, he perseveres and does his best.

Of course, secular saints are usually victims. You know and we, the audience, know that the greedy neighbours (great to see Yves Montand at the end of a significant career and Daniel Auteuil at his beginning) have sealed the well that belongs to him, conspiring against Jean, hoping that he will give up because of lack of water, sell his property cheaply to them. They set up a neighbour, as well, to goad him.

It is, literally, the death of him. Here is a good man, trying to do his best for his family, acting with dedication and integrity, unaware of the powers against him, defeated, dying. Yes, a secular saint.

One of the reasons at the time for considering Jean in this way is that I read a book by Edith Pargeter (many of us knowing her better as Ellis Peters the author of the wonderful mediaeval mysteries with Brother Cadfael, thankfully all filmed as telemovies in the 1990s with Derek Jacobi), *The Heaven Tree*. Its hero is Harry Talvace, a genial man, a gifted stone carver who builds a cathedral, becomes the victim of intrigues. I think it was he who alerted me to the secular saint in Jean.

I think you would want me to pay a tribute to Gerard Depardieu, the most ungainly of leading men, but an actor who has created such a range of characters, both evil and good. And, of course, for those of us who are, unfortunately, more limited in our human virtue of forbearance, there is the vengeance satisfaction of his daughter in the second part of your drama, *Manon de Sources*.

Dear

HOMBRE

If I were caught in a competition as to which was the better Paul Newman film, *Cooled Hand Luke* or you, I would very reluctantly give up my devotion to *Cool Hand Luke* (letting go of my memory of Luke's "failure of communication", his smiling surrender to the old man/God who was not there in the church, and too many eggs) and you would be my choice. I'm always surprised that the two of you were made in 1967.

I remember thinking at the time (and this was before I started reviewing) that there was some ambiguity in your title. While it is the Spanish word for man, it is sometimes used as "hey, man", "yo, man". But, somehow or other, there is something more archetypal about *Hombre*. Maybe it came from studies of English theatre, which we were doing at the time, but my favoured translation would be Everyman.

This was the mid-1960s, remembering all the changes that we had gone through, were going through. The way we saw the world at the beginning of the 1960s, at least those of us who lived in Western culture, was with beginnings of dissatisfaction, wanting to break free of what came to be seen as the ordinariness, even the complacency, of the 1950s. And, the way that we saw the world by 1970 was in many ways revolutionary – just letting some things come to mind: war in Vietnam, the Civil Rights movement, the expansion of drug taking, the hippy movement and flower power, the changes in the churches, especially the Catholic Second Vatican Council.

I noticed that some commentators referred to you as a 'revisionist Western'. Perhaps that was one of the important movements in cinema in the 1960s, revisionist American westerns – more than egged on by a slew of what came to be called spaghetti westerns, the Italians, often filming in Spanish locations, working with their own perspectives of the cowboys, the Indians, the outlaws and the violence of the West.

I hope you don't mind if I put in a good word for *Devil's Doorway* and *Broken Arrow*. When I was at school, we were alerted that Hollywood was having another look at how Native Americans, the 'Red Indians' were being portrayed on the screen. Instead of the marauding and cruel enemy, there were beginnings of presenting the famous Indian chiefs, the Indian Braves in a more humane light. I remember being told this in 1950 when we saw James Stewart working with Jeff Chandler as Cochise in *Broken Arrow*.

By 1967, here was Paul Newman, a white man, John Russell, raised by the Apaches, permeated with their culture, finding himself at odds in the West, with white men and women. He is taciturn. Has inherited a property from his father. Is caught up in a situation not of his making, and tested. He is set up as an Everyman.

You are a stagecoach story, harking back to the classic of 1939. A mixed group of characters is travelling Arizona, caught up in robbery, betrayals, demands for heroism. Another image for the stagecoach could have been 'ship of fools'. On the coach is a robber, is a corrupt reservation agent and his snobbish wife, a crooked sheriff, a Mexican, and the sympathetic owner of a saloon. Under siege and in danger, it seems that the person who could save this group is John Russell. But, he runs the danger of losing his life. And the question is, are the stagecoach passengers worth it? John Russell will die.

And here we get into semantic difficulties, especially with the emergence of inclusive language in recent decades (a personal lament from me that still, especially in public oratory and debate, exclusive language is still so prominent). There is no tradition, unfortunately, for Everywoman. Everyperson is pretty awkward. And so, with reference to him and his, I mean her and hers as well.

And that is one of the questions for an Everyman figure, for the Everyman to evaluate his own worth, to consider the value of each human person even though the estimate of value might turn out to be almost-worthless, to consider the inner drive to save, the inner drive (which frequently and tragically often fails) to give up one's life for another.

And your great value, certainly revisionist concerning presentation of Native Americans on screen, is the traditionally religious but 1960s-revisionist man or woman, heroically self-sacrificing.

Dear

DISTANT VOICES
STILL LIVES

The impact that I felt while watching you in the late 1980s is still with me. I was very moved during your first part, invited to be cheerful in your second part. And, in writing to you, I am trying to probe something of why that might have been.

One of the immediate things that comes up is how sad you are. This is very true of *Distant Voices*, and your World War II setting in Liverpool. There is more joy and hope in *Still Lives*, but still some inherent sadness.

I was wondering why I identified so readily with the characters. And now I'm wondering whether it is your picture of life in Liverpool, the working class family, Catholic, and whether as an Australian of Irish descent I feel at home with your characters even though their lives were, in fact, quite different. I wonder whether some of them or their parents or grandparents migrated from Ireland to Liverpool and there are remnants of sad 19th century Irish memories, memories of oppression.

While we did not have such experience of the war here in Australia, somehow or other, I resonated with the hardships of the time, the uncertainties, young men going off to war, living with the bombing raids, again the sadness of the women. Actually, the sadness is quite compounded by the role of the father in the family, what the Irish call a hard man. In fact, he was something of a tyrant, dominant and violent, and I can still see Pete Postlethwaite's unusual face, even fierce, in his often unrelenting interactions with his family. When he dies, he is mourned by his family but they are truly relieved. But, most of all, I can still see the face of Freda Dowie as the mother, a woman of patience, religiously stoic, supportive of others, sadness but interior strength.

Director, Terence Davies, had difficulties in completing you and your second part, *Still Lives,* was filmed two years later. It is the same family, the early 50s, peace but rationing, humdrum but hope. And the atmosphere of the hard dead father still hovers.

But, another reason why you are so memorable is that so much of your running time is devoted to music and song. I remember enjoying the songs, most of them familiar, sharing the atmosphere of the men and women in the pub, bonding as a local community, singing, hoping...

While you know your songs, someone else reading this letter may not have come across them so I found a list and thought I should include them in a PS, as the song says, thanks for the memory.

I did not know your director, Terence Davies, at the time of your release but you prepared me for his next film, his autobiographical *The Long Day Closes*, the story of an innocent young boy and his family in mid-1950s Liverpool, the love for songs and the Hollywood musicals, again a Catholic family, devout, church scenes that brought those years alive again, and the little boy, unaware that he would have to make decisions about his sexual orientation. An autobiographical wistfulness. Davies had difficulties at times in raising money for further films but he made many to admire, Edith Wharton's *The House of Mirth*, Terence Rattigan's *The Deep Blue Sea*, the story of Emily Dickinson, *A Quiet Passion*.

Davies described you as a mosaic of memories. I was certainly caught up in the emotion of these memories and their sad and happy nostalgia.

PS, here is a list of your songs:

- "There's a Man Goin' Round Takin' Names" - Jessye Norman

- "I Get the Blues When it Rains" - Marcy Klauber

- "Oh, Mein Papa" - Eddie Calvert

- "Roll out the Barrel" (Beer Barrel Polka) - Jaromír Vejvoda

- "A Hymn to the Virgin" - Benjamin Britten

- *Pastoral Symphony No.3* - Vaughan Williams

- "Love is a Many Splendored Thing" - Mantovani

- "Up the Lazy River" - Hoagy Carmichael

- "Galway Bay" - Tommy Riley

- "Taking a Chance on Love" - Ella Fitzgerald

- "Finger of Suspicion" - Dickie Valentine

- "My Yiddishe Momma" - popularised by Anne Shelton

- "Brown Skin Girl" - King Radio

- "Back in the Old Routine" - Wilson Stone

- "I Love the Ladies" (Traditional)

- "Buttons and Bows" - Jay Livingston, Ray Evans

- "If You Knew Suzie" - Joseph Meyer & Stephen W. Ballantine, George Buddy De Sylva

- "I Wanna Be Around" - Johnny Mercer – sung in the 1950s by Julie London

- "O Waly, Waly" - Peter Pears

- Theme from Limelight, Charles Chaplin

- The Isle of Innisfree – Dick Farrelly.

Looking back now on that list, it does seem like going back in ancient history. Ah, yes.

Dear

NO WAY OUT

I wasn't necessarily going to include you in these letters but, thinking about you, remembering, I decided I should write.

One of the things that I like in watching films is the experience of the unanticipated twist. We are going along satisfactorily, enjoying the murder mystery or whatever drama it is, then the dramatic rug is pulled from under us. We enjoy the discomfort, the intellectual and emotional shock, the relish of the discovery and having to readjust our response to the novel or the film.

And that, back in 1987, is what I experienced as I watched you.

Looking back, who was to know that this kind of Cold War espionage thriller would become rather out of date, not in the sense that the stories were not interesting – just think John Le Carré and the continuing popularity of his books and film versions – but that particular era, from the 1940s to the 1990s, soon became part of history. The Iron Curtain was a severe reality – although the Soviet Union infiltrated the US with sleepers. Did the US do the same in Russia?

Reinforcing that, the memory came back of travelling on a Greyhound bus to Vermont in October 1989, sitting up the front to get the best view of the fall leaves and colours, listening into a conversation between the driver and two men sitting across the aisle, who turned out to be British sports coaches (I forget which sport) working in West Germany. The driver asked whether they thought the two Germanies would be reunited. They thought yes, but not for a number of years. And then, almost immediately, the Berlin Wall came down and the Soviet empire was doomed (or at least possibly to be transformed by Vladimir Putin).

You had a very interesting and enjoyable plot. This was the era of Kevin Costner as movie hero (he had just played Eliot Ness in *The Untouchables*). Here he was a Navy Commander, working with the Secretary of Defence (Gene Hackman). There are sexual complications, the Secretary and his relationship with his mistress, the naval officer also in relationship with her – and then the Secretary accidentally killing her. The two men build up a narrative where a Russian spy, Yuri, is to be blamed for the murder. And the naval officer is to head the investigation. So far, so American version of John Le Carré. A reader looking over my shoulder may be thinking that they have might have seen you since it all seems familiar but they may be remembering Gene Hackman as the US president, again involved in a murder, being investigated by Clint Eastwood in the version of David Baldacci's *Absolute Power*.

I had enjoyed seeing you when I reviewed the film at home so that when it appeared on US cable television in 1989, where I was staying in a parish Presbytery in New York City (the immigration officer in San Francisco thought I meant I was Presbyterian when I responded to his request as to where I was staying as a Presbytery – I had to learn that in the US this was actually a Rectory!), I was ready to watch you again. I recommended you to one of the assistant priests, a very proper man, to say the least, and it suddenly dawned on me that the sex scene between the Secretary and his mistress might be a bit too explicit for him. We worked out a compromise. I explained the plot so far, waited until the potentially offending scene was over, called him in and he enjoyed the rest of the film!

Here I'm caught in a dilemma. You know your plot. You know the twist. You know the solution. But that reader looking over my shoulder who has not seen you may be enticed to want to watch you. So the main thing to say is there is a very good twist which makes us rethink what we have been watching. And for those who have seen the film, my clue for memory is one of Agatha Christie's earliest novels which dumbfounded all the readers when the murderer was finally revealed.

There is even now, decades later, a frisson of excitement when I remember your twist and what it meant.

Dear

ROMERO

Not long after you are released in 1989, I had the opportunity to interview your director, John Duigan. I was particularly interested because I had what I see now was a privilege to attend an early preview and meet your producer, Father Bud Keiser, the Paulist priest who produced so many *Insight* programs for American television, dramas with inspiration, featuring many Hollywood stars who were his friends. When deregulation occurred for American television, no legislation to screen religious programs, he moved to feature films. One of his great ambitions was to make a film about the martyred Archbishop of San Salvador, Oscar Romero, killed in 1980 – and declared a saint by Pope Francis in 2019. So, course, you have a most worthy subject. I asked Father Keiser why he had chosen John Duigan to be your director, John Duigan not being a religious man, not a believer. Father Keiser had been impressed by a number of his films, especially his story of the Philippines and Catholic lay workers during the Marcos era, *Far East*. He considered Duigan a man of humanity.

In the new Parliament House in Canberra, there are photos and quotations from a number of film directors, including John Duigan. His quotation helps us appreciate why he was so willing to make this film about Archbishop Romero. His quote runs:

> It's not so much film per se that's interesting to me, it's film as a vehicle for ideas, and for exploring human psychology and personality, and love and political oppression or whatever it is. (On the wall under John Duigan's photo in Parliament House, Canberra.)

Duigan was also pleased to tell me that, at that stage, you were the only film to have been screened for the American Congress. It was a period of trouble in Central America, Nicaragua, the Sandinistas, so you were particularly relevant for American politicians but also for Catholics around the world, concerned about military dictatorships and persecutions of ordinary citizens.

We all appreciated, especially, the performance by Raoul Julia as Romero, an unexpected nomination to Archbishop of San Salvador, something of a bookish man, with more than a touch of the conservative. But as he entered into his ministry in the later 1970s, and with his friendship with the activist, Father Grundy, also martyred, he became a fearless opponent of tyranny, using pulpit and radio to challenge the government, urging, even commanding them to stop the repression.

Your final minutes are very moving, from the gunmen drawing lots as to who would do the shooting, the approach to the church, the celebration of Mass, the dramatic portraying of Romero's being assassinated as he lifted the chalice (actually a dramatisation because he was killed after Communion – and, a number of Catholics, ideologically opposed to Romero and his stances, condemned the whole film as a fabrication because of this).

That final scene is one that I regularly use for workshops on Christ figures, an obvious choice, of course. But I wanted to tell you about an occasion during the 1990s. The senior students at a Catholic high school had been to a screening and I was to follow-up, drawing out their reactions to you and their reflections. I decided that I would show your final sequence again – and was very surprised, though perhaps I should not have been, with a number of the girls in the class sobbing as they saw again the death scene that had so moved them during the previous screening.

I am sure that I am going to be watching your final scene yet again in future seminars. I hope so.

Dear

SCHINDLER'S LIST

Almost immediately, you became a dear and significant film for all those who experienced or remembered the Holocaust. Who could not be moved by your storytelling, the sadness of those rounded up by the Nazis, interned and murdered in the camps, the survivors, their relatives, their descendants, and those of us who needed to know and, when possible, feel the experience of the six million Jews...?

When Steven Spielberg won the Oscar for best film and Best Director, 1993, he spoke of not being ready to make you ten years earlier, needing more time to reflect and mature. And, with the impact of making you, he moved on to the project of a collection of video interviews with survivors, keeping alive the memories and with the hope of: never again.

At the press preview in the Paramount Theatrette, I found myself sitting next to one of the survivors and his wife. And then, he became one of the characters. And, the most moving moment for me, bringing home the reality, that final sequence where your characters, accompanied by the real-life survivors, including the man sitting next to me, were filmed placing stones on the grave of the righteous Oskar Schindler in Jerusalem. That memory is at this moment coming back to me emotionally and I hear the strains of John Williams' plaintive score, its sadness and lament.

The transition from your opening with the colour of the lighted candle and its then being extinguished moving to the powerful black-and-white photography for the next three hours, was the best choice for the audience to enter into such a grief-stricken, black and white world. And, always, the symbol of the little girl with the red coat, escaping down the streets, and the digging up of the bodies and the revealing of her red coat. And, then, your climax, colour again, signs of hope in the Schindler grave sequence.

For me, you are the Holocaust film, though I still remember the agony of *Sophie's Choice*, the musician in *Playing for Time*, and the pathos of the two young boys in *The Boy with the Striped Pyjamas*. But you were an immersion in the survival in the ghettos, the rounding up of the Jews, the train journeys to the camps, the hard work, slavery, and the reality of deaths, the ovens and the smoke.

As drama, you had three central characters bringing alive the facets of this experience. Liam Neeson was persuasive as the entrepreneurial playboy, Oskar Schindler, mixing with the powers that were, discovering the realities of those who suffered, discovering his deeper self, conversion experience that led him to capitalising on his factories, the workers, the Jewish workers and saving them. Ultimately, losing his money and reputation, he found his true self.

Ben Kingsley was also marvellous, in a quiet way, as Stern, efficient manager, making his lists, finding the workers, saving the Jews – but humiliated and downtrodden by the Nazis.

And I will never forget Ralph Fiennes as Goeth, the arrogance and sadistic superiority of a pragmatic Aryan ideologue, living on whims, consciously comfortable while watching others suffer, arbitrary in his judgments, shooting with intention, shooting at random. A Satanic figure if ever there were.

I was very glad that Thomas Keneally contributed so much to the film, his Booker Prize winning story, *Schindler's Ark*, the Schindler facts and the Jewish lists, those saved (but don't tell him that I never finished his book, too many statistics and details, better the film for me).

Spielberg (with the exuberance of John Williams' scores) was a great entertainer, *Jaws, Indiana Jones, ET, Close Encounters, Jurassic Park*... But, after making you, he tackled a great number of serious themes, just remembering slaves and freedom in *Amistad*, World War II and D-Day in *Saving Private Ryan*, the Olympic Games massacre in *Munich*,

Lincoln, the Pentagon Papers and Richard Nixon in *The Post*. Just a few.

But, I think you are his first serious and lasting monument.

Dear

CALLE MAYOR

You were the first Spanish film I ever saw. And, even after fifty-five years, some moments are literally alive in my memory. But what has stayed with me is the overall impact you made and, as well, the situation in which I first saw you.

Let me tell you first about the situation. It is 1963 or 1964. The Gregorian University in Rome, a Jesuit institution, suddenly offered a course called Filmologia, a day a week over four weeks. It was led by a Jesuit priest, Enrico Baragli, his specialty being communications and who specialised in cinema. He had contributed to the first document produced by the Second Vatican Council, a declaration on media, *Inter Mirifica (Amongst the Wonderful Things...)*, 1963. For someone who was a keen film watcher, it was an opportunity not to be missed.

You were one of the films that Father Baragli showed us. Another film, Italian, of which I have happy memories as well was the crime comedy of inept thieves, *I SolitiIgnoti* (which could be translated as *The Usual Suspects*). Another point about our course was you were screened in a commercial cinema – something which was not permitted for clergy in those years in Italy (even the word 'communication' was bandied about but I'm not sure that that was true!). We did see films in those years but in a special cinema, Oratorio di San Pietro, adjacent to what was then The Holy Office. So more than something of a special atmosphere when we saw you.

I should mention to you also that one of the points that Father Baragli made concerned where we should sit in a cinema for the best effect. In we went and sat in our accustomed places (fortunately we did not genuflect out of habit going down the aisle to our seats as, we have been told, some clergy actually did). Father Baragli then told us we were sitting too far back, too far behind the optimum place and position. He recommended a distance about a third of the auditorium from the front and the screen and, optimally, centre-row. He spoke of an equilateral triangle, the best physics for viewing a film. I have adhered to that practice for more than 50 years. And recommend it, urged it to others. And I found that audiences, even reviewers, sitting too far to the back, miss out on a lot of immediacy of the film's impact. (To try it out, I would suggest sitting way back for a horror film or for a creepy thriller and experience has shown me that the audience is not, or minimally, horrified or terrified – still sitting rather unmoved in their seats.)

I have been telling you about the situation. I should tell you about your impact. A synopsis on paper would look very small, even familiar. A small Spanish town in the mid-1950s, the main street/the calle mayor, the place for people to promenade, gossip, watch the passing parade. Middle-aged men, rather bored, drinking and egging each other on with dares. And, a middle-aged woman, Isabel, 35 and living with her mother, unmarried and feeling more desperate that she was going to finish up as a spinster (having already achieved the status of wallflower). She is played by American Betsy Blair (just after her Oscar-nominated performance as Ernest Borgnine's wife in *Marty*). She has a luminous screen presence but that description would be a great surprise to her forlorn character.

Then comes the cruelty and the pathos. One man, Juan, is urged to date her, lead her on, propose to her. This he does, although it begins to have a questioning effect on him. But Isabel blossoms, delighted, happy, prospects of a happy future. Then, yes, the man is unable to tell the truth to her but a friend does.

There have been many such stories but I will never forget the pain, the deep hurt, a sense of loss, an experience of bewilderment, betrayal, the destruction of her feelings, deadening of emotions, no future. And, you have one of those classic endings, Isabel, close-up, looking out a window, not going out of the town in a train that might lead her to... She is bereft.

Just before I began this letter, I thought I should Google you. Perhaps we were told at the time, but I see that you were Spain's selection for Oscar nomination for that year (though not a final nominee). And then, in 1996, I see you were voted the ninth top Spanish film on the occasion of the centenary of cinema. Belated congratulations.

I have always been thankful to Father Baragli for selecting you for our course and for opening my eyes to Spanish cinema, to a humane sensitivity.

Dear

THE LADYKILLERS

We really enjoyed seeing you in the mid-1950s. At school, we had seen a number of the Ealing Studios comedies, many with Alec Guinness. You are a kind of culmination of these comedies and Alec Guinness starring in them, a man of many characters and many faces (and, within two years, winning an Oscar for *The Bridge on the River Kwai*). Of those many films, I thought it best to write to you.

The word 'Ladykiller' denotes something of a macho approach of too-self-confident men towards what used to be referred to as 'the ladies' now, more appropriately, 'women'. The criminal crew here are definitely not ladykillers in that old, rather sexist, sense. Their approach is much more literal.

One of the main reasons for your charm, despite the possibility of her impending murder, is the presence of 76-year-old Katie Johnson. Stories are told that the producers wanted somebody a bit younger – but their alternative choice actually died before production. Just as well (the casting, not the death) Katie Johnson got the part because she actually won a BAFTA award for Best Actress. She is certainly memorable, the dainty old lady with a touch of the daffy, long skirt, umbrella, hat pin, old-fashioned and genteel way of speaking.

She is a very good example of the old lady who cried wolf. Down she went to the police station, urging action on all kinds of scenarios, ultimately not being taken notice of by the busy sergeants. (Ironically and humorously, this paid off because when she brought the stolen money to the police station, for them it was another wolf-cry and they did not examine the bag with the loot – she could keep it, excitedly forgetting her umbrella and confiding in the police that she could afford another one!)

Katie Johnson's leading man, the principal ladykiller, was another tour-de-force performance by Alec Guinness, and for those who have not seen you, not to be missed! He is the sinister Professor Marcus, a touch ghoul-like, crooked smile, very noticeable teeth, thinning hair – and, it was said at the time, modelled on Alastair Sim. I don't know whether Alastair Sim would be quite flattered by the comparison, but Guinness does remind us of him in many ways!

The cover of the criminals, definitely more-than-motley lot, was that they were musicians, rehearsing (Boccharini and then Hayden), one with a violin case containing you know what. I have always enjoyed Cecil Parker in his dithering roles like this one here. Danny Green could always play the dumb character. Herbert Lom had no difficulty in looking sinister. And, that's right, the youngest of the criminals was played in a very early role by Peter Sellers – not one of his best, not necessarily signalling how successful he would be over the next quarter of a century. Actually, the cast also has cameos by Kenneth Connor as a taxi driver and Frankie Howard as The Barrow Boy. Not a bad catalogue of British comedians. Oh, and at the station there was that most regular of British policeman, Jack Warner.

I probably should have noted at the beginning, but you would have been well aware of it, that you are not just a comedy. You are a black comedy, full of ironies, capitalising on the humour of grim situations – even attempts on poor old Katie Johnson's life, and even the successive deaths of the gang.

The setting was near King's Cross station in London, so the scene of the crime, the scene of the house, not too far to the robbery and for the escape. That meant also the atmosphere of trains, open carriages into which bodies could be dropped, eerie smoke emissions, and large signals that could be relied on to hit villains on the head, propelling them over the rail, into those open wagons. Oh, sorry to any readers who haven't seen you (pity!), I've included some spoilers.

One unusual thing about your screenplay and direction is that they were by Americans. Director Alexander McKendrick had spent some time in Britain and made some of those Ealing Studios comedies, including another favourite, Alec Guinness *in The Man in the White Suit.* And your screenplay was written by William Rose, startlingly winning an Oscar nomination for a small-budget British comedy. He too had spent time in England, writing screenplays there and then in the United States. Great credits all round.

In case you didn't watch the Coen Brothers US remake with Tom Hanks, my advice would be, 'Don't'. It is the equivalent of a cinema sacrilege!

Dear

TO KILL A MOCKINGBIRD

It is only just now that I discovered that the American Film Institute declared that Atticus Finch was the 'Greatest American hero of the Movies of the 20th century'. Quite an accolade. And a tribute to Gregory Peck for bringing him to the screen so persuasively, and his winning an Oscar for Best Actor. I see also that playwright and screenwriter, Horton Foote, also won an Oscar for his adaptation of Harper Lee's classic novel of 1960.

I came to see you rather later than earlier. And I can't quite remember when I saw you but it would have to be some time in the 1970s or early 1980s. I'm fairly sure that I had read Harper Lee's novel before I saw you. Which meant that I was rather primed with your reputation, eager to see you, eager to see the embodiment of Atticus Finch. You didn't fail.

But seeing you later reminded me of what was happening in the United States when you were released in 1962. There were still far more than vestiges of segregation in the South, on the importation of the slaves, their hard lives, experiences of backbreaking work and oppression, injustice and lynchings – Governor George Wallace and his stances were soon to come to the fore in presidential campaigning in Alabama. 1962 was also the Kennedy era, stronger movements for Civil Rights, the year before the March on Washington and Martin Luther King's dreaming and dream. I would think that you contributed to something of these movements and changes to come.

But you took us back into the 1930s with a picture of bigotry and cruelty. There are still images in my mind of Brock Peters as Tom Robinson, Black labourer on trial for rape, the jury not listening to the evidence, finding him guilty, his subsequent murder by the father who had abused his daughter.

You made your message of racial harmony and equality through the drama of the court case and its consequences. But, you communicated your message through Atticus Finch and through his children, Mary Badham and Philip Alford as Scout and Jim.

Thinking about Atticus Finch as the American movie hero of the 20th century reminds me of Atticus' presence in the court, his defence, the quality of his speeches and arguments, the strong tone and passionate vigour of Gregory Peck's voice, his demeanour, is insistent: a character of authenticity and integrity.

But there is also Atticus Finch, the father, communicating this integrity to his two children and their discovery of racism and violence, seeing how well their father helped all those in need, sharing dismay at the guilty verdict, and then they themselves, the night of the Halloween party, also attacked violently by the abusive father – and introducing the pathos of their being rescued by their reclusive neighbour whom they used to spy on, Boo Radley (Robert Duval's first film) and their recognising and respecting him.

So here is the fictional town of Maycomb, Alabama, standing in for Harper Lee's hometown in Alabama, Monroeville, where she experienced events like these during her childhood, writing about them so vividly in her novel, a novel which has found itself on so many curricula, for literature, social studies, human rights issues...

I also saw that in 1995 you were selected for preservation in the United States *National Film Registry* by the *Library of Congress* as being "culturally, historically, or aesthetically significant".

Yes – and not only in the United States, everywhere.

Dear

THE SEARCH

You have been in my memory for a long, long time because I saw you at primary school probably the year after you were released. I think I would have been nine or ten. I can still see images, hear the music, remember – re-experience – the sadness.

I have just being looking at some notes I made when I saw you decades later. I see I used the word 'poignant '. But you are far more than that. Even 'most poignant 'does not do justice to your humanity and your impact.

World War II was only three or four years over when I saw you. Not sure at this stage how much of an impact the war had made on me – I do some remember some ration books and hearing that a submarine was in Sydney Harbour but I was at school on August 6th 1945 and have no recollection of hearing about the dropping of the atomic bomb on Hiroshima. Nor on Nagasaki on my sixth birthday. So it was films like you that began to shape my understanding, my images of the war.

You were filmed on locations in West Germany. I'm still dismayed when I see films of the Blitz and the devastated buildings in London. And I'm still even more dismayed when looking at films that roam through the ruins of bombed German and Austrian cities – Berlin, Dresden, Hamburg, and of Vienna in *The Third Man*... How could people survive? And, more importantly, how did they survive, shelter, food and water, the search for lost family members...?

Your scene when the Czech family was sitting at the meal and there is a knock at the door and the parents taken. Then, the little boy, Karel (Ivan Jandl receiving an Oscar for the best juvenile performance 1948), caught up with children in the camps, not speaking German, wandering the ruins after the Allied victory, the droves of wandering children, the little French boy explaining and the pathos of his drowning, Karel being a Catholic but unable to communicate this and his being shipped with the Jewish children. And the children's screams and their wanting to escape from the ambulance, thinking that it was an SS and to take them to the camps.

I can still see Karel's mother and her search, wandering the cities, broken roads, grieving, her contact with Mrs Murray and her practically giving up, deciding to work with the children. And then, the tension for audiences, especially seeing lost children, her passing Karel and not seeing him, our fears that she would never find him, tears that they finally find each other.

One thing I realised about the actress, Aline McMahon who portrayed Mrs Murray, was that she made such an impression – the way she looked, her expressions, so kindly – that in later years when I saw her in films from the 1930s, she looked too young and I couldn't reconcile her with the actress who had so impressed me. And, of course, this was one of Montgomery Cliff's first films.

And now, writing this letter to you, thinking back, moments of reminiscing, I realise a powerful identification with Karel searching for his mother. With my mother dying in 1947, our sadness rather stoic in those days, even as children, and her being-in-heaven focus of our grief, there must have been quite an impact when I first watched your story, a child deprived of its parent, fears and bewilderment, and what it was like to be sad at such a young age.

Dear

MR SMITH GOES TO WASHINGTON

I am writing to you during an election campaign, having just spent an hour or more listening to four representatives of major parties in Queensland, the television program, Q and A. It began with an audience member asking the question whether courtesy would prevail with no bagging of the opposition and its policies. Three were polite but a senator, from a party that I've never voted for, continually interjected, held up and waved his promotional pamphlet, began to shout louder and louder, badgering the member to whom he was ideologically opposed (to say the least)..., the host always in danger of losing control of the senator. It made me realise that I've been interested in films about politics, especially American politics, for as long as I can remember.

Then I began to wonder what it was about politics that intrigued me, whether it was the elaboration of policies and the motivations behind them (very worthy) or whether it was the rough-and-tumble of arguments, oneupmanship, spurning of opposition, witty expressions of brutal bludgeoning (less than worthy). My conclusion: it must be the theatrical experience, the dramatic twists of politics.

I had been intending to write to you and I had been wondering why. You are one of Frank Capra's masterpieces, films of hope but, over the decades, declining optimism. You were released in 1939 just after the outbreak of war in Europe. It was to be more than two years before the bombing of Pearl Harbor and America entering the war. Franklin D. Roosevelt was president and, in the wake of the Depression, he was rolling out his New Deal. Surely some optimistic moments. But, there you are, backgrounds of political patronage, an atmosphere of political corruption, money deals and protection, lies and knives out, political stabbings in the back, political slitting throats.

But, here is the image of the good American, Smith, the ordinary man, Jefferson in memory of constitution and presidency. And he is something of a country bumpkin, from the sticks or, as we might say, from the bush. He is a man of integrity, works with scouts, wants to promote education and welfare at the local level. And, of course, he is Jimmy Stewart, tall, sometimes a touch dishevelled, earnest, sometimes bumbling, very much an aw-shucks kind of man. Not born to be a politician! But, promoted, coming to Washington and plunged, one might say, into the depths.

They used to describe Americans visiting Europe as "innocents abroad". So here is an innocent in Washington. And he is played by perennial bully, Edward Arnold, manipulating corruption. Educated and respectable-seeming senator, Claude Rains, has been dominated, the respectable face of corruption – who, thank goodness, has some final moments of redemption.

So eighty years ago, politics was just the same as today – or, putting it more properly, politics today is still the same as it was.

Mr Smith is rather overwhelmed by his predicament, by people badmouthing him (despite the help that he gets from Jean Arthur), misjudging him.

And then there is the filibuster – and I am wondering when I first heard this word and saw it in action. Most probably, watching you. For Jefferson Smith, talking for 25 hours to gain some kind of respect, for some kind of self-vindication, and then collapse. That was a real filibuster.

So I admired your themes, found them fascinating. Your extensive cast of veteran actors was admirable and Sidney Buchman's dialogue well worth listening to.

And James Stewart had many wonderful roles in a 50 year career (think Hitchcock, for example) but your director, Frank Capra, provided him with two of his best.

I have written to you instead of to *It's a Wonderful Life* because of the politics. Everybody quotes *It's a Wonderful Life*, its screening for Christmas (even The Gremlins watched you, but raucously!) and in the aftermath of World War II everyone talks about its hope, optimism and Clarence the Angel. But, to my memory, when James Stewart tries to kill himself and goes into the ugly and corrupt alternate version of Bedford Falls, I'm overwhelmed by these images of pessimism about human nature and society.

To end this letter, you have made me think of American politics during my lifetime. I've counted that there have been thirteen presidents after Roosevelt, some moments of high, many moments of low, from Jimmy Carter to Richard Nixon. As I write, Donald Trump is still there – who knows!

Dear

THE FISHER KING

I remember being quite excited when I first saw you. Terry Gilliam was a significant small-screen, big-screen presence, his being a member of the Monty Python team, talented animator, leading audiences on fantastic journeys, ranging through the history of Western culture with *Time Bandits*, into surreal society in *Brazil*, the oddity of *Baron Munchausen*. These were, whether comic or tragic, exhilarating mixtures of the real, the surreal, the fantasy and the fantastic.

I know Terry Gilliam spent years working on his interpretation of Don Quixote, seemingly tilting at windmills, a failing but eventually combining the Don's life and quests with those of a contemporary film and commercials maker, with even more imaginative and creative knights and chivalry, power and betrayals, *The Man who Killed Don Quixote* – but, somehow or other, it was far too much for me to take, let alone enjoy. Which brings me back to you, a fine example for me, of Terry Gilliam's imaginative fact and fantasy.

And here you are in New York City at the beginning of the 1990s doing the same thing.

But how could you combine the myths and legends of chivalry with the life of a radio shock jock, merciless in his talkback, ruthless as he misread desperate callers – and then the victim of tragic events that he set in motion? It seemed quite a stretch for him to finish up as The Fisher King. It seemed that there would have to be a lot of repentance and atonement, if he were to be worthy to find the Grail.

Your engaging screenplay by talented writer, Richard La Gravenese, provided the perfect answer, going back to ancient stories, stories of rulers and courts, the ever-present butt of courtiers' attention and lack of attention, the conscience of the King, the fool, Fool with a capital F.

This is one of the roles that Robin Williams was born to play, drawing on his manic radio personality in *Good Morning, Vietnam*, with the seriousness of his mentoring, his Oscar-winning performance in *Good Will Hunting*. I don't know whether you have come across the documentary made about the life of Robin Williams and his career, a probing of his personality, his hyper-personality. It had the evocative title, *Come Inside My Mind*.

In the light of his life and career, his performance as Parry here is something of an exemplification of his mind, his life, his comic speed and zest, excitement, his depression and manias, the exuberance and its toll leading him to take his life.

In a sense, his character here, Parry, has died with the death of his wife, the victim of the shootings instigated by the shock jock. He has withdrawn into his afterlife, many moments of purgatory, moments of hell, symbolised by the Red Knight, a monstrous and vindictive and pursuing giant through Central Park. But, there are some moments of heaven, especially in his attraction towards the withdrawn Lydia, that life might not be completely over.

Terry Gilliam has an affinity for the holy Grail with the pursuit by the Pythons. Parry has a fixation about the location of the Grail, in a wealthy New York building. In his dealings with Jack, and Jack's partner, Anne (remembering that Mercedes Ruehl won an Oscar for her performance), their helping him to meet the timid Lydia as a competition winner at the video shop, a date at a restaurant. All this is part of Jack's withdrawal from life, his doing penance. But, now, Jack has to scale the walls, go on his quest, invade the building, rescue the Grail, return in triumph. He is redeemed – and Parry, the wise fool, initially a victim of The Fisher King, rehabilitating him.

What is left for Parry and Jack is to be at peace with themselves, at peace with human nature, lying naked on the grass, contemplating the stars. Is that what the recovery of the Holy Grail means?

Dear

THE EGYPTIAN

Is it ever too late in life to make a confession? I'm not confessing a sin to you but rather confessing that you were one of my favourite films during my teen years. I saw you at 15 – someone might ask did I not know any better! So I'm not exactly repenting (although I gather that some critics think I should) – and, indeed, I'm not really in need of absolution or a need for atonement. But, thinking about you makes me reflect on my lifelong cinema interests and tastes, especially when I was a boy.

It was great to be a boy in 1954-1955. At least in the world of, as we used to say, "going to the pictures". Why this period? Cinemascope, of course. We all saw *The Robe* (even seeing it a second time as we walked the three miles from boarding school into the Empire, the picture show, in Bowral – and walked back). Lots of wide screen, lots of action adventure, encouraging our spectacle imagination, my appetite for the spectacular, from the Khyber Rifles to the South African veldt.

So I'm wondering what it is about you that appealed to me and to my, as I characterised it, spectacular imagination or my sensibility prone to spectacle. I was only too happy to be transported to ancient Egypt. Egypt looked wonderful (with Oscar-nominated Leon Shamroy's photography). Ancient palaces, pharaohs, palace intrigues, invading armies, local taverns, a sympathetic visiting doctor. And a quite spectacular cast, Victor Mature who had been both Samson and Demetrius the gladiator, Jean Simmons who was to be Spartacus' wife, Peter Ustinov after Nero in *Quo Vadis* and before *Spartacus*, a majestic Gene Tierney, and a lot of all those character actors, like Henry Daniell, who could embody the sinister without effort, a high priest here. I do remember Edmund Purdom and only now realise that Marlon Brando was to be Sinuhe, the Egyptian. Brando might have been more subtle but Purdom was, at least, pleasant.

So, you see, I'm already enjoying the reminiscing. And surprised that you were directed by Michael Curtiz (just a decade after *Casablanca*).

Interesting, as I think back, that even in those days we must have had some sound religious education at school because the parallel with Sinuhe and his humble origins seemed a most obvious reference to Moses, his birth, his being saved, his promotion in the life of the Court of Pharaoh. And, perhaps with too much smug satisfaction at our religious education, being most impressed that that most mild of Pharaohs, Michael Wilding's Akhenaton, was a monotheist. To devout us, most obviously, he was a good man, a man of virtue, even reluctant to go to war, definitely on the right religious track long before Moses at Mount Sinai, let alone the coming of Jesus.

Which meant, as I now confess to you, that I really enjoyed seeing you, coming back to school and sharing our enthusiasms, as a group of us did with the pictures we saw during the holidays, recounting the stories, sharing the high points.

Which also means that, while I did see a range of films during school holidays and I had the task – which I thoroughly enjoyed – of choosing the film program for the year, I had a soft spot (too soft?) for travelling back into spectacular history (*Sign of the Pagan* just rushed to mind, Jack Palance as Attila the Hun with Jeff Chandler combating him – maybe not the critically greatest but I really enjoyed it, always glad I saw it). In fact, I have always had a memory penchant for locating historical events and placing them in their appropriate chronology.

So I like you very much because I like history coming alive. I like locating ideas, themes and meanings in their historical context – and, of course, I have loved reading, but can you beat two hours or more immersed in the colour and the larger-than-life re-creation of an era? I suppose you can, really, but you will always hold a special place as one of the films that reinforced my imaginative love for the spectacular.

Dear

IKURU

A straitjacketed life. Then a terminal illness. This is the fate of Kanji Watanabe. Your film *Ikuru/Living*.

In writing to you, I'm also acknowledging the wonderful career of your director, Akira Kurosawa and what I consider his exalted place in 20th century Japanese cinema. I presume a lot of his samurai action tales would be receiving admiring letters. Also many of his crime stories. I was tempted by the beauty of some of his later films, his moving into colour, his interpretations of Shakespeare, his portraits of Japanese life and traditions, his touches of the mystical in the early 1990s. But, because of your deep humanity, you kept coming to mind.

I didn't see you when you were first released in the early 1950s, after Kurosawa's breakthrough with *Rashomon* and before *The Seven Samurai*. In fact, I can't remember when I saw you, but your sad, then hopeful, tale of Mr Watanabe is a film I treasure.

I'd better tell you that I saw you well before I reached Mr Watanabe's age. And while there was empathy at first sight, it was not that I needed reassuring in some midlife crisis nor the facing of a cancer (that was to come much later when I was in my 70s). No, it was the performance of Takashu Shimura', the deadening routine of his bureaucratic job for 30 years, the neglect by his children, his not even being able to tell his son that he was terminally ill, they all made an arresting impact.

In retrospect, it would seem as if World War II and the defeat of Japan had not occurred. Or, as if the experience of the war had bypassed Mr Watanabe. There he was, sitting at his desk, expecting that this would be his life forever, that this was what life was like. And, while he dealt with people, he could not galvanise any personal initiative to promote the transformation of a cesspool into a playground.

I know what it's like when a doctor tells you, across his desk, "it's cancer". You have to do some immediate thinking, begin assessing, imagining, rationalising, and wondering... There is an ominous phrase, 'impending death'. I'm always grateful to have come out the other end. But this was not the case for Mr Watanabe.

You show his bewilderment and ask us to share it. He discovers that his son is more preoccupied with inheritance and so he does not tell his son the truth. You rather shocked me when you showed what Mr Watanabe decided to do – literally go out on the town. He sings a song – pre-karaoke.

But he realises that club life is too shallow a solution. He meets a young woman associate who seems to be rather happy in life, very uncomfortable with his attentions, but, when he questions her about her happiness, her making dolls, she replies that by doing this work, she feels she is playing with the children.

I wondered, as everyone with a terminal illness does, whether we will have some moment of conversion. Your answer is quite a resounding yes, a personal conversion and transformation, but no opting out of – there's that phrase again – 'impending death'.

Mr Watanabe, you reveal, discovers (or re-discovers) his humanity, putting all his efforts into providing that playground. And, a blend of hope and irony, his straitjacketed co-workers are amazed at what is done, wondering whether he knew he was ill, even making good resolutions after they hear that as he died, he sat on a swing at the playground and sang the song from the club. But you remind us that so often the result of good resolutions is not keeping them.

You are a realist film, admiring humanity and humane qualities, but realising that, with most of us, a conversion and acting for the better, does not come easily. But, you hope it could and does.

Dear

THE NUN'S STORY

You might be very surprised to learn that I'm beginning this tribute letter to you with laughter. Laughter is certainly not something that anyone would immediately associate with you and your story, a beautiful story but a very sad story about a nun in a religious community.

Here is the laughter episode which might take you back. In 1961, the cinema manager in the town in Queanbeyan, just across the border from Canberra, invited members of religious orders to attend a special screening. A group of us were senior seminarians at the monastery in Canberra, adjacent to the Drive-in cinema on the north side, a terrible temptation to glance across to the screen when we were supposed to be recollected – although, it did provide a service, when in the late 1960s, the Superior was in such a rush to get out before everyone else, thinking that James Bond had happily married Tracy in *On Her Majesty's Secret Service*, had to be rushed to the window to see the actual ending – sad! Of course, that's not the laughter story.

So one Saturday morning, there was a theatre full of nuns and us. And, as you progressed, the titters and giggles burst into laughter. I don't know what the poor manager was thinking at such a response to his generous offer for the screening. You may well be wondering what we were all laughing at. Probably best to tell you that it was self-conscious laughter, seeing up there on the screen very strict religious practices that we had experienced in the previous years, during the 1950s. They mirrored what we had gone through – and, at this stage, behaviour we were trying to come to terms with, trying to discern the values, trying to pass beyond the rigidities of formation and community life. Even as I tell you this, I really do hope that some of the sisters did explain to the manager the reasons for our reactions and that we really did appreciate the opportunity to see you.

You are the last of the old stories of nuns (unless for re-creations of past history). Ingrid Bergman, Loretta Young, Jennifer Jones, even Anglican Deborah Kerr in *Black Narcissus*, belong to an era that was ending (except for those communities, bound rigidly to the past, or even some contemporary communities who still yearn for this kind of strict life). In good faith, you went into production in 1958. But that was the year that Pope Pius XII died, the end of an era. A new age began with the election of Pope John XXIII and his springing on an unsuspecting church an ecumenical council, the encouragement of renewal and updating, aggiornamento. So you were released when John XXIII was Pope.

Obviously, I saw you again later in life and have a great admiration for you. Although your setting was Belgian, and then into the Congo, especially in the 1930s, your story was quite universal. Your technical advisors were very accurate. You have the look of a monastic community, the sisters in their habits, the large numbers, scenes in the chapel, scenes in the refectory, the practice of Chapter of Faults, the acknowledgment of imperfections (seeming trivial in retrospect) that were publicly confessed and a penance imposed. I have just remembered that some of the loudest laughter came from the scene where Audrey Hepburn, perfectly embodying the novice nun, even the spoken intonations, had to kneel in front of the tables in the refectory and kiss the feet of the sisters. Pretty absurd in thinking about such asceticism in retrospect. We laughed in 1961, anticipating the demise of this kind of practice.

In 1961, we were actually studying at Australian National University and our religious superior, in somewhat ponderous tones, told us that it would be a tragedy were we to fail any subject. And then, on the screen, there was Sister Luke, Audrey Hepburn looking pious and demure, being told to fail her medical examinations for the sake of humility. That looks even worse now, an erroneous spirituality, a blind obedience, allegedly God's will through the will of the Superior but actually a Jansenistic/Puritanical whim of the Superior.

Looking back, such formation processes, in the name of humility and spirituality, the sacrificing of one's will, that the presumption that one's will was always in the wrong, seem false. But, they had a very long tradition. The danger was that a religious who, even in undoubted good faith, stayed within those patterns of living out their vows, remained infantile.

Then, in the aftermath of changes from the Second Vatican Council, and in the light of changes in social consciousness – and some boundaries-breaking yearning for freedom – large numbers of men left the priesthood, men and women left religious life, not always easily, but having to struggle through release from the arbitrary imposition of whims, the harsh asceticism, the lack of opportunity to reassess commitment until it seemed too late. Many left. But, for good reasons (and sometimes very poor reasons, a kind of nesting) many stayed.

Sister Luke found her challenge in her medical vocation, in her service in the Congo – and in her decision to leave her congregation, along with the sadness and loneliness that she packed her bags, went out a Convent back door, alone out into the world and, in middle age, to a new life.

But you are a great film, mirroring the past, offering a great challenge to members of religious orders to look more deeply into their commitment.

Dear

BRUCE ALMIGHTY

Oh my God. That used to be a prayer – I hope it is still a prayer for many. But in recent times, OMG is just a texting exclamation of surprise, awesome!

Which means then that Oh my God needs some kind of rehabilitation or that in an increasingly secular world, we need some sense of God's presence, or something of transcendence in our lives and in our world, even if we don't "believe in God". It means that God probably needs a lot more credibility these days. At times, he is just absent and, day by day, people don't notice. But, then, he suddenly seems to exist when people experience tragedy, especially in illness and pain, untimely deaths, natural disasters that take their toll. Where is God? Why didn't God intervene? If God is a loving God, how come that he allowed this...?

These are philosophical and theological questions, psychological questions too, needing empathetic listeners, allowing anger and grief, and maybe having to live with no easy, ready or platitudinous solutions.

Actually, that sounds a fairly heavy introduction in a letter to you, one of my favourite comedies. I'm not sure that anyone in 2002, with memories of Jim Carrey as *Ace Ventura, Pet Detective* or *The Mask*, would associate him with deep God questions. But, it is to the credit of your director, Tom Shadyac and his zest in writing and directing, that this is the case. The treatment is light but, for those who enjoy the film and its divine speculations, some God-directions are to the fore.

Jim Carrey is Bruce, getting towards middle age, not making much progress in his media work, not the most patient of people, with a nice girlfriend aptly named Grace (Jennifer Aniston), he goes into that exasperated martyr mode – what has God got against him! He becomes hypersensitive on that point, even blaming God for cars splashing water on him as they speed past.

Many of us really enjoyed God as a short, nearly hundred-year-old, cigar-smoking George Burns, *Oh God!* (And two sequels, including George being able to offer God's Satanic shadow side). But in these days, if there were to be a ballot for who would be a convincing God-presence on screen, I am sure that Morgan Freeman would be near the top, or at the top. He has a gravity, tall and distinguished, venerable grey hair and the perfect speaking voice.

There is always that distraction that the Hebrew people had an explicit commandment that there be no images of God, although the Ancient of Days in Daniel 7, seated in majesty, is a visual exception. But, in the Christian tradition, reinforced by Michelangelo, God is pictured as an old man (and shades of William Blake). Maybe, in those days, they served as the equivalent of Morgan Freeman.

So the quarrelsome Bruce receives an invitation to visit a company building, Omni Presents, and distracts the janitor, the general caretaker, dressed immaculately in white, though for racial consciousness these times, God is black. And sounds perfect.

I know that God is supposed to be omni-everything but he claims not to be omni-healthy, is getting a bit worn out and needs a holiday. So what better than to hand over to a God-conscious complainant. Bruce reckons he knows how God should intervene so he accepts the job. But he forgets that God is not supposed to be narcissistic and he indulges in all kinds of jokes and meanness (from parting his soup like the Red Sea to putting a spell on Steve Carrell having a verbal breakdown on air – and that is also one of the funniest scenes in movies). God is not supposed to be lascivious either, but Bruce is a bit creatively leering towards Grace.

As you might guess, Bruce will discover that being God is no easy task, even to managing all the prayers and requests coming in and deciding how they might be handled. He and God gather on the top of Mount Everest for a literal summit. Looks as though not everyone can be satisfied – but God has made the stipulation to Bruce that he can't interfere with human free will. Humans can still make choices, free to do so (wrong and destructive choices).

So you become the popular cinema, multiplex-style, equivalent of a sermon, if not theology class, illustrated. How long your lesson lasts is something of a problem. Many commentators, many parents, worry about the undue influence of the cinema, especially on the young, fearing violence and pornography. However, you and the biblical and current faith-based movies are a constant reminder that the influence of the cinema, especially the cinema of the good, even of the holy, can't be having as much good influence otherwise, think how quickly and easily we could become good, let alone holy.

But, while you are there, you are something of a theological tonic (but, of course, quickly rejected by those who are antipathetic to tonics).

You know Tom Shadyac tried it again but not nearly so successfully with *Evan Almighty*. Perhaps Steve Carrell as Evan was not so susceptible. But it's always a pleasure to see Morgan Freeman-God.

THE VISITOR

I thought you were a fine film, small and modest but significant, a film that could be well recommended all-round. You have a strong impact, emotionally, and you provide a welcome challenge to an audience's sense of humanity.

If we were to be asked to name a post-9/11 American film, New York-based, helping people to continue to live in hope with tragedy, cope with the threat of terror (and not just making a war against it), welcoming the stranger, especially those who look and sound different (and of middle eastern appearance), I would choose you.

I have admired Thomas McCarthy as an actor, had been very impressed with his modest film, *The Station Agent*, with Peter Dinklage. And, of course, he directed *Spotlight* (Oscar-winner for Best Picture, but irritating at times as if *The Boston Globe* journalists discover the scandals of sexual abuse all by themselves, not acknowledging that other countries had been tackling the issues before they did – but, *Spotlight* was still a devastatingly alerting film).

When you were screened in England, I was coming from a press preview in Soho and there was Thomas McCarthy, stuck in the street, looking at a guidebook or a roadmap. I was glad to have the opportunity to say hello, to offer him some words of admiration, then be a Good Samaritan and point out how he would get back to his hotel. And I was sorry that I did not have my camera with me to get a souvenir and prove that I had met him! But, that's just about me, better back to you.

Richard Jenkins has to be one of the most reliable and versatile of older American actors. Always good to see him on screen and in such a wide range of characters. He is the star (about time, one might say) and he did get a non-Oscar nomination as well as other nominations and awards. For purposes of the screenplay, it is significant that Jenkins plays Walter, a sixtyish white male, straight, reasonably affluent, middle-class American. He symbolises the US character that post 9/11 – or any time – must be challenged. Thomas McCarthy noted that he had Richard Jenkins in mind when he wrote the screenplay.

You show him as a widower who lectures at a Connecticut college, but who has withdrawn into himself and into the stale routines of academia. His main attempt to come out of himself, to learn to play the piano (his late wife was a concert pianist), comes to nothing.

After a conference, when he returns home to his apartment, he finds two illegals occupying his New York apartment (they have been swindled by a conman). He is shocked but he is a decent man and offers them some temporary refuge. Then, music again. You show him being rewarded by learning that Syrian Tarek (a charismatically genial Haaz Sleiman) plays drums. It is wonderful (and encouraging for those who are not as young as they used to be and who sometimes feel stuck in their ruts) to watch Walter open up as a person as he shares the life of the two and learns to play the drums himself.

But that you also portray an atmosphere of tension. Tarek and his Senegalese companion (Danai Gurira) are continually wary about being picked up by the authorities and subjected to detention or, even worse, deportation. When Tarek is suddenly detained, it has a profound effect on Walter who makes many efforts on his behalf. Tarek's mother (the dignified Hiam Abbass of *Lemon Tree*) comes to New York and, as she is helped by Walter as they go to a lawyer and as Walter visits Tarek, Walter warms to her and is introduced to a completely different world.

Actually, I needn't be telling you this; I'm just taking the opportunity to remind myself.

In this war against terror period, you show that authorities are necessarily on alert but overly suspicious – and many officials seem to assume that rudeness and rough treatment is a way of combating terrorism. The treatment of Tarek neglects some basic human rights. Walter is shocked at this. Thomas McCarthy doesn't let his audience go contentedly out of the cinema. You have a pervading melancholy ending.

I must have been in a proselytising mood when I finished my review at the time of your release: 'It is a pity that so many moviegoers' budgets are eaten up by the big blockbusters which they enjoy when they could also invest in a moving and satisfying film like this one'.

And I still hope that many people will discover and watch you.

LEMON TREE

I have seen practically all the films of your director, Eran Riklis, his taking us into various stories of Israel and, so often, including Israeli-Arab characters, Palestinian characters. Which means that there is always some edge. Given the histories of Palestinians, of Jews and Israelis during the 20th century, there must always be some tension in the drama, some tension in the audience response, some hopes that there might be resolutions, many disappointments that they have not yet been achieved.

Your story is a strong case in point.

I remember some years ago listening to a friend speaking about the construction of the wall in Israel which he referred to as a fence. It was a bit of a shock some years later when I visited Israel and saw that the word 'fence' was quite an underestimation. I stayed a night at the Tantur Institute, an ecumenical and inter-faith study centre, which overlooked the wall, which turned out to have the height of many fences. We intended to visit Bethlehem which meant going down to the border, going through the stiles for passport control, coming out on the other side, amazed at the close-up height of the wall, looking at the pictures and artwork, and wending our way to Bethlehem. Passport control was more stringent on the way back. And then I remembered your story.

Hiam Abbas is an actress I have long admired. She has a very dignified screen presence, hasn't she? And this is important for the role that she plays, Salma, a Palestinian woman with a lemon grove, right on the border in the West Bank. The lemon grove is part of her heritage and this is a story of how it is threatened. One of the ministers in the Israeli government, the Minister of Defence, owns a mansion at the border. Security is a top priority with the Minister and his advisers suggest that the grove is a security threat, any terrorist threatening being able to advance close under cover of the trees. They have to go or be severely pruned – or at least the number must be lessened.

So, as the Scriptures have long offered as a symbol of unequal struggle, this is a David and Goliath story. Audience sympathy is all for Salma as she is decides to challenge the threat to her grove. She is well supported by family and friends. She goes to authorities in Ramallah, needing help because she does not read Hebrew. A young Israeli lawyer becomes her advocate. And, step-by-step, tenacity by tenacity, her case eventually arrives at the Supreme Court in Jerusalem. On the one hand, very objective and logical participants decide in favour of security and the Minister's safety. On the other hand, those who are moved emotionally, including sympathy from the minister's wife, want Salma to win.

You are a film that has great power to move an audience because you are an Israeli film taking up personalised issues of human rights. Sadly, as with the history of the past decades, you do not come up with a peaceful solution. Rather, there is sadness – and the lyrics of Peter, Paul and Mary's song and their sadness:

Lemon tree very pretty and the lemon flower is sweet, but the fruit of the poor lemon is impossible to eat.

And, as I was in the van going down from Jerusalem to the airport in Tel Aviv, news came of rockets being fired from Gaza on Israel, then the protective defence, the retaliation...

Dear

O BROTHER WHERE ART THOU?

I am greatly indebted to you. Let me tell you about an episode at the Cannes Film Festival in 2000.

The head of the Vatican's Pontifical Council for Social Communications, an American, Archbishop John Foley, a very dignified and proper man, had been invited to be a guest of the festival in 1997 but had to withdraw on the occasion of the death of his mother. He was able to accept the invitation by 2000 and had agreed to be present at a screening. And the film chosen was you. I was very apprehensive, especially because of the previous film from your directors. That was *The Big Lebowski* full of what rather proper Americans referred to as "cuss words". (It contained that memorable comment on four letter conversation when Sam Elliott, the narrator of the story, sat at a bar near Jeff Bridges The Dude, cussing more than apace, suggests that he swore too much – and the famous reply of The Dude, "what the fuck you mean?"). I was anticipating much embarrassment all around.

But God was on our side. God was on your side. You are a very sweet and entertaining film, not a cuss word to be scandalised at. I was amused the next morning in the sacristy before Mass when an American TV crew interviewed the Archbishop, mentioned that he had seen a Coen Brothers film – perhaps expecting a bit of moral turmoil – asking his opinion. Interestingly, many American churchmen consider the moral implications first and the interest and entertainment aspects second. The Archbishop replied that he had found nothing objectionable in the film and, then, that he enjoyed it very much. Day saved.

Which does mean that, unlike some of the other Coen Brothers films, you are a pleasure for most audiences. Your title comes from the plaintiff's song from the depression and, here we are, in the 1930s, three would-be musketeers working in the chain gang (just like those gangs in 1930s movies), planning an escape, roaming the countryside, getting into all kinds of adventures and scrapes. We are told that you are an American 1930s play on Homer's *The Odyssey*. And there are many entertaining references and parallels as our trio try to make their way home through the American southern states, George Clooney as Everett being a rather Clark Gable-looking Odysseus, with John Turturro as the troubled Pete and the engagingly slow-witted Delmar played by Tim Blake Nelson.

You compel your audience to ask whether you are making out of three prison escapees and their adventures the equivalent of epic myth. Or are you implying that, when it is all boiled down, Odysseus and his companions were much the same as convicts on the run?

John Goodman plays a kind of Cyclops, menacing the trio. They are also distracted down by the river with Sirens playing and singing – and some immersion baptisms (Peter and Delmar with Everett exposure getting on doubts about religion and God). On the way, there are deceiving relatives and crooked politicians, a governor who may or may not have reform in mind. And the goal is for Everett to get back to his wife, Penny (of old, Penelope), who has not been as faithful as her predecessor and has taken up with a villain who is revealed as being a member of the Ku Klux Klan, torturing and burning. So, of course, themes of racism.

I enjoyed seeing you so much, much beyond the gradual growing relief from apprehensiveness about Archbishop Foley's language comfort zone. In fact, thinking back over all the characters and episodes, I finished my review with a recommendation-invitation: 'And how you can get all that into one film, well, you will just have to go and see'.

PS. If you are in contact with any of the other Coen Brothers films, especially *Burn Without Reading, Hail Caesar, A Serious Man*, those early gangster films, in fact all of them (except *The Ladykillers*) mention that I would really have liked to have written to all of them.

Dear

LADRI DI BICICLETTI, BICYCLE THIEVES

You are a wonderful film. Everyone agrees – and have done so since you were first released in the late 1940s. I am addressing you by your Italian title. In English-speaking countries, including the United States, you were correctly translated as *Bicycle Thieves* – but, in an anomaly, your American poster had Bicycle Thief. While it is true that Antonio, the father, does steal the bike. He is so devoted to his son, Bruno, who shares his anguish when they have been robbed, and is momentarily dismayed, but then puts his hand in his father's hand as they trudge the streets, bicycle thieves and solidarity.

I can't remember when I first saw you but you were an overwhelming experience. On paper, this seems very strange, references to you as a masterpiece (although that sounds very dignified and grand in English while the derivation of the Italian word for masterpiece, capolavoro, indicates the talent and effort combined, 'top work'). And, you are a capolavoro for your director, Vittorio De Sica. In fact, he had quite a number of masterpieces, interestingly so many films in his early years focusing on young children, like *Shoeshine* and *Miracle in Milan*, but, I suppose, he is remembered for his heyday in the 1960s and his being inspired by Sophia Loren and Marcello Mastroianni.

You have a great advantage in having been made in the period of the acclaimed Italian neo-realism. You are out on location in the streets of Rome, we the audience accompanying you through the streets and alleys, right there, if not feeling quite at home, then knowing that we are really part of Rome. And, your cast, ordinary people rather than professional actors. Perhaps they had some basic acting instincts but they allowed themselves and their performances to be shaped by an empathetic director.

I suppose in saying this to you, I am joining all those who see you as a masterpiece but also those who are amazed that a comparatively brief film, black-and-white photography, simple plot with high emotion, simple characters with their hard lot in life, can stand competitively and without embarrassment in the masterpiece stakes with, say, Lawrence of Arabia.

If ever there was a film about father-son relationships, you are that film. This is the day that Antonio, with his wife Maria at home, goes to get a job putting up posters around the city (and De Sica pays some tribute to Rita Hayworth and her popularity during World War II with posters of

Gilda), accompanied by his young son, Bruno. But, to get the precious job, he needs a bike. Maria takes in washing, they sell some of their linen. Hope.

But there are rogues in Rome as you show us, rackets and black market, stealing bikes and Antonio condemned before he really starts. So much of you is the search for the bike, we the audience identifying with father and son, anguish, a mixture of hope and hopelessness, asking the police with little help, chasing an old man through the church to get some information, a session with the so-called holy woman, sanctifying fortune-telling.

One of the things I wonder about you is how much Vittorio de Sica was affected by Italy and the experience of the war, and of Mussolini himself, his dictatorship power in the 1920s, the nation depending on him, then the humiliation of his downfall, the degradation of his execution. As with Antonio and Bruno, their mutual loving relationship, the moment of humiliation and desperation, Bruno ashamed of his father – is this reading too much subtext into your screenplay and de Sica's interpretation?

As with so many Italian films of these decades, thinking of Fellini, for instance, and his collaboration with Nino Rota, you have a musical score by Alessandro Cicognini, sad, evocative, completing the neo-realistic mood and look. So sad.

Dear

THE NINTH DAY/ DIE NEUNTE TAGE

You are an important film for me, personally. Not so much immediately personal but significant. I will say something to you later in this letter about the connection.

When you were first released, I remember critics commenting that there had been not many films about priests interned in the Nazi concentration camps. They quote a statistic of about 3000. While there are powerful scenes here in Dachau, especially setting your tone with the crucifixion and crowning with thorns of a Polish priest, the drab lives of priest convicts, attempts to get the wherewithal to celebrate Masses without the guards knowing, this story goes beyond Dachau for the nine days, of the title, to Luxembourg. But then back again to three years of Dachau internment.

Your central priest, Henri Kremer, is played by the gaunt German actor, Ulrich Matthis who, a year later was so credible as a sinister Joseph Goebbels in *Downfall*.

If someone were to be looking for an alternate concentration camp film, you can be recommended.

And the question is, who is Father Henri Kremer? He is based on a Luxembourg priest, Jean Bernard, who wrote a memoir of his experiences in 1946, *Pfarrerblock 25487* (translated as *Priestblock 25487: a Memoir of Dachau*). And, so, the further question needs to be asked, who is Father Jean Bernard?

He came from Luxembourg, born 1907 (died 1994), ordained in the early 1930s, involved in the developments in Catholic media in Belgium and Holland, especially OCIC, L'Organization Catholique Internationale de Cinema. He headed the central office in Brussels for six years until it was closed down by the invading Nazis in 1940. He contributed to the development of the organisation and its moves to becoming international. However, with World War II, the office was in abeyance.

As regards your plot and storytelling, Jean Bernard was arrested in 1941 and interned in Dachau. However, suddenly in January 1942, as shown with Henry Kremer in your screenplay, he was released from prison, sent back to Luxembourg to persuade the Archbishop, who had moved out of the city and was not cooperating with the regime, to publish his support the Third Reich. If Kremer did not return after the allotted nine days, every priest in Dachau would be executed.

Jean Bernard never revealed why he was sent back to Luxembourg and so your screenplay is quite an interesting speculation. The ecclesiastical situation is complicated in terms of support and collaboration with the Reich. Jean Bernard also had a brother, an industrialist, who was collaborating with the regime. The screenplay also has quite a number of discussions between the SS officer (August Diehl) who had been a seminarian but was now trying to persuade the priest to convince the Archbishop. So, there are a number of sequences between the priest and the Archbishop, the days passing, the pressure mounting.

Of course, it would be very interesting to know what actually happened but Jean Bernard kept that to himself. Instead, the Archbishop gives the priest an envelope to hand to the Nazi authorities with his answer. The page inside the envelope – is blank, not a word. And the priest goes back after the nine day limit to years in prison.

Actually, I haven't explained the connection. After World War II, Jean Bernard resumed his work with OCIC, becoming its president from 1947-1972, controversial years in terms of growing international cinema, the developments of so many new national cinemas, controversies about moral issues. Jean Bernard defended the church diplomatically when OCIC awards were given to Pasolini's *Teorema* in Venice in 1968 and to Schlesinger's *Midnight Cowboy* at Berlin in 1969. precarious moments, but OCIC survived. And the connection, though not having ever met him, I was his fourth successor as president of OCIC.

The Secretary General of OCIC and I were invited to your premiere in Luxembourg itself, proud moments, especially, when your director, Volker Schloendorff, introduced you, paid great tribute to Jean Bernard and his life and work and dedication to the media.

You were not originally on my Dear Movie list. It seemed too personal a connection. But now, having written to you, I'm glad I did (and I hope I have always followed well in Jean Bernard's footsteps – moved as I have been when looking at his documents in the archives, admiration for his values, humanitarian sympathy, and practical common sense in dealing with church cinema issues).

Happy to say you are a fine tribute to him.

Dear

THE BOOK OF ELI

I have been wondering when 'post-apocalyptic' entered our vocabulary about futuristic films. It certainly has proliferated over the last 10 to 15 years. I wonder was Coppola's *Apocalypse Now* a trigger for the imagination and use of the word. In fact, that same year, 1979, saw the first of the *Mad Max* films, Australia making a claim for the post-apocalyptic. And one of the publicists referred to it as "Apocalypse Pow!". There has certainly been a lot of the pow since then. Including yourself.

I quite enjoy some post-apocalyptic films but I prefer those with human characters rather than monsters emerging from earth hell-holes or sweeping like aliens from the sky, or some mysterious phenomenon which people wrongly call 'supernatural'. You certainly fill the bill and, with Denzel Washington as your star, quite an amount of respectability – and this was before he became action tough in *Equalizer* action dramas.

Do you know Ray Bradbury's apocalyptic story, *Fahrenheit 451* a François Truffaut film from 1966 (and remade for television in 2018)? Your screenplay seems to be a variation on the theme. For Ray Bradbury, books combust at temperature 451 – and, in a future fascist society, the fireman's role is not to put out the fires but to light them, book conflagrations. And there were rebels, individuals who memorised the books and went out into the wilderness communities. I remember one individual pacing and opening with "It was the best of times, it was the worst of times..." And so into Dickens' *A Tale of Two Cities.* I remember that the screenplay didn't include anyone who had memorised *Genesis* or *The Gospel of John!*

Which leads me to note that you have made more than compensation! Your futuristic outsider, Eli, has memorised the whole Bible. And you give him a unique post-apocalyptic mission, to travel across the devastated American landscapes, mechanised, but looking and acting like a 19th century gunfighter. (You may have been an audition for Denzel Washington and the *Equalizer* action shows with his more than adept wielding weapons, especially his samurai sword.) His destination is San Francisco where he can deliver his recitation of the Bible, where it can be transcribed, typeset, printed and distributed and offer some hope for the surviving humans.

Your production design is most impressive, the lonely and ugly desert with its remnants of past civilisation. And Eli has to stop in a town which serves as a microcosm of what has gone wrong with the world. There might be physical destruction but there is also moral destruction, Gary Oldman as Carnegie, a warlord in a rather tinpot town, wanting to find the book so that he can wield its power. And, sexist and misogynist, he puts pressure on his blind mistress and urges her daughter, Solara (Mila Kunis) to seduce Eli to discover his secret.

So you present Eli as something of a biblical prophet, bringing God's Word into a disrupted world, almost Jesus-like, the Word incarnate. Eli is something like a futuristic John the Baptist, challenging, critical of society, not afraid of communicating in the fire and brimstone vein. And while Carnegie wants to have his head on a plate, urging Solara to be sexually provocative, this futuristic Salome becomes a disciple, aiding the prophet. And what about that very weird post-apocalyptic episode where Eli and Solara are hosted by an elderly couple who turn out to be menacing cannibals – and their names being, archetypal link, George and Martha.

It is not exactly a spoiler but I do want to compliment you on your hopeful ending, the irony of the Bible that Eli memorised being written in Braille (and Carnegie's blind mistress thwarting him because she had forgotten how to read it). Eli delivers, both book and himself, mission accomplished, and a death in peace.

Religious themes, especially explicit biblical themes, sometimes serve as symbols for post-apocalyptic films (after all where did Apocalypse come from, Ezekiel, for instance, in the Jewish Scriptures, the Book of Revelation in the Christian Scriptures). Just after you were released, there was an action adventure with Paul Bettany called *Priest*, with some post-apocalyptic clerical machinations. I would have liked some more.

And I wondered where your directors, the Hughes Brothers, got their motivation from – after all, they had made some African-American action films, *Menace II Society* and *Dead Presidents*, then turned their attention to Jack the Ripper, *From Hell*, then Allen went solo with American crime films and Albert went way back to prehistoric times with *Alpha*.

So you had unexpected plotlines and themes – but, after all, isn't that characteristic of the post-apocalyptic!

YANKS

I feel I owe you something of an apology. While you were one of my favourite films of 1979, you had slipped from my immediate consciousness while compiling my *Dear Movies* list. And, coming towards the end, thinking about including *Sommersby* and the presence of Richard Gere, suddenly there you were – and I'm writing to you.

It's forty years since you were released and you seem to have disappeared. While reviewers enjoyed you, your box-office, especially in the United States, was very poor. What a pity, so many audiences missing out. The Americans looking at the title perhaps wanting a story set at home rather than having to go over to Europe, to be stationed/stuck in England as so many Americans were. Many of the British saw these Yanks as very brash and there was that saying at the time that Yanks were, "over-paid, over-sexed and over here". Of course, when America entered World War I, Irving Berlin's famous patriotic song, with lyrics by Yankee Doodle Dandy himself, looked at it from the other side of the Atlantic, "Over there". And perhaps an ominous threat: "The yanks are coming (repeated!)".

Speaking of American songs, your credit song has just played in my memory, one of those yearning, more than a touch plaintive songs, "I'll be seeing you... In all the old familiar places...

I'll find you in the morning sun
And when the night is new
I'll be looking at the moon
But I'll be seeing you

Dear oh dear. I suppose that's pretty sentimental. However, the lyrics and the melody bring to mind the word 'romantic'. I think you are one of those films, rather near the top in fact, that brought home to me that I am, if not exteriorly and in manner, then interiorly, a dedicated romantic. I realise that my eyes can moisten fairly readily, not just at romance but also at appreciating a happy outcome, happy ending – and I just remembered talking with other reviewers and their wiping a film (rather than a tear) because they thought the ending was contrived and soppy and asking them whether they would like at the end of a day's work to go home and find their spouse and children all slaughtered on the kitchen floor rather than receive warm greetings, hugs and kisses, happy meal together...! (That certainly sounds like an emotional outburst!)

The other distraction I had was a television skit by Carol Burnett demonstrating how men can manoeuvre their arms and hands to flick a tear from their eye as unobtrusively as possible, the rapid finger towards the eye as if briefly scratching, an arm over the head providing an inadvertent brush with the eye…, a slight shift of hand that, they hope, other patrons won't notice. A complaint: and now some of the cinemas put on the auditorium lights at the beginning of the credits, not giving us enough time to avoid being seen, moist-eyed, by those around us.

While watching you and, especially at the end, my eyes were romantically moist. You immediately drew the audience in with images of the English countryside in the 1940s, the quieter way of life, exterior propriety – but then the revelation that it masked surging emotions which led to affairs, pregnancies, war widows.

While two of the relationships of the three in your screenplay were familiar enough, it was the relationship between Richard Gere and Lisa Eichorn that moved me at the time and which has stayed in my memory. This was early Richard Gere, a genial young man, a cook, ordinary, pleasant and courteous. And Lisa Eichorn, just looking at her, was just wonderful, her beauty, her manner, her voice and tone, the perfect 'English Rose', as they used to say. (And quite a bit of a shock to find that she was actually an American actress.)

With the title and its tone, you are a memoir of American and British involvement in the war, in a sense quite far from Churchill or Montgomery, far from Eisenhower, yet experiencing their decisions for deployment, the training, for sending men into action and, so frequently, to injury and death. John Schlesinger was a deft director for a number of classic films – but I would think that so much of your impact comes from the writing of Colin Welland, who had contributed to a number of television series, but an Oscar winner for another journey into the British past two years later, *Chariots of Fire.*

As I've mentioned, you don't seem to turn up in re-release or on television schedules. But, after forty years of romantic memories, when I can, I'll be seeing you...

SOMMERSBY

I was just mentioning to *Yanks* that in thinking about writing a letter to you, Richard Gere sprang to mind and the delight in remembering that *Yanks* was one of my favourite films of 1979. Move forward another fourteen years and there is Richard Gere again, and you, another favourite.

And having confessed to *Yanks* that I'm a romantic at heart and eye-moisture prone during screenings, I would affirm that you are also a fond, romantic favourite.

You have a considerable historical background. Your original story was set in the 16th century in France, *The Return of Martin Guerre*, from 1982 with Gerard Depardieu and Nathalie Baye. And the story was adapted for musical theatre by the team who worked on *Les Miserables* and *Miss Saigon*, Alain Boubil and Claude-Michel Schonberg. Unfortunately, I've never seen it.

You have brought the story to the United States, the 19th century, the period of the Civil War and its aftermath. The setting is in the South – a farming community. Your narrative plays out against the changing seasons, seen in their beauty, seen in their harshness, seen in the hard work of crops growing, crops harvested. You draw your audience into your narrative. We are immersed in your setting and in your life – and with your characters.

I was just looking at some of the comments about your impact from bloggers on the IMDb. Talk about divided responses! Except for unanimous praise for Jodie Foster and her performance. But I wanted to mention one of the main difficulties that was raised, the credibility of the plot, the contrived aspects of the plot, seen as quite improbable or inconsistent and so to be dismissed.

I would prefer to go along with my emotional response to the whole film rather than be restricted by logical and critical analysis. The point of the narrative is that it highlights the central puzzle, what might be called *The Return of Jack Sommersby*, his life before he went to war, the tensions of his marriage to Laurel, the effect of the war on him, the resumption of his life on the farm and of his marriage, the response of the townspeople. If I were to be uncharitable, I would be tempted to call the intellectual quibbles about your plot, 'nitpicking'. But I have to concede that the realist audience does want everything to be clear, logical, avoiding any overtones of the mystical.

It's hard to remember whether, on first viewing, I actually thought that Jack was not Laurel's husband or when was the moment I began to be suspicious or made my decision that he was not. In a way, the point is that Laurel had managed the farm during her husband's absence, did not have good memories of him, that, perhaps, he had changed deeply with his war experience, that he was a new Sommersby, he was what she needed and could fall in love with. You ask us to share Laurel's experience and not argue with her whether she believed Jack or not, not for her to list her reasons for and against.

Again, some of the realists have great difficulties with the court case (mentioning the improbability of a black judge, noting that judges do not pronounce verdicts and that is the role of the jury...). But what you raise is more emotion (at least in me) as Jack goes to court. What happened to him during the war? Crime or war action? Should he be considered guilty? Is he guilty in his return and its consequences? And the anguish for Jodie Foster, her presence, testimony – and the gallows?

So, you leave us at the end with Laurel, the pain of her first marriage, the acceptance of Jack Sommersby, love for him even to death, and yet another absence looming for her life.

I remember experiencing you as a moving film. I still do.

Dear

TRUE CONFESSIONS

Interesting that two films which draw on a famous murder case in Los Angeles in the 1940s, investigations, scandals, the mystery unsolved in those years, could both suggest some kind of sharing of ideas, and confession, with a seal of secrecy, confidentiality in their titles, *True Confessions* and *LA Confidential*. If I were asked to nominate a film about the Black Dahlia mystery and the LA police force, then *LA Confidential* would be the obvious choice. But, I would nominate you, *True Confessions*.

In past decades, before Church sexual abuse became an extraordinary focus of attention: the often irreparable harm done to victims, the campaigns by survivors, the Catholic Church, along with so many other institutions, having its conscience examined in public, when asked to nominate my best film on priesthood, *True Confessions* was the answer. And as I've said, there is and has to be now the focus on institutionalised sexual abuse. But in recent years, they have been the two excellent candidates for best film on priests – and I have written to them as well – *Of Gods and Men, Calvary*.

Which means then that I look at you primarily in the light of a portrait of a diocese and clergy. Another observer, someone in law enforcement, would look at you in the light of a portrait of police and detectives. Someone else would profitably look at you in the light of American social change, especially in cities. Your screenplay, with John Gregory Dunne working with his wife, Joan Didion, adapting his novel, is something of a film for all seasons.

As a letter coming from me, you will not be surprised that I'm going to focus on the portrait of the Church. Your 1947 LA setting comes before the Church-changing Second Vatican Council. However, with your sombre religious ending, it is 1963, the year of the second session of the Council. You span an era of what might be called old-church to an emerging, changing church.

Your title! I remember when I first noticed it that the confessional did not come to mind. Rather, there was those popular magazines, going behind the movie sets, prying into the life of the stars, their 'true confessions'. In many ways, you do have a prying look at the city where Hollywood dwells, but you go very deeply.

Just a word about the church if I might before confession and conversion.

For audiences, and there were audiences back in the 1980s who put the Catholic Church on a pedestal, you offered an instant shock. A priest had collapsed and died in a brothel. The hierarchy had to find a way to avoid scandal. How would 'the faithful' respond to such news? And there soon followed problems with corruption in the building industry, lay Catholics involved there (and again dubious sexual connections) especially with contracts for the building of diocesan schools. And, in worldly diplomacy, how do you deal with anticipating and avoiding scandal – hold a banquet where the builder is named and feted, 'Catholic layman of the year'. And then quietly sacked.

On the one hand, your story about the church is, one might say, juicy. On the other hand, it is depressingly disedifying.

In this context, the portrait of the cardinal of Los Angeles, played with austere superiority and pomp by Cyril Cusack, has to take responsibility but he has an ambitious young Monsignor, Des Spellacy, to do all the negotiations, to get jobs done, to maintain the cover.

So, as regards portraits of priests, there is the cardinal, a prince of the Church, more in the line of Machiavelli than of Jesus, the Good Shepherd. I should mention that there is a good priest, old school, pastoral, relegated to the boundaries of the diocese – and played by Burgess Meredith, reminding us that he had a similar fate as a priest in Boston archdiocese in *The Cardinal*.

But, of course, for me, the focus is on Monsignor Spellacy. This has to be one of Robert De Niro's best performances, just after his Oscar for *Raging Bull*. (And De Niro was to portray priests in *The Mission* and *Sleepers*.) Monsignor Spellacy is the epitome of the career clergyman, socially presentable, collaborating with the authorities, ambitious to become the authority, going through the motions of priesthood but losing the core of his commitment, his call to holiness, his call to be a holy and good man in ministry.

For those who are interested in law enforcement, they would be telling you about the portrait of the Monsignor's brother, Tom Spellacy (and a fine performance from Robert Duvall), impatient, becoming a bagman for crime payoffs to the police, disappointed.

But, if murder will out, so scandal will out.

The latter part of your screenplay focuses on the monsignor's re-awareness experience, some re-conversion, the renouncing of ecclesiastical ambition, going out to one of those parishes on the boundaries. There are quite a number of confessions. The building magnate confesses to the monsignor who refuses him absolution. Tom confesses to Des – and Des confesses to him. And as Des goes through the pattern of the Sacrament of Penance, an examination of conscience initially forced on him, an awareness of an acknowledgment of sinfulness, his being heard, judged, forgiven, experiencing a change of heart and going into the desert to be a committed priest, his atonement, he finds his true self.

Of course, there have been thousands of committed priests around the world at any one time but you are a reminder that if a priest succumbs to being put on a pedestal for whatever reason, including his own ascending the pedestal, he needs integrity in his conscience and understanding, authenticity in every detail of his life.

The sounds a bit like a homily or a conference for a retreat for priests. I'm only partly sorry!

Dear

THE END OF THE AFFAIR

I've just been writing to *True Confessions*. Graham Greene was a film reviewer back in the 1930s and I wondered whether he had seen *True Confessions* in his old age and what he would have made of it. My guess is that he would have liked it, resonated with its themes, been fascinated with its portrait of a priest. Sometimes his characters choose to go "into the void" but with you there is a reminder of what sinning is but that repentance is always possible, and holiness emerges from unlikely situations for unlikely characters.

You begin in the rain. Overcast weather – whether in real life or in the soul – is the season for Graham Greene. Sunlight is so often a subsidiary season. And that is certainly true in your story.

I should tell you that one of the main reasons for writing to you is that you have been a film that I have relied on for seminars over several years. I have written to Vera Farmiga's *Higher Ground* because I wanted to use that film in the course for Spiritual Directors. It wasn't available at the time. After some serious thought, I decided that you were the film to use.

You may be wondering how this worked out in action. Those doing the Spiritual Direction program were all mature age men and women, mostly lay people, but a number of priests and nuns as well. At our Heart of Life Spirituality Centre, there are fine conference rooms and it seemed a good investment to finance a DVD player. So, the opportunity to watch you followed by the participants working one-on-one with each other. One was to be in the role of the spiritual director, listening attentively, no manipulating, enabling the client to speak, reflect, discerningly draw conclusions. And the client was bringing to the director the experience of watching you, being affected by your dramatisation of sinful behaviour, of an awareness of God, of bargaining with God for the life of another, ready to give up a relationship forever. Then the two participants reversed roles.

Clearly, I have seen you a number of times but am still amazed at the number of faith experiences, questioning of God, fall and repentance, that you treat so explicitly. Your Irish director, Neil Jordan, brings a background in Irish Catholicism to his screenplay and interpretation of Greeneland (and, if you are wondering about aspects of his Catholicism, could I recommend *Breakfast on Pluto* and *The Butcher Boy*).

Your character, Maurice Bendix (Ralph Fiennes at his most intense) is a writer who is bewildered by the sudden breaking of a passionate relationship after a bomb explodes on the building where he and Sarah Miles (an Oscar nomination for Julianne Moore) had their rendezvous. But we, the audience, are privy to what happens, that lapsed Catholic Sarah prays aloud on her knees that if God spares Maurice, she will not see him again. Greene's is a puzzling God and hears her prayer – both sides of the prayer.

In your version, Sarah does meet Maurice again and they travel to Brighton, Sarah failing anew and in the full light of what she had promised God. But Greene actually believes that grace is limitless (even for Scobie making a decision that would send him to hell in *The Heart of the Matter*), although in his earlier *Brighton Rock*, there is no evidence of repentance, grace or forgiveness for Pinky.

When Maurice hires Parkis, a private detective, to discover the truth about Sarah and Parkis finds her diary, Maurice reads it in disbelief. Not only has she terminated the relationship, she has gone to a priest for instruction in her faith (Jason's Isaac performance is so stern I would not like to have gone to get instruction from him). And, she is terminally ill.

Greene published his novel in 1951, back in the old days of Catholicism, back in his old days of Catholicism when his life began to mirror that of Sarah's. But, completely unexpectedly, even for me, was Sarah's miracle. She had touched the severe birthmark on the face of Parkis' son. He is healed. Saints intercede with God for healings. They are required if the church is to declare someone a saint.

After going through the ordeals with Sarah, empathy and sadness, that Graham Greene would canonise her is something of a hopeful shock. God's grace.

Dear

HABLE CON ELLA/ TALK TO HER

Fortunately, I have a DVD copy of you so I decided to have another look before I wrote you this letter. I am glad I did because in some ways I had quite a different perspective on it from all those years ago.

And I wanted to write to one of Pedro Almodovar's films because of his significance as a long-staying director in world cinema. I see that he made a number of short films even before Franco died. But, after Franco's death and the consequent Spanish sense of liberation, he became quite cheeky and satirical in his small budget comedies. Gradually, more serious issues entered into his films even though there was always the comic touch. I was glad that he won an Oscar for your screenplay – and I notice that you had so many nominations and awards, especially in Europe.

When I first saw you, I was intrigued by your central character, Benigno, with regular Almodovar actor, Javier Camara. All Almodovar screenplays have touches, or more than touches, of the bizarre. He finds offbeat aspect of human nature (*The Skin I Live In*), unanticipated relationships (*All About My Mother*), paedophile infatuations (*Mal Educacion*). But, you have one of the strangest.

Benigno seems a simple soul, and that is the opinion of other members of the staff at the hospital where he works. As we meet him, he has spent four years tending a ballet dancer, Alicia, injured in a car accident, and in a coma. He is completely devoted to her, night and day, attending her, washing her, comforting her, limit charges and exercises, and, as your title suggests, talking to her. For Benigno, Alicia is alive. He encourages friends, including her ballet mistress, to come for conversations.

Then there is the disturbing element, Alicia is found to be pregnant – has Benigno's preoccupation become infatuation, has he gone beyond the bounds? And, what will happen to him as he is accused, sent to jail, pines for Alicia, wonders about the birth of the child, cannot live without her?

That theme was absorbing as well as disturbing, sympathy for Benigno but our being upset by him – he says that the authorities have called him a psychopath. The 'psycho' part of the word is low key in his attitude and leads audience to focus on the 'path', the pathos of his lonely existence.

However, watching you again just now, knowing Benigno's story, I was really surprised how much of the focus, even more of the focus, was on the journalist, Marco (an impressively sombre performance from Argentinean Dario Grandinetti – who had played Pope Francis in the 2015 film, *Francesco, el Padre Jorge*). As always, Almodovar's stories have plots, subplots, interplots and the journalist's story has him involved with a female matador, Lydia, brutally mauled, also in a coma, Marco visiting her and encountering Benigno and Alicia.

I had forgotten the sequences of Marco visiting Lydia, remembering the past, her injuries, the story of her breaking with him, his travelling the world writing his travel books, his returning to Madrid and discovering what had happened to Benigno. I was impressed by the warmth of his friendship, his devotion, his advice in the past to Benigno who told Marco that he wanted to get married – to Alicia. Marco's experiences have been sad. He is upset by his visit to the prison, distraught at Benigno's death – but Almodovar has decided that the future need not be sad.

By the way, you have all kinds of Almodovar riffs which add to the enjoyment and the complexity – I particularly enjoyed the TV interviewer still clinging to Lydia and still bombarding her with embarrassing questions as Lydia angrily walked off the set as well as Benigno's landlady complaining vigorously that the media had not been to interview her. Early, there are contemporary dance sequences, with Pina Bausch and her company, indicating themes as well as offering comparisons to the choreography of arena bullfighting. And, at the end with Alicia awake, Marco and Alicia meeting, watching the dance, about to resume the dance of life.

I'm not sure that my letter does you justice but I found you moving each time I watched you.

VOZURASHCHENIE/ THE RETURN

You caused quite a shock at the Festival in Venice, 2003. Not that you were shocking. Rather, you were a film by a first-time Russian director and had been programmed in the early afternoon, not the best hour for a press preview, especially in terms of reviewers who are otherwise occupied at the time, interviews – and lunch. Then the word quickly went round about how impressive you were – and your reputation increased, you won a number of awards, including the Catholic organisation prize, and then the Golden Lion. No more obscurity.

I felt a certain critical pressure to write a letter to a Russian film director like Eisenstein or Tarkovsky (although for me Tarkovsky is both mystical and mystifying). I notice that one blogger praised you but with a backhander: "brilliant – but not in the league of Tarkovsky"! In fact, your director, Andrei Zyvagintsev, with his four succeeding films – and I will mention their names in case another reader happens on this letter and decides he should see them – powerful portraits of aspects of contemporary Russia, incisive, not always hopeful: *The Banishment, Elena, Leviathan, Loveless*, the latter having some links with your children and parent themes.

In fact, you were such a success that you won an award from the Templeton Foundation who, for ten years, made an award to a European film. Trinity and All Saints campus of Leeds University hosted an evening with your director, a screening followed by Q&A and I had the pleasure of chairing it – not the easiest because English was not yet Andrei Zvyagintsev's second language! But he was a gracious, if somewhat timid, guest.

It is interesting to note that while you were the director's first film, he was almost forty at the time of making you. So, while a first-timer on the screen, he brought a great depth of personal experience. In many ways, your plot outline is very simple, the father absent for twelve years, two boys brought up by mother and grandmother, the father's return, taking the boys on a holiday but continually and fiercely forcing their masculinity, clash, rebellion, tragedy.

And while there is little dialogue, the performances speak volumes. This is the communication of body language, not learning the details about where the father has been, prison perhaps, on shady business, or just sick of being with his family. And the boys' performances are most impressive as well, the older boy and a desperate desire to bond with his father, to please him, to measure up to his expectations, finding this more and more difficult to fulfil; while the younger brother is quietly resentful and rebellious. (Others who might read this letter may not be aware that the actor playing the older brother, Vladimir Garin, was drowned, sadly, two months before your release.)

No family is the same but so many share similar anxieties, pressures, falling out of love, resentment because of expectations. You are a very Russian version, unfamiliar in many ways to international audiences, rousing both curiosity and comparisons. And you have distinctive landscapes, Russian forests, becoming more remote from the towns, lakes.

In fact, we are so drawn into your action that we too become desperate with the boys, puzzled about what their father is asking of them, anxious with them to prove themselves, finally agreeing with them that their father is asking too much.

But you leave the audience with extraordinary poignancy, the father dead by accident, the boys placing him on the boat – and then its drifting out from the shore beyond their reach. And as the father moved beyond that reach, there is a desperate cry, released after suppression, of the younger boy calling out to his father.

You are a film of humanity, of humanity wounded, of humanity struggling.

Dear

Z

You made an enormous impact on me when I saw you in 1970. I don't think I had seen such a powerful political film, especially one portraying recent events like those of Greece in the 1960s, and you had a touch of the mind-blowing. You drew significant audiences – and then you won the Oscar for Best Foreign Language Film of 1969.

Looking back, I now realise your impact as I remember that I co-wrote, with the editor of the magazine in which I reviewed, *Annals*, Father Paul Stenhouse, quite a long article in June 1970. The title was *Z: HE LIVES*. And, at the end of that year, writing a book called *Films & Values*, with an opening section on *A Searching Age* and sections on *Future Shock, Loss of God-Values, Lost Pharisees, Lost Atheists, Open Humanism*, and then the main section, *Ten Films in the Search for Values*. I have already written letters to two of them, *Midnight Cowboy* and *2001: A Space Odyssey*. There was a chapter on you headed *Change*, fourteen pages exploring your themes.

I was impressed by your director, Costa-Gavras, and followed his career with exposés of urban guerrillas in

Uruguay, *State of Siege*, the Vichy government in *Section Speciale*, Chile in *Missing*, American racism and Nazi memories in *Betrayed* and *The Music Box* in the 1980s and his film version of Rolf Hochhuth's play about Pius XII, *The Deputy*, called *Amen*. For me, significant contributors to films dramatising politics.

This letter, I'm afraid, is going to sound a little preachy. But I am asking your indulgence to allow me to look back on how I thought 40 years ago (and, I hope, still do).

To situate my response, here is the opening paragraphs of the article in *Annals*:

> Demonstrations in our streets, the Moratorium, Police and nonviolence, May 1970. Condemnation and rebuttals: Communist, Right-Wing, US, Liberation. Australia, although distant from the intensity of the world scene is stirring in its placid semi-apathy. What of our presence in Vietnam, conscription, napalm, guerrillas, torture and massacres and corpses floating down the Mekong River?
>
> Many consciences are at work and people are awakening to find themselves on the Right or the Left, with a brand attached 'made in Russia' or 'made in the USA'. There is a great need for Australians today to focus on this alertness. (And

then a page exploring how you are part of this alertness.)

I'm going to skip to the final paragraph but you can work out how you contributed to that 1970 exploration. By the way, in 1970, we were stuck (as, unfortunately, so many journalists and public figures still are) in exclusive language, the presumption that 'man' covers everyone, including that 51%, women.

Man's social history is the interaction of Left-wing and Right. The Western world claims it is Right. Z is an indictment of an extreme which claims stability, Christianity and God for its support. It seems also to assert that Christianity has been inextricably linked with a rigid orthodoxy which easily resorts to violence to impose itself. Z is an excellent film, a moving and timely alert to our own social attitudes.

In the chapter in *Films & Values*, some paragraphs, in retrospect, as if I was being carried away! Like this:

The identification of themselves with God makes the Right-wing view all critics and political enemies as kinds of devil-enemies. It transforms the campaign to maintain the *status quo* into a crusade.

Later, in an attempt at some balance,

Z, while it takes a stand on the Left of the political centre, nevertheless criticises the impatient and violent attitudes of some of its members. It implies that an extreme Left-wing man is as violent and as blind as an extreme Right-winger.

Since this is beginning to sound a bit like a diatribe, I'd better draw this letter to you to a close, but let me reassure you that this is a tribute to the impact you had back then as a film and as a provocateur.

Man's social history as the inter-action of Left and Right. The Western world has claimed and still claims that it is Right. Z is an indictment of an extreme which claims stability, Christianity and God for its support. It seems also to assert that Christianity has been inextricably linked with a rigid orthodoxy which easily resorts to strong-arm tactics and measures to impose itself.

This was written in the era of so many military dictatorships, in the middle of the Vietnam war, uprisings in South America, independence movements in Africa. And Jihadis were yet to come.

NASHVILLE

I was so enthusiastic about you back in the 1970s that I decided you were a perfect film for screening for a group of educators during their sabbatical year. A flop, I'm afraid. In fact, one of the participants came up to me afterwards with a disapproving frown. "That says more about you than about the film." Because she was a friend, the situation was rather gob-smacking – the "well, shut my mouth" kind of gob-smacking. I found it too difficult to explain to her why she was wrong! And she wasn't in the mood for listening.

In fact, she was voicing something of the Australian response to your first release. I'm still amazed, as I look back, that you lasted only one week in the cinema in central Melbourne. However, when word of your reputation in other countries got around, especially with many Oscar and Golden Globe nominations, the distributors gave you another chance.

But right from the first viewing in that first week, you were, and still are, one of my favourite films.

Somebody described you as a "satirical musical comedy-drama". That barely covers it. I just checked what I said in my review: "a sardonic metaphor of modern America: the bizarre aspects of recent politics, violence and assassinations, the clashes of the strata of society, proud tradition, public enthusiasm, sentimentality, selfishness, the pleasing ordinariness of people". Perhaps I should stop there!

No, there needs to be a tribute to your screenwriter and director. Your writer was Joan Tewksbury who went on a visit to Nashville at the request of your director, Robert Altman, made notes about her visit and this formed both the structure and the detail of the screenplay, events over five days, the interplay of many subplots as Nashville was hosting a rally for a presidential candidate. And there was huge cast. Interesting about Robert Altman's career. Up to the year that he turned 45, he had worked in television and smaller budget films. But that year, 1970, he had great success with M*A*S*H. And, over the next 35 years, he became something of a byword for a filmmaker who could interweave multiple plotlines, with large casts, finding cinematic techniques for the complex interactions. In fact, someone coined the word for this kind of filmmaking, 'Altman-esque'. (Googling provides an item explaining the dictionary meaning.)

When I think about you and the social context of the mid 1970s, I realise that it was only just over 10 years since the assassination of John F. Kennedy, that 1975 saw the end of the Vietnam war, that Richard Nixon had resigned over Watergate the year before, and that the United States was revving up for the celebration of its bicentenary. There are traces and memories throughout your screenplay. Nashville, city and film, can be seen as a microcosm of the United States, 1960s and 1970s.

One of the extraordinary things about you is that there are about 25 key characters, a great number of women who portray singers, were the reigning stars of the city, singers in religious worship, singers trying out their hand at composition, waitresses who thought they could be successful but weren't. Amongst the men there were the candidate (heard but not seen), political wheeler dealers and publicists, husbands, a Vietnam veteran, and a sinister young man with a violin case. One of your characters is a chattering BBC reporter and your screenplay uses her as a means for introducing and identifying so many of your characters.

Violence and assassination were in the air and, ultimately, the sinister young man shoots the favourite singer of the city. American guns. American violence and deaths.

And the music, of course. After all, what is Nashville known for! Many of the cast wrote and performed their own songs, enabling them to move into the atmosphere of country music. And Keith Carradine won an Oscar for one of his songs, 'I'm easy'. There is music and singing in a Catholic service, in a Protestant service, in a black Protestant service with a baptism. Nashville is the city of the Grand Ole Opry, performances there as well as in Opryland USA.

I think your favourable reputation has grown over the decades and many see you as an impressive standout in Robert Altman's career, a career that has many standout films. My critical friend from the 1970s is long since dead – we did have conversations about her judgmental condemnation both of me and you, but, sadly, no conversion experience resulted.

The best summary word that we can offer is, Altmanesque. And that's a fine compliment.

Dear

SECRETS AND LIES, VERA DRAKE, ANOTHER YEAR

While writing these letters, I have been wondering what film I should leave readers with. I have re-interpreted my *Dear Movies* aim in writing a joint letter to *Grand Torino* and *The Mule*. It enables me to cheat now, so to speak, with a much less burdensome conscience by writing to three films in one.

After all the reviews and commentary about you, you must be highly conscious of the fact that you are Mike Leigh films. That you are excellent Mike Lee films and have nominations, awards, and favourably critical reviews to back this up. And I choose you three because you embody all Mike Leigh's qualities, his interests and perceptions of society, relationships, happiness and sadness (often in that order). By writing to you, I am not excluding his lavish historical excursions into British history, Gilbert and Sullivan in *Topsy Turvy*, the painter *Mr Turner*, industrial uprisings in *Peterloo*.

I was always impressed by hearing that Mike Leigh frequently used an improvising method to create his screenplays, your screenplays. I remember hearing this about scenes in you, *Vera Drake*, where cast members were assembled, given some basic information about their character and its relationship to a particular scene, but no more information as to the development of the character later in the film. Leigh listened, took notes, shaped his treatment on what he had heard and experienced, wrote a precise screenplay for the cast to perform. So while you are all Mike Leigh screenplays, you contain a great deal of the insights and experiences of the cast.

You, *Secrets and Lies*, were rather overwhelming when I first saw you, and I still have many images of Brenda Blethyn, a bewildered woman, suddenly discovering her daughter, her black daughter, shock, but a movement towards recognition and love. You have many other characters, but this is the powerful focus in my memory.

An anecdote. Mike Leigh visited Australia in 1996 to promote you. Later I heard that he could be very tetchy even in the middle of a conversation. When I mentioned to him that the Ecumenical film organisation had given its prize to you in Cannes, he suddenly put me off guard by telling me, rather snappily, that he would have much preferred we had given a prize to his film of three years earlier, *Naked*.

What can response can you give to that! Later, I went to see his *Happy-Go-Lucky* not believing that he could make a film with that title and that content!

If ever there was a powerful film about abortion, it is you, *Vera Drake*. I have screened both of you, *Secrets and Lies* and *Vera Drake*, in seminars exploring values and relationships, qualities of life. Some people hearing this are scandalised that I should screen a film in which the central character is an abortionist. But, as embodied by Imelda Staunton, she is a good woman following her lights, trying to help women (and the setting is Britain in 1950s) but experiencing the law coming down on her, the shocked reaction of her family, the audience moved to an emotional analysis as well as principles analysis, that serious moral issues require depth consideration rather than mere, even a good-intentioned, sloganising.

In fact, this all came up in our Catholic organisation jury at the film festival in Venice in 2004. We voted to give the prize to you but then the Italian members vetoed the award (it was their country) saying that the Catholic Church would be the target/victim of the media. This was not quite true because, during the festival, a Vatican spokesperson wrote a newspaper article about you in the vein of my previous paragraph. And, as chair of the jury and making remarks like those I have, I was quoted (favourably) in

American *Variety*. You were never reinstated for the prize – but it seemed important that it be put on the record that you were the winner.

Secrets and Lies, you won the Palme D'Or in Cannes. *Vera Drake*, you won the Golden Lion in Venice.

And, something for you, *Another Year*. You also screened in Cannes and received an award from the Ecumenical Jury. One of your main values is that you are quieter, more focused, lower-key than many of Mike Leigh's films. Once again, you are both happy and sad.

As the title indicates, your action takes place over a year, in each of the four seasons, mirroring something of the experiences of your characters. At the centre, we have a happy couple, older, wiser, trying to help others – with the danger that they can seem to others, if not to themselves, patronising or condescending. There are other relations and friends. But more and more assuming the centre is an unmarried middle-aged woman, no great self-image, searching and hoping, helped but, perhaps, patronised. And, as with the other films, the principal exploration is of female characters, this time played by Leslie Manville and Ruth Sheen.

In a way, you are a film about ordinary people in the suburbs or a small town, microcosm of the wider world and its even more dramatic problems. And we have Mike Leigh to thank.

In writing to you, I am signing off in this series of Dear Movies letters – coming down, in a good sense, from heightened dramas, spectacle and fantasy, music and comedy, to the ordinary, sometimes humdrum, world in which most of us live.

But, sometimes to escape, sometimes to explore, sometimes to be challenged, we can always 'go to the pictures', turn on the TV or download a movie, delving into images of secrets and lies, going ahead to live another year.

FILMS LISTED IN ALPHABETICAL ORDER

2001: A Space Odyssey

Amadeus

Anna Karenina

Another Year

Apocalypse Now

Babette's Feast

Bad Lieutenant

Bicycle Thieves

Big Fish

Book Of Eli

Born On The 4th July

Boys Are Back

Bram Stoker's Dracula

Browning Version

Bruce Almighty

Calle Mayor/ Main Street

Calvary

Cardinal

Castle

Chant Of Jimmie Blacksmith

Citizen Kane

Clockwork Orange

Court Jester

Cries And Whispers

Dead Poets Society

Des Dieux Et Des Hommes/ Of Gods And Men

Devils

Django Unchained

Distant Voices, Still Lives

Double Indemnity

Edward Scissorhands

Egyptian

End Of The Affair

Evil Angels

First Reformed

Fisher King

Gallipoli

Godfather

Gran Torino

Gunga Din

Happy Deathday 2 U

Higher Ground

Hombre

House That Jack Built

Ikiru/ Living

Importance Of Being Earnest

Interiors

Jack Reacher

Jean De Florette

Jesus

Jesus Of Montreal

Jesus Christ Superstar

Jirga

Ladykillers

La Strada

Lawrence Of Arabia

Lemon Tree

Les Miserables

Life Of Brian

Man Who Knew Too Much

Midnight Cowboy

Modern Times

Mr Smith Goes To Washington

Mule

Muriel's Wedding

My Fair Lady

Nashville

Neiges De Kilimandjaro/ Snows Of Kilimanjaro

Night At The Opera

Neunte Tage/ Ninth Day

No Way Out

Nun's Story

O Brother Where Art Thou

On The Waterfront

Outlaw Josey Wales

Pride And Prejudice

Priest

Raining Stones

Return

Richard Iii

Romero

Salo, Or The 120 Days Of Sodom

Schindler's List

Search

Secrets And Lies

Silence

Singin' In The Rain

Sister Act

Sommersby

Sorry To Bother You

Talk To Her/ Hable Con Ella

Third Man

To Kill A Mockingbird

True Confessions

Under The Moonlight/ Zir-E-Noor-E Maah

Vera Drake

Visitor

White Palace

Wit

Wizard of Oz

Yanks

Year of Living Dangerously

Z

WHEN THE FILMS WERE FIRST SEEN BY THE AUTHOR

Seminary Years, Australia

    Double Indemnity
    The Nun's Story   2

Seminary Years, Rome

    The Cardinal
    Calle Mayor
    Lawrence of Arabia   3

1965-1970

    My Fair Lady
    Hombre
    2001: A Space Odyssey
    Midnight Cowboy
    Z   5

Sometime in the 1970s

    La Strada
    Mr Smith Goes to Washington
    Modern Times
    Ikuru
    To Kill a Mockingbird
    Bicycle Thieves
    Singin' in the Rain   7

The 1970s

The 1980s

The 1990s

Jesus of Montreal
Edward Scissorhands
Born of the Fourth of July
White Palace
Sister Act
The Fisher King
Bram Stoker's Dracula
Bad Lieutenant
Muriel's Wedding
Sommersby
Schindler's List
Raining Stones
Priest
Secrets and Lies
The Castle
The End of the Affair   16

The 2000s

O Brother Where Art Thou
Wit
Under the Moonlight
Talk to Her
Bruce Almighty
The Return
Big Fish
Vera Drake

Lightning Source UK Ltd.
Milton Keynes UK
UKHW020251080223
416610UK00016B/2196